THE NEW CITY

MODERN CITIES

3

JEAN-FRANCOIS LEJEUNE, EDITOR

UNIVERSITY OF MIAMI SCHOOL OF ARCHITECTURE

C R E D I T S

Editor
Jean-François Lejeune

Editorial Board
Roberto M. Behar
Andres Duany
Jorge Hernandez
Elizabeth Plater-Zyberk
Ramon Trías

Translations
Jean-François Lejeune
Roselyne Pirson
Ramon Trías

Graphic design
Jean-François Lejeune &
Suzanne Perez
  (on the basis of
  Vol. 1 & 2 designed by
  Jacques Auger Design
  Associates, Miami Beach)
Collaborators: Debbie Al-
  Ahmari, Greg Lorusso,
  Fay Bernardo

Production
Jacques Auger Design
  Associates, Miami Beach

Redaction
University of Miami
School of Architecture
1223 Dickinson Drive
Coral Gables FL 33146
Tel: (305) 284-5258
Fax: (305) 284-2999

Distribution
Princeton Architectural Press
37 East Seventh Street
New York, NY 10003
Tel: (212) 995-9620
Fx: (212) 995-9454

Printing
CS Graphics, Singapore

Acknowledgements
The editors acknowledge the
help given by the following
persons and institutions for
the elaboration of the present
issue:

The University of Miami
School of Architecture,
particularly Elizabeth Plater-
  Zyberk, Dean; Jorge
  Hernandez, Associate Dean;
  Leonor Pol (Librarian);
Stiftung Bauhaus Dessau,
  particularly Rolf Kuhn
  (Director) & Harald Kegler;
The Wolfsonian, Miami Beach,
  particularly Peggy
  Loar (Director), Pedro
  Alvarado (Librarian);
The Bass Museum of Miami
  Beach, particularly Diane
  Camber (Director), Ruth
  Grim (Curator);
Philippe Brandeis (Jerusalem);
Jean-Louis Cohen & Monique
  Eleb (Paris);
Giorgio Grassi Studio,
  particularly Simona Periti;
Henry Green, University of
  Miami Judaic Studies;
Dawn Hugh, Historical
  Museum of Southern Florida;
Peter Katz (San Francisco);
Michael Kraus, Akademie der
  Künste (Berlin);
Caroline Mierop (Brussels);
Rodolfo Machado (Machado &
  Silvetti Architects);
Stefanos Polyzoides (Poly-
  zoides-Moule Architects);
Viviane Rodriguez, Metro-
  Dade Art in Public
  Spaces (Director);
Dennis Russ, Miami Beach
  Development Corporation;
Gabriele Tagliaventi & Elisa
  Abati, *A Vision of Europe*,
  Università di Bologna;
Kenneth Treister (Miami).

Software & fonts
Quark-Express 3.31 on
Power Mac 6100-66.
Typeset in Bodoni and Zürich.

Price per copy
United States: US $30
Other countries: US $35

Previous volumes
Volume 1 (Foundations,
1991): out of print.
Volume 2 (The American City,
1994): out of print (Winter
1996).

Internet address
http://www.arc.miami.edu
Vol. 1 (Foundations) & Vol. 2
(The American City) are
available on the Internet at the
above site (Winter 1996).

ISBN 1-56898-058-2

Front cover:
Tato (pseudonym of
Guglielmo Sansoni, 1896-
1974). *Tato (Aeropittura) –
Sorvolando Sabaudia*.
Postcard (Roma: ediz. d'arte
v.e. boeri [1935]}, 4 1/8 x 5
13/16". Courtesy Mitchell
Wolfson, Jr. Collection, The
Wolfsonian, Miami Beach,
Florida and Genoa, Italy.

Back cover:
Theodor Overhoff, architect.
Am Achteck in Siedlung Hohe
Lache, Dessau. Photo
Junkers-Luftbild-Zentrale,
1921. © Anhaltische
Verlagsgesellschaft mbH
Dessau.

Page 1:
Paul Schmitthenner, architect
and planner. Drawing of the
central square, Staaken.
From: Franz Oppenheimer &
Fritz Stahl, *Die Gartenstadt
Staaken von Paul
Schmitthenner* (Berlin: Ernst
Wasmuth A. G. , 1917).

This page:
Bauhaus Dessau with Junkers
G 38 plane. Photo Emil Theis,
1930. © Anhaltische
Verlaggesellschaft mBH
Dessau.

PUBLISHED WITH A GRANT FROM THE GRAHAM FOUNDATION FOR ADVANCED STUDIES IN THE FINE ARTS (CHICAGO)

THE NEW CITY

MODERN CITIES

C O N T E N T S

4 ESSAYS — **MODERN ARCHITECTURE & TRADITIONAL URBANISM: PATRICK GEDDES & THE PLAN FOR TEL AVIV**
Neal E. Payton

26 — **MIAMI BEACH AS URBAN ASSEMBLAGE: A UNIQUE CULTURE OF HOUSING**
Allan Shulman

50 — **FROM HELLERAU TO THE BAUHAUS: MEMORY & MODERNITY OF THE GERMAN GARDEN CITY**
Jean-François Lejeune

70 — **FERNAND POUILLON (1912-1986): NEW FOUNDATION OF THE CITY, NEW FOUNDATION OF A DISCIPLINE**
Alberto Ferlenga

94 — **APARTMENT BUILDINGS IN CASABLANCA: TYPES AND LIFESTYLES (1930-1950)**
Monique Eleb

106 — **HENRI PROST & CASABLANCA: THE ART OF MAKING SUCCESSFUL CITIES (1912-1940)**
Jean-Louis Cohen

122 CHARTER & EDITORIAL — **FIN DE SIECLE/CHARTER FOR THE NEW URBANISM**
Introduction by Jean-François Lejeune/Congress for the New Urbanism

132 PROJECTS — **HOUSES OF STONE: A BERLINER PORTFOLIO**
Hans Kollhoff & Helga Timmerman

144 PROJECTS — **THE NEW WILLIAMSBURG, VIRGINIA**
Charles Barrett, Frank Martinez, Frank Caruncho, Ana Alvarez, Andres Duany & Elizabeth Plater-Zyberk/de la Guardia Victoria, Trelles Architects/Maria Fleites, Cesar Garcia-Pons/Roberto Behar, Jaime Correa/Jorge Hernandez, Francis Lyn

150 BUILT WORKS — **MANIFESTO FOR AN ORDINARY BLOCK: THE RECONSTRUCTION OF THE RUE DE LAEKEN IN BRUSSELS**
Introduction by Caroline Mierop; Houses by Joseph Altuna, Sylvie Assassin, Javier Cenicacelaya, Barthélémy Dumons, Jean-Philippe Garric, Philippe Gisclard, Marc Heene, Michel Leloup, Valérie Nègre, Liam O'Connor, Marie-Laure Petit, Nathalie Prat, John Robins, Iñigo Saloña, Gabriele Tagliaventi; Dan Kiley, landscape architect

158 ESSAY — **THE RECONSTRUCTED STREET OR THE EXACT NAME OF THINGS**
Maurice Culot

164 ESSAY & BUILT WORK — **ARCHITECTURE ON THE STAGE: GIORGIO GRASSI & THE RECONSTRUCTION OF SAGUNTO'S ROMAN THEATER**
Essay by Alberto Ustarroz/ Giorgio Grassi and Manuel Portaceli, architects

176 BUILT WORK — **THE BIGGEST "M" IN THE WORLD**
Roberto M. Behar & Rosario Marquardt

178 PROJECT — **THE 836 OVERPASS IN MIAMI**
Monica Ponce de Léon & Nader Tehrani (Office dA)

184 BUILT WORKS — **NEW TOWNS NEAR BERLIN: KIRCHSTEIGFELD-POTSDAM/GARTENSTADT FALKENHöH/WASSERSTADT OBERHAVEL**
Rob Krier & Christoph Kohl/ Helge Sypereck/ Jürgen Nottmeyer; Hans Kollhoff & Helga Timmerman; Christoph Langhof, Klaus Zillich, Heike Langenbach

PATRICK GEDDES (1854-1932) & THE PLAN OF TEL AVIV

MODERN ARCHITECTURE & TRADITIONAL URBANISM

Neal I. Payton

Modern architecture and traditional urbanism of streets, blocks, and squares have usually been seen as antithetical. Modern architecture, so often implicated as a degenerate component of decent urbanism, has been all but ignored by connoisseurs of the traditional city and recent advocates of the "New Urbanism." The pilotis and the horizontal strip window, two of the icons of International Style architecture, are now emblematic of a failed generation of urban planning proposals and of a hopelessly naive architectural avant-garde. Meanwhile, a whole new avant-garde, while perhaps admiring of the challenge to traditional Beaux Arts formality offered by the modernists, publicly eschews its sociological component, and going further, doubts the likelihood of predicting and democratically controlling any process of urban development that results in a traditional spatial milieu.

These characterizations have led to the strict architectural codes advocated by the proponents of traditional urbanism and the *real Politik* pessimism of the current avant-garde. Yet this dichotomic view cannot be supported further in light of the conflicting evidence offered by a variety of cities that have lately been discovered by historians and aficionados of architecture and urbanism: Tel Aviv, Miami Beach, Copacabana, Casablanca, etc. Among these, Tel Aviv, clad almost exclusively in International Style architecture, reveals a level of pedestrian friendliness, spatial integrity, functional variety, and neighborly feel that even the most ardent proponents of the "New Urbanism" can applaud. In the context of a tightly controlled and binding plan, such as the one Patrick Geddes provided for Tel Aviv in 1925, extreme anti-urban propositions become unfeasible.[1] This suggests a rethinking of both the common wisdom regarding the effect of modern architecture on town life as well as the pessimistic pronouncements concerning the impossibility of planning, particularly in those places that, like Tel Aviv, were or are being built with a minimum of means for a rapidly expanding population.

As a modern city in a part of the world often overlooked in traditional scholarship on International Style architecture, Tel Aviv has until recently received little attention among historians of twentieth-century architecture. Responsibility for the city's relative obscurity is due, in part, to the shoddiness of its early *shikunim* or housing blocks. Not so much "machines for living" as Le Corbusier may have advocated, these constructions, built originally without elevators, were crudely fabricated walk-ups that aged poorly and rather rapidly. Lacking the pristine finish and formal sophistication of the early Dutch experiments in Rotterdam or Amsterdam, the overly exuberant Hollywood-inspired detailing of Miami Beach, or the rationality of the *Neues Bauen* Siedlungen in Berlin and Frankfurt, Tel Aviv was relegated to a city of second or even third class status, making it unworthy of any scholarly interest among historians and practitioners of urban design *(fig. 2)*. Indeed what little was written about the city's plan or physical appearance, most of it by Zionist visitors or provincial boosters, was at best apologetic and often took a harshly critical position.[2]

Underneath the scruffy facades, however, lays a city that in its early stages was built upon a progressive ideology typical of the early 20th century. Its founders were Zionist immigrants who were both conversant with the ideas of Ebenezer Howard and distrustful of the traditional European cities from which they had emigrated.[3] The emphasis on the land and "return to the soil" embodied in Howard's text found a sympathetic audience among these pioneers whose own ideology embraced similar concepts. The idea of discrete satellite towns with their own centers connected to each other, was also appealing, as was the soft socialism inherent in the work. Exemplifying one of the parallels between the two movements, Lewis Mumford pointed out that the Zionist project, as detailed in Theodor Herzl's *Altneuland* (Old Newland) outlined a form of political association— the *Genossenschaft* as a free and voluntary society— whose principles were roughly embodied in the First Garden City Association conceived in England almost concurrently.[4]

The original development of Tel Aviv, a sixty-family dormitory suburb of Jaffa originally known as *Ahuzat-Bayit* (meaning Housing Estate), has been explored in other accounts *(fig. 3)*.[5] However, it is

Opposite page:
Fig. 1. Aerial photograph of contemporary Tel Aviv (© Ofek Aerial Photography, Israel).

Fig. 8 (see p. 7). Patrick Geddes: Concept of the Valley section. From Peter G. Hall, Cities of Tomorrow (New York: B. Blackwell, 1988).

important to reiterate several points. As part of the Zionist project to colonize Palestine,[6] its design was to help create "a new Jew, a new society, a new environment, ultimately, a new nation."[7] Among its characteristics it was to be as "green" as possible with a manageable density. Industry would be zoned out of the center of town and everyone would have access to small gardens. As the first planned Zionist town, it was to be a model capable of attracting Jewish capitalists to the colony of Palestine for investment and permanent settlement (fig. 4).

Unlike the prototype from which it derived, Tel Aviv was not destined to be a dependent of another city. While it was indeed founded in 1909 as a suburb of Jaffa, inter-ethnic violence in 1921 convinced the Zionist settlers that their place was elsewhere. The purely subservient character of the garden suburb was therefore modified as expeditiously as builders could allow. In retrospect, the Zionist ideological element at the root of the Tel Aviv suburb assured from the outset its complete autonomy: It was to be occupied exclusively by Jews; it was to be outside of Jaffa and at some distance away; and it was to have a public building program whose central focus was the Hebrew Gymnasia (or high school) in which Hebrew nationalists from all over the world would come and study.[8] The lack of a syna-

gogue in the program suggests the secular nature of the undertaking with its emphasis on the Zionist national aspect rather than on religious faith.

Background

Rapid Jewish immigration and several haphazard expansions (fig. 5) assured that by 1925, when Sir Patrick Geddes was commissioned to prepare a "General Town Planning Scheme," Tel Aviv's status as a full-fledged town was complete.[9] Having outgrown its progenitor (which today stands as a tiny vestige), this "English garden suburb" planted within a foreign culture and climate would become, it was hoped, a true "garden city," with one major difference. The urban nucleus or, in this case, nuclei, from which it drew its citizens and industry were not twenty or thirty miles away. Instead, thousands of miles separated Tel Aviv from its mother cities in Poland, Russia, Germany, and England. Convenience as well as national pride necessitated a civic and cultural presence never required by its antecedents.

Indeed, the selection of Patrick Geddes to design the extension of Tel Aviv was based on just such aspirations. Geddes (1854-1932), the Scottish botanist, sociologist, and town planner, had established his sympathies with the Zionist cause as early as 1910 as a

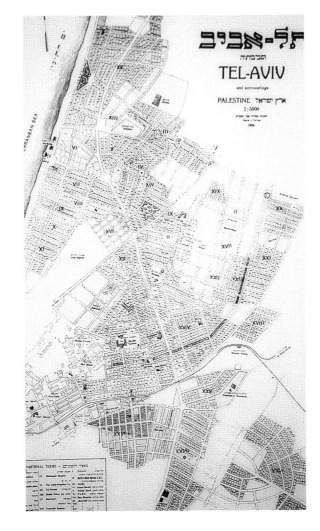

result of contacts made at the Town Planning
Exhibition that he helped to organize.[10] Geddes had
used the exhibit to put forward his agenda, in fact his
manifesto, for a new urbanism. Along the way, he took
critical aim at the latest proposals from the United
States, particularly those of Daniel Burnham, laying out
a theme that he would return to fifteen years later:

*The question has to be asked, how far do these
imperial plans, whether in old Versailles or new
Chicago really meet the needs, either of industrial life
on the one hand or the industrial worker on the other?
And above all, granted that they fully express the
greatness of Caesar, what do they provide for the coming child?*[11]

Less than a decade after the exhibit he was to
receive the first of several fruits provided by his new
acquaintances: the commission to produce a plan for
a new university in Jerusalem, i.e., the Hebrew
Univer-sity on Mt. Scopus *(figs. 6, 7)*. More projects
were to follow including works on the Carmel area of
Haifa, Talpioth (a suburb of Jerusalem), and other
sites in Palestine.[12]

The commission to plan Tel Aviv, however, was
Geddes' *pièce de résistance*. Destined to be a new town
built upon progressive urban planning techniques, it
was also to be a living and working model for the rest of

the world; one that would attract support from and
instill pride within the Jewish community in the
Diaspora. What made Geddes a seemingly perfect planner for this particular project was his belief in the existence of a relationship between the social and cultural
structure of the community and the physical environment, as well as his ability to map it and to act upon it
as it existed. His argument derived from French geog-
rapher, Paul Vidal de la Blache (1845-1918), who
championed the survey method that Geddes was to
employ in his famed 'valley section' *(fig. 8)*. Urban
form, architecture, and all human settlement and cultural activity, Geddes argued, derive from a region's
resources and geography.[13] Extending this line of reasoning he employed French sociologist Frederic Le
Play's (1806-1882) composition of Place-Work-Folk
(a trilogy that was to have special significance in Tel
Aviv) to solidify his own notion of anchoring human
settlement to the natural resources of a locale.[14]

As wanderers in the Diaspora, the settlers of the
"hill of spring" (translation of Tel Aviv) had been
placeless, separated culturally and physically from
their own roots *(fig. 9)*. Yet, as Geddes understood, and
contrary to the belief of his own clients, this region was
not a tabula rasa, but had been continuously inhabited
for millennia. This fact, he argued, offered clues to the
returning Zionists on how to resettle their homeland and
to return to the essence of their culture. For Geddes, the
regional survey "gave understanding of an 'active expe-
rienced environment' which 'was the motor force of
human development,…the seat of comprehensible lib-
erty and the mainspring of cultural evolution.'"[15] Near
the end of his career, the design for this utopian project
represented for Geddes the unique opportunity to wed a
nation with a landscape—to make place in the most
existential sense of the word.

Even with Geddes' connections and well-estab-
lished ideologies, two other factors were critical in his
selection. One of these was undeniably his international stature. Geddes was not merely one of a group of
planners in Britain and the United States interested in
realizing a singular vision for the city, but a theoretician of substantial import. An early proponent of the
concept of "regional planning," he commingled it with
Howard's Garden City ideal to create what was at the
time, a radical charge for a nascent profession. The
township of Tel Aviv had already begun work with local
architect Richard Kaufmann whose enmity they risked
incurring when they denied him the contract due to
their learning of Geddes' availability (his arrival in
Palestine was, ostensibly, to attend the inaugural ceremonies of the Hebrew University).[16] The town fathers
presumably believed that Geddes, as progenitor of the
regional planning movement, would not only bring his
unique vision of a city to bear, but also place Tel Aviv,
to the attention of the world simply by his association
with the project.

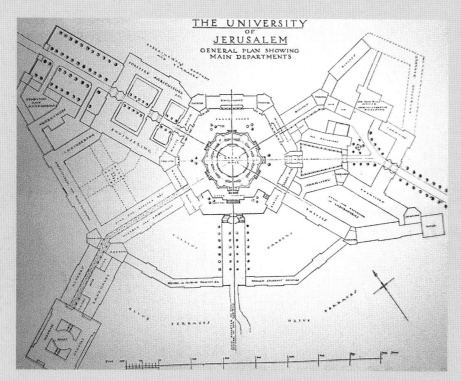

Top & Center:
Figs. 6 & 7. Design for the Hebrew University in Jerusalem on Mt. Scopus by Patrick Geddes, and Frank Mears (© The Office of Sir Frank Mears, Edinburgh).

Opposite page:

Top left:
Fig. 9. Plan of Tel Aviv-Jaffa in 1925. The area on which Geddes was primarily involved is north of the developed area stretching northward to the river (© Map Library, Department of Geography, Tel Aviv University).

Bottom left:
Fig. 10. Cover page of Geddes report showing only known drawing of original Geddes plan (© Archives of the Municipal Engineer, Municipality of Tel Aviv-Yafo).

Right:
Fig. 11. The 1932 plan of Tel Aviv (rendered by the author, Neal Payton). Area in gray indicates the limits of the Geddes plan. This plan differs strongly from the final 1938 "Geddes Plan." It is however the oldest plan on file with the Tel Aviv municipal authority.

The second factor that appealed to the town's founders was Geddes' pragmatism in the practice of his ideology. Town planning, for him, was not an experiment outside the economic and social conditions of modern society. His interests were in what could be achieved within the given constraints to create a higher civilization. By this reasoning he was a realist, positing to achieve, not a Utopia, which by definition was never to be attained, but a working model for an economically viable model community.[17] Tel Aviv was to be such a place. It lacked the patronage of an inspired individual, like Raymond Unwin at Letchworth and Hampstead Garden Suburb. Rather it was to be planned for an ideologically motivated yet ultimately bourgeois constituency. Geddes must have seemed the perfect fit.

The Plan

Geddes spent two months of intense work in Tel Aviv and five additional ones of preparation in Edinburgh. The result was a lengthy (sixty-two pages of single-spaced text) and detailed report that consisted of historical facts, recommendations, flights of poetic license, and romantic diatribe addressing such issues as roads, railway lines, port installations, open space, parks, public buildings, commercial zones, general building questions, and other odds and ends that he was moved to discuss. The cover page of the report revealed the only visual image embodied in the text: a crudely drawn skeleton plan showing the network of primary and secondary streets that he proposed (fig.10).

The Town Planning Department elaborated the scheme immediately and produced a final map, tentatively approved by the municipality by the end of 1925 (fig. 11).[18] Sensing, at age seventy-four, that this commission represented a unique and perhaps final opportunity to put his entire philosophy of regional planning as an act of civic improvement into practice, Geddes could hardly contain his enthusiasm:

I am impressed by the life of Tel Aviv—the real live Jewish city, free from the mutual inhibitions which are so tragic enough in Jerusalem (and everywhere else!). Here now is the mass of the youth of Israel, needing education! Goodness knows I'm not going back upon universities as the main interest of my life, but here are demands no universities yet require, a new sociology and civics, a needed ethics and ethopolitics, a psycho-biology and so on."[19]

What Geddes was proposing was a town plan that would embody a continuous and lifetime education in civics, botany, horticulture, history, and so on. Implicit in his remarks was a final critique of the town planning strategies advocated by Burnham and other proponents of the City Beautiful Movement, a critique he had begun at the Town Planning

Top:
Fig. 15. Diagram of a
superblock. From Hermann
Josef Stübben, Der Städtebau
(Stuttgart: A. Kroner, 1907).

Center:
Fig. 16. Garden City Tennants'
Cottages, Pixmore Hill,
Letchworth. From Raymond
Unwin, Town Planning in
Practice (London: T. Fisher
Unwin, 1909).

Bottom:
Fig. 17. Geddes plan for Indore,
East suburb. While geometrical-
ly purer, the block structure at
the north anticipates Tel Aviv
(© Geddes Archive, University
of Strathclyde).

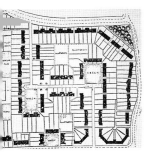

Exhibition of 1910. Only a city plan that was wedded to regional planning of the "neotechnic" age—a time characterized both by industrial decentralization and Geddes' 'valley section'—offered that possibility. Anything short of that offered only incremental improvement, at best.[20]

The diagrammatic plan itself consisted of two major north-south streets running parallel to the Mediterranean, extending from Allenby Street to the Yarkon at the northern end, as well as three lesser north-south arteries. Running east-west was a series of parallel streets creating a more or less rectilinear grid of very large blocks. One of Geddes' important contributions centered on his interpretation of the "super block," a concept which was already in use at that time and had been discussed by important urbanists such as Unwin in his pamphlet *Nothing to be Gained by Overcrowding* (1912). By including secondary streets within his version, Geddes departed from the model as it was typically applied. Seeking economic arguments to buttress his advocacy of the "superblock," Geddes wrote to his protégé, Lewis Mumford, asking for examples of the large block system in the United States. The clarity of Geddes' ideas can be discerned in his departure from the model Mumford suggested in reply:

As soon as I got your letter from Tel Aviv I asked Clarence Stein to send you the report of the Community Planning Committee; you will note that the Diagram at the end of the report deals with your very problem, and gives statistical proof of the economy of the large block. It was a customary way of planning in America around Boston, at Longwood and Brookline, and because of it, those two suburbs have kept their rural character much better than most of the other adjoining towns. Moreover, the big block gives you the opportunity to produce charming little dead-end streets as in the diagram. It is interesting that the very careful investigations of Stein and Wright should have brought them back to the same solution: the current age of Transportation sacrifices to its roads the money and space that should go into gardens.[21]

Geddes rejected the cul-de-sac model that Mumford advocated and instead provided an inner perimeter of streets within the block connecting to the exterior of the block in a pinwheel fashion *(fig. 12)*. Thus each block could conceptually be understood as a rectangular ring with its center left void either for neighborhood gardens or for civic structures. In order to discourage through traffic along the interior streets the latter were not aligned across superblocks. Thus these streets could be made one-way and narrower than the typical cul-de-sac, the latter requiring two-way traffic and a place to turn around. Unfortunately, only a few of the centers were ever realized as gardens or repositories of civic structures, the ideal model having given way to the realities of land ownership and real estate values *(figs. 13, 14)*. Although the municipality was able to get

the British Mandate to legalize expropriation, a real estate crash and the virtual bankruptcy of the city in 1926 prevented the purchase of much of the needed public land.

From the outset the significance of these green spaces as the nuclei of public life had been clearly understood. For example, the perimeter of one of the few blocks developed in the Geddesian manner, Ginat Nachum Zemach, was originally settled by teachers through an informal arrangement facilitated by the union to develop a neighborhood that would foster support for education and educators on a 24-hour basis.[22] Given the ease by which this urban arrangement supported many of the communal aspirations of the early Zionist settlers of Palestine and the degree to which it seemed to promote a greater sense of community than might be found in more standard platting patterns, it is curious that the organizational scheme was not more widely adopted elsewhere.[23] Geddes' use of this model probably came from Camillo Sitte or from the urbanist Josef Stübben, whose 1907 book *Der Städtebau* concentrated more on practical concerns and techniques of city design *(fig. 15)*. He may have been further influenced by English town planner Raymond Unwin's use of the pattern, especially at Letchworth *(fig. 16)*. Prior to planning Tel Aviv, Geddes himself had already employed a similar strategy in Indore, India, deriving its form from 'model' plague camps *(fig. 17)*:

…the improvement of these Plague Camps must be considered from more than the present temporary point of view…. It is evident that each of these Camps is a Garden Suburb in the making. Thus readily and within a comparatively short time, there may be extended to large areas outside Indore, and by means of these Plague Camps essentially, the conditions which are so admirable a feature of French manufacturing and commercial towns.[24]

Geddes understood that such a block prescription was more than picturesque. He recognized the multi-faceted utility of the central spaces resulting from this pattern, arguing that they would "do much towards renewing the values of village social life," provide an outlet for "organic waste matter, which provides such a problem and an expense in every large town," and, when used in a network or a chain as he proposed in Tel Aviv, reduce traffic congestion by providing "room for vehicles to wait, thus doing away with most of the inconvenience and delay of minor traffic streets."[25] The street sections that were described but not drawn in the plan—that aspect was left for the township authorities themselves to prepare—included the width of "sidewalks, pavements, plantations and lines of building, etc." Geddes may have discounted most of Eric Mumford's advice, but he took heed of the last sentence, "the current age of Transportation sacrifices to its roads the money and space that should go into gardens."

Geddes himself had made similar arguments in India when critiquing the plans of the British engineers: "The reduction of congestion is the most common and plausible excuse for the creation of new wide thoroughfares.... The new [wide] street will only too readily destroy any remaining social character within an area." He further wrote that "the best way in which congestion can actually be reduced is by the creation of open spaces."[26]

Accordingly, the roadways produced in Tel Aviv as a result of his plan were surprisingly narrow. While the principal north-south street, Dizengoff, had a roadbed of 31-feet and a building face to building face width of 85-feet *(fig. 18)*, a typical east-west through street had a roadbed of 22-feet with a face to face dimension of 74-feet. The interior streets, comprised of two principal types, were even narrower. One had a roadbed of 20-feet, thus allowing parking on both sides with one lane of one-way traffic *(fig. 19)*; the other had a roadbed of $16^{1/2}$-feet—technically allowing one-sided parking and one lane of one-way traffic—with a face to face width of 50-feet. As might be expected, autos move quite slowly on these narrow streets rendering them ideal for residential use *(fig. 20)*.

Typically, a front yard, sometimes quite lushly planted, was included within the dimensions cited above. It ranges in width from 10 to 13 feet depending upon the type of street. These yards are always defined by either a wall, a fence, or a dense screen of planting such as a hedgerow *(fig. 21)*. Additional street trees further define and tighten the apparent width of streets and create a surprising feeling of intimacy. The only exceptions to this rule are at a few corner locations where shops prevail and at the two major north-south thoroughfares which are exclusively commercial on the ground floor, the yard area having been paved *(fig. 22)*.

At the southern end of one of the two principal north-south thoroughfares, Dizengoff Street, Geddes proposed a hexagon-shaped urban space. Rather than simply borrowing an element from Baroque town planning—which is what it came to resemble, built as a circle, albeit with markedly differing architecture *(fig. 23, 24)*—Geddes placed a highly symbolic significance in the six-sided polygon. He had previously used a circumscribed Star of David as a ceiling motif at Hebrew University, and he stated about the Dizengoff Square project:

This plan too I had also reached independently, and on architectural grounds of sound construction (as old as the bees) and on symbolic grounds as well, since a six-sided figure alone lends itself to the full notation of Life: Life organic, life social and life moral also (…). I know not how far this modern scientific—and I trust not unphilosophic—mode of expression of Life, with its six

Top:
Fig. 21. Contemporary view of typical sidewalk condition. Photo Neal Payton.

Bottom:
Fig. 18. View of Dizengoff Street, circa 1936. Photo Eric Matson. Eric Matson Collection (© The U.S. Library of Congress).

Top right:
Fig. 23. Views of Kikar Dizengoff (Dizengoff Circle). Photo Eric Matson.
Eric Matson Collection (© The United States Library of Congress).

Top left:
Fig. 19. Contemporary view of Hirschenberg Street. Photo Neal Payton.

Center left:
Fig. 20. Contemporary view of Gottlieb Street, one of the narrowest streets. Note the cars parked legally across the curb line. Photo Neal Payton.

Bottom left:
Fig. 22. Contemporary View of Dizengoff Street. Photo Neal Payton.

factors (of environment, function, organism; organism, function, environment) may correspond to that of the traditional interpretations of this ancient and venerable symbol of the hexagon star; but I cannot think there can be discord between them.[27]

The architecture

Generally, villages and suburbs based on the English Garden City model were outfitted with traditional domestic architecture, reminiscent of the local vernacular. However, the cultural backgrounds and affinities of Tel Aviv's population as well as the source of the city's funding suggested something else entirely. In light of the fact that immigrants arriving to the new city during the 1920s were almost exclusively Jewish and came primarily from Eastern Europe, and with the knowledge that his work was funded by Zionist organizations in England and the United States, Geddes assumed that the local vernacular of Arab villages would not necessarily provide an image capable of satisfying his patrons' desires. The text of his plan betrays his awareness of the mine field within which he tread when addressing the question of style for this model village:

The present, magnificent recovery of classical Hebrew as the spoken language of the Jews in Palestine is of course a first step toward re-Orientalization; but others are needed. Without recommending any more adoption of the Arab Architecture, either in its simplest form in the hillside village — excellent though this is in its way — or still less desiring the over elaborate magnificence of later developments of the Arabian style as in Cairo, it is important to realize that this architecture and decorative art, at their best, are second to none in the world.... There is no discredit, but the very reverse, in learning all we can from this style of architecture, just as we have had to do from the Romans.[28]

Geddes hired a Western educated "Jewish architect," as he was quick to point out, who was also familiar with "Oriental architecture," to do some sketches for buildings with a "distinctly Oriental treatment." He argued that "such drawings...express beginnings towards the formation of a distinctly Jewish style."[29] Geddes' text belied a dissatisfaction with the bulk of architecture being produced by the local Jewish professionals. His protégé, Mumford, addressed that distaste in a return letter to Geddes:

Fig. 24. View of Dizengoff Circle). Photo Eric Matson. Eric Matson Collection (© The United States Library of Congress).

As for the wretched Jewish architecture that still crops up, I'm doing what I can: I made a long and careful analysis of the Jewish tradition…. There are plenty of capable Jewish architects, but I suspect that inveterate nepotism of the Jews is responsible for some of the atrocities.[30]

Besides such general stylistic recommendations Geddes provided little of substance in the report to base a new architecture. He did advocate the holding of an annual architectural exhibition to educate both the architects within Israel as well as the general public. His only other architectural recommendation within the text of the plan found him praising the original plan of Herzl Street with its termination in the Gymnasium, and lamenting that nothing since then had been of that quality.[31] In private, Geddes wrote letters and negotiated "behind the scenes," either on behalf of various architectural solutions or of particular architects. These were the methods he truly used to influence the status of architecture in Tel Aviv:

I found a talented young man D. Moed, a Belgian Jew whose enthusiasm for Oriental Architecture has given him two years in… Cairo where he has designed… a great £100,000 new mosque! I got permission from the Mayor of Tel Aviv to engage him for two or three weeks to make sketches and perspectives (rather than elevations) for my new museums, theatre, library and for Tel Aviv as it is for future![32]

Geddes' advocacy of a style manifested itself in words, in the illustrations he had commissioned to accompany the plan, and in a list of architects of whom he approved. However, it never appeared as a specific and enforceable set of rules, i.e., as the codification of a style. Indeed his desire to see an "oriental style" for Tel Aviv did not revolve around "marketing" the concept. Nor did it result from any nostalgia he might have harbored for streetscape. Rather it represented his reading of an authentic response to climate and culture. His advocacy was not so much for a style than for an ethic—one that grew out of a Ruskinian love of craft combined with a neopositivist belief in progress, particularly as a result of the metaphoric application of Darwin's theories of evolution to the production of architecture. Thus, the absence of any specific architectural code or methodology allowed any number of possibilities to occur, or more aptly, to ethically evolve. One imagines however that the view of Tel Aviv circa 1925, that he kept in his own collection, is illustrative of the scale of streets—albeit with larger front yards—and the type of domestic architecture he foresaw (*fig. 25*).

Nonetheless, Geddes' failure to be more specific on the question of architectural style was either naive or representative of his ambivalence about the modern movement. While some have suggested his lack of familiarity with the movement as the cause, the evidence does not bear this out. As Geddes was beginning his work on Tel Aviv, Martin Wagner and Bruno Taut were producing a modernist scheme for Berlin-Britz. Likewise, Ernst May, who had worked with Unwin in 1910 on Letchworth and later on Hampstead, was commencing his work on the garden districts of Römerstadt and Praunheim outside of Frankfurt, employing almost exclusively a modernist vocabulary.

Even if Geddes was not specifically aware of these German experiments, the winds of architectural change were universally apparent and reflected in the journal to which he was a regular contributor and subscriber: *Garden Cities and Town Planning*, the mouthpiece for the Garden Cities and Town Planning Association. By 1925 numerous pages had been devoted to modernist schemes.[33] Particularly interesting was the publication of an image of the "Square de l'hexagone." It was reprinted from *L'habitation à bon marché* which gave an account of "La Cité moderne," Victor Bourgeois' housing district built in the suburbs of Brussels (1922), and may have provided a model for Geddes' deployment of the hexagon at Kikar Dizengoff (Dizengoff Circle).[34] Geddes' familiarity with contemporary architectural trends was even more apparent in his correspondence:

…though I cannot yet find the right collaborator from among Jewish architects here or elsewhere, I do not despair of this. All so far as I can yet discover, are on quite other lines than ours—those of their neat countries and capitals they came from—with a strong mixture of the 'cubistic' kind of jokes which throw away the old forms of beauty without yet reaching a new one! They're to be fit in warmly with my view—that we must develop for Jewish architecture by great simplicity—of Arabian tradition….[35]

By the time of Geddes' receiving the commission for Tel Aviv, the modern movement had already influenced Zionist settlements in Palestine. Neutra had issued a proposal for the Library at Hebrew University (which Geddes and his son-in-law, Frank Mears, eventually designed three years later) and, together with Mendelsohn, had been very active in Haifa. In addition, members of the Zionist establishment had already let it be known that they perceived, among their colleagues and constituents, a bias toward German- and Russian-trained architects and away from English ones. The case for Geddes' ambivalence about a trend that he clearly anticipated in Tel Aviv but did not fully understand was exemplified, ultimately, by a letter in which he cited an article by Mumford. Geddes excerpted his protégé's characterization of the dilemma in achieving a "Jewish architecture:"

To search out the valid and vital elements in Jewish Culture and to establish them securely in the midst of the Machine Age—this obviously is no easy task for the architect; indeed it is only as the Jewish Community itself approaches a revolution that he will be able to embody it tentatively in his buildings.[36]

The gardens

Another potential explanation for Geddes' lack of specificity in regard to architecture is simply that it was not
as important to him as was the landscape of Tel Aviv, a
subject to which he devoted considerable energy in the
report. The combination of the city's growth into more
fertile areas with building restrictions limiting construction to one third of the total area on any given site,
allowed, in Geddes' view, for the possibility of lush,
fruit-growing gardens. This was an image that proved
irresistible, and the text of his plan, which tied a
romantic image of Jewish culture with his own idealistic view of the ethics of gardening and horticulture,
indicated that:

> To unite economic efficiency as fundamental with
> ethical idealism as supreme, this surely of all characteristics
> of Jewish culture, is one of the most distinguished…. Tel
> Aviv assuredly may be so, surely must be, a living and
> contemporary evidence of this harmony of thought
> and action. And towards this in all directions, what
> better beginning than by spreading over this whole
> city, its verdant and expanding banner, fruit-embla-
> zoned in purple and gold.[37]

The "garden city" was a Zionist's dream come
true. It reconciled both the biblical admonishment to
"sit under one's vine and fig tree"—and nowadays perhaps park under one (fig. 26)—with the modern
Zionist's aspiration for a nation of farmers with the
necessity for some form of urban settlement, supporting
agricultural trade and subsidiary industries. Thus,
Geddes argued, Tel Aviv was not simply to be one garden city among others, but it was to be peculiarly, the
"Fruit-Garden City," "Almond City," "Orchard City,"
"Vine and Fig Tree City," "Orange City," and many
more. Although it was not the first time nor place for
which he was to project such a vision, in Tel Aviv it was
to be met with a sympathetic audience.[38]

And so the stage was set, or so it was assumed,
for a rather extraordinary and unique undertaking: the
building, on unfettered ground, of a new kind of city,
unencumbered by existing property distinctions that
prevented adequate sun and air and without the rub-
ble of a decaying European past. It was to be a city
founded on ideological impulses and adapted, somewhat, to modernist sensibilities.

The implementation

The skeleton plan was embraced by local officials in a
surprisingly short period of time though it took significantly longer for British authorities to grant final
approval.[39] Nonetheless, work on executing the plan,
albeit with some modifications, began almost at once,
even before approval was received. Some of the streets
were altered to accommodate powerful or uncooperative
land owners. The difficulty of maneuvering around or
removing tent cities which had sprung up as a response

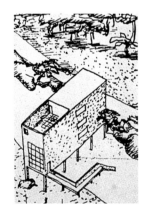

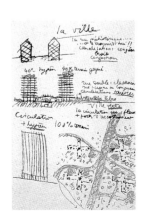

to the shortage of housing caused further alterations. However, the most significant modifications to the plan were made as a response to the massive immigration that occurred in the 1930s.

Between 1930 and 1933 the population of Tel Aviv almost doubled, jumping to 80000, and in 1934, that trend accelerated so that by 1937 its population had almost doubled again to 150000.[40] In spite of his enthusiasm, Geddes did not imagine the extraordinary growth that actually occurred, no doubt because he did not foresee its driving force, Hitler's rise to power in Germany. Yet, his underestimation of the city's success should not be interpreted, as city planner Yossi Shiffman has claimed, as having resulted from Geddes' design of his new town plan "as a suburb near Tel Aviv."[41] In light of Geddes' own words when he described his activities in the city, "I'm really townplanning Tel Aviv just now...,"[42] it is clear he viewed his efforts far more significantly than the city's bureaucrats.

As a result the final plan (officially approved in 1938, twelve years after its first publication, and known popularly as the "Geddes Plan") differed significantly from Geddes' actual plan. Shiffman explained:

The faults in the new plan did not occur in the first years of the buildout because there was minimal building and development. However, in 1932 a lot of development began and very quickly it became clear that this plan no longer met the needs of the developing city. The need for fixing the road system, the building laws, and the land use zoning was obvious.[43]

Not only was the street layout changed from its original inception, but the resulting buildings also differed markedly from the initial conception, though not by design. For example, the platting that was done at the time of the Geddes Plan was of a width sufficient to allow for the emergence of ample green around each single-family house. Rather than Geddes, it was Tel Aviv's founding father, Meir Dizengoff, who more accurately envisioned the demand for housing in the new city. Standing atop City Hall in the early 1930s he is purported to have declared, "Here will rise a New York of the Middle East."[44] Indeed, densities were to increase dramatically above what Geddes envisioned, reaching more than eighty units per acre.

Despite the density, Tel Aviv was not to be New York. Like in Miami Beach, a city to which Tel Aviv is commonly compared, developers were able to create large parcels by assembling lots. This practice often resulted in the development of building morphologies that enclosed a form of semi-public space. However, builders rarely developed more than one lot at a time. Responding to Geddes-inspired legislation regarding platting, building height (three stories, later raised to four on wider streets), front yard requirements, lot coverage, and side yard requirements, the predominant building type emerged: a three- to four-story apartment building on a narrow lot (fig.27).

Essentially, it occupies a form that fills out the legal building envelope; its long dimension is perpendicular to the street and with just enough frontage to suggest enclosure.[45] These structures are regularly spaced, of a consistent scale, and contain porches or balconies to support life in the interstitial realm. Coupled with the walls, fences, and hedgerows, they produce a coherent, pedestrian-scaled city of neighborhoods where gardens and buildings coexist to enclose the public realm. However, as a result of the raised height limit, the spatial character of the side and rear yards appears much harsher and less pleasant than Geddes would have desired. Somewhat more apparent to the casual observer than the just described evolution of the building morphology is the radical stylistic transformation that accompanied the implementation of the plan and which is commonly attributed to the shift that took place after 1932 in the immigrant pool, tipping the balance from Eastern Europe to Germany.

The International Style

The rise in the numbers of German and Austrian immigrants was indeed a critical agent in the city growth's requirements for financial capital and technical expertise. Similarly, many of the new immigrants, particularly architects, were "children of the avant-garde movements" and thus early proponents of the Bauhaus and the International Style. Yet, these facts do not, in themselves, give a sufficient explanation for the popularity of modernism in Tel Aviv.

From 1930, the planer, white, and stripped down surfaces, the horizontal window bands, and the buildings raised on pilotis took the city by storm and quickly came to embody and to renew the freshness of vision, and the utopian rhetoric that had captivated the imagination of Tel Aviv's earliest arrivals. Ironically, such aesthetic devices hinted at an architecture consistent with Geddes' own vision of a decade earlier, if not in character, then in characteristic and in type. Geddes himself had advocated three-story houses open on the ground floor so that fresh winds from the sea could stream into the city. Furthermore, in an earlier literary sketch of Palestine, he had taken note of the "plain walls" and "flat roofs" of Arab hillside villages, and in their "contrast and composition of masses and voids" Geddes saw architecture "in its very essence."[46] Within the hot, humid, and ideologically charged seaside city of Tel Aviv, Le Corbusier famous seaside sketch must have seemed prescient (fig.28).

Indeed, Le Corbusier's "white city" was a style and concept uniquely suited for the new Mediterranean city. His drawing of the history of the street became the unconscious operative diagram, albeit strictly mediated by the traditional urban structure and land ownership (fig.29). Until recently, most critics viewed the results of this construction activity in Tel Aviv with unsympathetic eyes, lamenting, for example, the erosion of the

Top:
Fig. 30. Zeev Rechter, Engel
House (1933). From Michael
Levin, White City: International
Style Architecture in Israel (Tel
Aviv: Tel Aviv Museum, 1994).

Bottom:
Fig. 31. Plan of typical apart-
ment building. From Gilead
Duvshani, I. Megidovitch,
Architect (Tel Aviv: Misrad
Habita-hon, 1993).

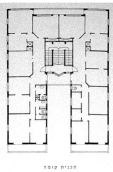

תכנית קומה

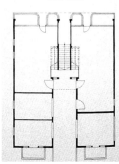

spatial quality of the traditional street.[47] In a view typical of this argument, one critic, writing on the history of
architecture in the city, referred to this aspect as a point
in time when a "far more anti-urban spirit began to
assert itself within the city."[48] Yet, the built reality is at
once more complex, and more successful.

Tel Aviv is a relatively non-hierarchical place
with few if any monumental buildings. The bulk of its
architecture is abstract (see pages 18-25) and displays
none of the elements typical of 'classically beautiful'
cities. Yet it is hardly chaotic or inert. Early decisions
regarding building mass, front yards, and mandatory
distances between buildings, allowed the city to be
understood as a coherent, pedestrian scaled assemblage
of well-defined neighborhoods where gardens and
buildings intermingle almost, but not quite to the point
of confusion. Perhaps, that condition exists in part,
because the young modernist architects that designed
the small apartment buildings using the exterior vocabulary of the International Style were doing so under the
patronage of speculative developers.

As an early example, Zeev Rechter's Engel
House seems, upon close examination, entirely consistent with the Geddesian vision, and consequently,
entirely urbane (fig. 30). The structure was configured
to organize a multivalent spatial experience, i.e., it
allowed for the enclosure and definition of the space of
its middle section, while simultaneously permitting the
extension of that space to the public realm beyond by
means of raising the structure on pilotis. The Engel

House was the first of many buildings in Tel Aviv to be
outfitted in such a manner. Indeed, the potentiality of
the raised building on pilotis seemed far-reaching, thus
leading Rechter and his colleagues to fight a successful
battle to change the building height limit from three to
four stories, ostensibly, to allow the ground floor to be
exempted. As a result of this new code, buildings were
very often raised above the ground.

In contrast, and no doubt due to the developers'
profile, the 'modernism' of Tel Aviv remained to some
extent skin-deep. Whereas the strip window and pilotis,
two of the elements of Le Corbusier's five points to a
new architecture, prevailed in the exterior architecture
of many buildings, their plans were rarely of the 'free'
type.[49] In fact, conventional bourgeois apartments generally lay behind the stylized exteriors (fig. 31). Even in
public buildings like the cinema and theater at
Dizengoff Circle, a traditional plan lies behind the
streamlined balconies of its facade. The planning
device of poché, more associated with the technique
of the French Hôtel than with ocean liners and modern architecture, seems to be the dominant instru-
ment of the plan (figs. 32, 33, 34).

Herein lies the paradox of Tel Aviv. At the core
of its founders' ideology and at the heart of their decision to engage Geddes was the distrust of the 'bourgeois' European city from which most city's immigrants
originated. Yet, Tel Aviv's development, unlike the
socialist Jewish agricultural settlements (kibbutzim)
being built concurrently, was decidedly "bourgeois."

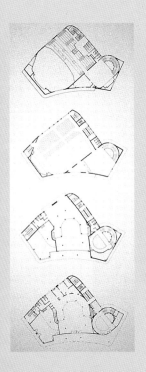

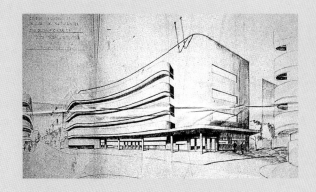

Furthermore, a "standardization of construction elements (formal and functional)…enabled contractors to
adapt the International Style" consistently, regardless
of or in the absence of architects.[50] The International
Style became Tel Aviv's vernacular architecture,
though hardly for ideological reasons. It was simply the
cheapest and most expedient manner in which to build.
It is for this reason as well that the raising of the height
limit narrowed the section of space facing the side and
rear yards to proportions that many find unacceptable.
Tel Aviv's most beloved admirers have offered the most
circumspect descriptions of the Zionists' utopia. For
example, a text of 1950 decries:

> To an unappreciative eye most of the build-
> ings look like packing cases with shoeboxes for bal-
> conies or, like technical studies in solid geometry,
> with a fixation on cubism; and the city as a whole
> has been likened to a run-down World's Fair, or a
> beach resort that tried to rival Miami, and just man-
> aged to top Far Rockaway.[51]

After these harsh words, this writer goes on to
idealize the peripatetic tempo of life in the city, liken-
ing it to the intensity of the blazing sun. Thus, despite
his embarrassment at the paucity of detail, he suggests
that an architecture more complex than one of plain
white walls and simple geometries, would be blinding
or exhausting.

The irony of such a criticism hints at one of the
city's greatest anomalies. In spite of its successful modernist urban landscape, Tel Aviv cannot be labeled as
beautiful, at least in any classic sense. Moreover the
city confounds post-modern expectations by supporting
a vibrant urban life, despite both the purported absence
of a 'traditional' architecture and the lack of a clear
hierarchy of architectural morphologies (there is only
one type of building form). Furthermore and somewhat

unexpectedly, its many buildings on pilotis do not
destroy street life, but rather provide another layer of
transition between interior and exterior space, between
public and private, which, when accomplished with
skill, further embellishes the realm of the street.

On the negative side, the city strains increasingly under the weight of a population and a density of
automobile traffic never imagined by Geddes. The
effects of that stress are all too obvious. Furthermore,
the lack of proper building maintenance and the shoddiness of some of the original construction have also
taken their toll. It is nonetheless a surprisingly pedestrian friendly city. Its cafe scene, its commercial
streets, and even its quiet residential neighborhoods,
support an intensity of public life that American city
planners can only dream of. It is the city in which most
new Israeli immigrants aspire to live.

A revived interest in the space of public life in
North America has led to efforts at reconstituting urban
milieus of such quality. The "New Urbanists" seek
nothing more than these qualities of place.[52] Stung
repeatedly, however, by attacks that proposals emanat-
ing from their studios are "passeist" or "nostalgic,"
many search for modern examples of the principles they
espouse. Tel Aviv awaits their analysis. It is a paradigm
of the New Urbanism. Yet it is not cloaked in garb that
reminds one of life in another era. It does not com-
memorate the grandeur of Berlin, Vienna, or Paris.
Nor does it recall in its architecture the intimacy of
the Eastern European *shtetl*. This story of a city built
according to a traditional plan without the supposed
imperative of architectural guidelines leads one to
reflect on the critical constituent of a humanely
designed city. Patrick Geddes understood it as the
plan—and its complement, the street section. His
legacy in Tel Aviv is an inspired one.

1. It is important to note that Geddes' plan for Tel Aviv, a proposal that eschews any fascination with the aesthetic of the machine and its ubiquitous urban component, the automobile, was produced in the same year as Le Corbusier's Plan Voisin, a proposal funded by and wedded to the automobile.

2. For example,"It must be born in mind that the architect was always desperately limited as to time and space. He had to utilize every inch of land and meet emergency with dispatch. With such phenomenally rapid growth, it can be understood that careful planning [in Tel Aviv] was impossible." Elias Newman, "Art Center of Israel," in *Israel: Life and Letters* (Feb-April, 1950 Vol. VI, Nos. 1 & 2): 24.

3. Howard's ideas were expressed in his book, *To-morrow, a Peaceful Path to Real Reform* (later known as *Garden Cities of Tomorrow*).

4. Lewis Mumford, "Herzl's Utopia," *The Menorah Journal,* v.IX, n. 3 (August, 1923): 163.

5. See Yossi Katz, "Ideology and Urban Development: Zionism and the Origins of Tel Aviv, 1906-1914," *Journal of Historical Geography*, 12: 4(1986): 402-24. See also Alexander Berler, *New Towns in Israel* (Jerusalem: Israel Universities Press, 1970); E. Cohen, *The City in Zionist Ideology* (Jerusalem: Hebrew University, 1970).

6. Ibid., 403-5. Fundamental to the tenets of Zionism was the right to develop and colonize Palestine, and construct a Jewish state in that location. In order to achieve this end, its socioeconomic agenda favored agricultural settlement, creating a new society rooted in the land, and not one based exclusively on trade and finance, a characteristic typical of Jewish society elsewhere. Nonetheless, there existed the recognition that trade and industry would also be necessary, but only within the context of "improved urban settlement."

7. Esther Sandberg and Oren Tatcher, "The White City Revisited," *Progressive Architecture* (August 1994): 33.

8. Katz, "Ideology and Urban Development," op. cit.: 406.

9. Letter dated May 6,1925 from Meir Dizengoff, President, Township of Tel Aviv to Professor Geddes asking for a fee proposal and time frame for completion. In the archive of the Municipality of Tel Aviv, File 3, Book 110, page unnumbered. Geddes was already in Tel Aviv at this point and had begun work in an unofficial capacity, as Dizengoff reports to the Assistant District Commissioner of Jaffa: "In April 1925 the Township of Tel Aviv had given over the elaboration of the general Town Planning Scheme to Professor Geddes," {Translation of Hebrew original, May 16, 1926 (Archive of the Municipality of Tel Aviv, File 3, Book 110, p. 7)}.

10. Geddes was not Jewish, but the exhibition that he and his associate Frank Mears organized brought him into contact with leading Zionists who were interested in his utopian proposals as they could be applied to a Jewish homeland. He thus moved easily in Zionist circles both in Palestine and in London. He maintained friendships with such ardent Zionists as American soap manufacturer Joseph Fels (and later his widow), Justice Louis Brandeis, Chaim Wiezmann, and Baron Philip Rothschild, among others.

11. Patrick Geddes, "Cities and Town Planning Exhibition" (text drawn from Geddes' catalogue to the first exhibition), *Cities in Evolution* (London: Williams & Norgate Ltd, 1949): 189.

12. See Gilbert Herbert and Silvina Sosnovsky, *Bauhaus on the Carmel and the Crossroads of Empire* (Jerusalem: Yad Izhak Ben-Zvi, 1993). I am grateful to Professor Herbert for his guidance early in this research.

13. Peter Hall, *Cities of Tomorrow: An Intellectual History of Urban Planning and Design in the Twentieth Century* (Cambridge: Basil Blackwell, 1990): 140.

14. The "Place-Work-Folk" trilogy was summed up by Lewis Mumford in the following manner, "It sees people, industry and the land as a single unit." "Regions To Live In," *Survey* (May 1, 1925): 151-2.

15. Hall, op. cit., 142. quoted from C. Weaver, *Regional Development and the Local Community: Planning, Politics and Social Context* (London: Wiley, 1984): 47.

16. Letter (in Hebrew) dated March 13, 1925 from Meir Dizengoff to Zionist Management, Mr. Friesland, Jerusalem, which states, "We are very happy that we will have the occasion of inviting Prof. Geddes to Israel. It is worthwhile to invite him to make plans for the buildings and urban spaces of Tel Aviv…. It is understood that we will pay him a good fee for this work. We think that we have to separate the plans of Tel Aviv and Jaffa…the work on Tel Aviv is much bigger than Jaffa." "Recently, we asked the architect Kaufmann to deal with this issue. We didn't make any contract nor fix a price. He came only once or twice and gave us advice about the place of the bridge. I inform you of this so that you will be able to arrange with Mr. Kaufmann so that he will not be angry with us, that we gave the work to Mr. Geddes. If Prof. Geddes stays only a month and not more it will be good that the professor gives general advice on the general plan and Mr. Kaufmann will work on the details. Anyhow, we really want to use the wide knowledge of Professor Geddes." {Archive of the Municipality of Tel Aviv, File 3, Book 110, p.20}. Ultimately, Kaufmann was engaged in 1929 to produce refinements to the "Geddes plan," though apparently, these were not significant.

17. Helen Miller (editor), "Introduction," *The Ideal City* (Leicester: University Press, 1979): 13. "Eutopia" was the term Geddes used for such a community.

18. Memo of May 16, 1926 from Meir Dizengoff: "…the final map was sanctioned by the Local Town Planning Commission on December 15, 1925. This map after it is approved by the CTPC…will serve as a map of 'The development of the Town.'"

19. Letter to M. Eder from Patrick Geddes May 2, 1925, Central Zionist Archive (hereafter CZA) (L 12/39).

20. If this seems a bit obtuse, perhaps Mumford's diatribe against many of the characteristics of older industrial cities would be enlightening: "No form of industry and no type of city are tolerable that take the joy out of life. Communities in which courtship is furtive, in which babies are an unwelcome handicap, in which education, lacking the touch of nature and of real occupation, harden into a blank routine, in which people achieve adventure only on wheels and happiness only by having their minds 'taken off' their everyday lives," quoted from Hall: 152.

21. Letter dated June 20, 1925 from Lewis Mumford to Patrick Geddes in the Patrick Geddes Archive, National Library of Scotland, File MS. 10575.

22. Interview, May 25, 1994 with Schlomo Chelouche, a 47-year resident of the area whose brother built many of the original houses fronting the garden.

23. While the pattern is repeated in newer parts of Tel Aviv, it is at a much larger scale destroying the intimacy of the garden spaces. The pattern is also briefly adopted in the neighboring town of Herzlia, but a perusal of the plan suggests that there too it was quickly abandoned as a strategy. The observation that the pattern results in a greater sense of community is personal and anecdotal, resulting from observations made of activities in the park.

24. Patrick Geddes, *Town Planning Towards City Development: A Report to the Durbar of Indore* (Indore: Holkore State Printing Press, 1918): 17.

25. Patrick Geddes, *Town Planning in Lucknow, A Second Report to the Municipal Council* (1917): 4.

Top:
*Street view and side alley.
Photo Allan Shulman.*

Center:
Plan of House Pelzmann (1934-35). See photo next page, top right. From Kamp-Bandau, Irmel, Tel Aviv, neues Bauen, 1930-1939 (Tübingen: Wasmuth, 1993).

Bottom:
Plan of house Cytak-Zeitig (1935). See partial view on photo next page, top left. From Kamp-Bandau, Irmel, Tel Aviv, neues Bauen, 1930-1939, op.cit.

26. Ibid.

27. Patrick Geddes, *Town Planning Report—Jaffa and Tel Aviv* (1925).

28 & 29. Ibidem.

30. Letter dated May 15, 1925 from Lewis Mumford to Patrick Geddes, Patrick Geddes Archive, National Library of Scotland, File MS. 10575. I have been unable to find Geddes' original letter to Mumford on this question.

31. Sadly, the lyceum has since been destroyed. On its site the tallest building in the Middle East was erected.

32. Letter to M. Chaikin from Patrick Geddes (undated, probably June, 1925), NLS Geddes Archive MS. 10517, f. 25. In a letter to M. Eder, Geddes further elaborates his architectural agenda, "I do not despair of converting some of them [Jewish architects practicing in Palestine], at least to our idea—essentially that of crystallizing the confused wealth of masses and domes of old Jerusalem towards an orderly presentment of the New. Thus Kornberg, (though I think you also will not find his style either pleasing or economical) has a strong touch of originality in his home, and has shown real constructive energy, as notably in his amphitheater.... Again, Kaufmann's garden villages, etc., are skillfully designed, also his new town of Afule. I've advised Mayor Dizengoff to get his new Hotel de Ville from Baerwald or Chaikin—or both in collaboration if they are open to this. For it would not do for us to be greedy and the spiritual edifices of the university are enough for us without the more temporal." {May 2, 1925, CZA (L 12/39)}.

33. Significantly, copies of the journal occupied Geddes' personal library {Univ. of Strathclyde Archives GED 18/1/309, issues of *Garden Cities and Town Planning* in the collection of Patrick Geddes}.

34. *Garden Cities* (June 1924):137.

35. Letter to M. Eder from Patrick Geddes, May 2, 1925, Central Zionist Archives (hereafter, CZA) (L12/39).

36. Letter to... from Patrick Geddes, August 3, 1925, Patrick Geddes Archive, National Library of Scotland, MS. 10517, f. 69. Geddes is quoting from Lewis Mumford, "Towards a Modern Synagogue Architecture," *Menorah Journal*.

37. Geddes, *Town Planning Report*, op. cit.: 48.

38. Indeed, ten years earlier and half a continent away he had asked, "Why not give to every village a new individuality, beauty, health, and wealth by planting avenues of fruit trees...and giving each household plot a group of fruit trees with its garden? The garden suburb is good, but how much better is the orchard village!" Patrick Geddes, *Report on the Towns in the Madras Presidency* (Cocanada: 1915):10.

39. Three months after Geddes was hired, the president of the Township (as Tel Aviv was then constituted), Meir Dizengoff, was already notifying the District Commissioner under the British mandate that "so as to make a quick parcellation of such lands it is essential that the roads in accordance with Prof. Geddes' plan be pegged out at once," and requested authority to do so. {From translation of letter dated July 15, 1925 from Dizengoff to Assistant District Commissioner, Jerusalem–Jaffa District; in the archive of the Municipality of Tel Aviv, File 3, Book 110, No. 15.} Another memo between the same two parties, dated May 16, 1926, again asks the Commission for approval of the Skeleton Town Plan. Yet another memo dated September 8, 1926 makes a third request (File 4, Book 7, page 17).

40. Population figures and immigration trends come from Y. Shiffman, B.SC., AMICE., Tel Aviv Municipal Engineer, "Tel Aviv the Metropolis: Towards a New Urbanity," *Palestine and Middle East Economic Magazine,* Vol IX, No. 5 (May 1937): 236.

41. Y. Shiffman, *Yidiot Iriat Tel Aviv* (The Municipal Newspaper of Tel Aviv) Translation by Rakefet Abramovitz.

42 & 43. Ibid.

44. Swet, Gershon, "The Man Who Built a City," *Israel: life and letters* (Feb-April, 1950 Vol. VI, Nos. 1 & 2). This quotation is the personal recollection of Swet. It is possible that in the writing about a meeting with the mayor when he is supposed to have made this remark, some twenty years earlier, the quotation may have been and probably was altered. If accurate, then it is indeed ironic coming from the man whose utopian idealism led to an initial vision of a garden city free from the corruption of the capitalist city he and his brethren were escaping.

45. There are notable exceptions to this. For example a U-shaped type also emerged where two adjacent lots were assembled, though more often than not the center space is merely a source of light for the apartments than an attempt to create a communal space. A rarer type is the garden courtyard resulting from an assemblage of individual lots and built as cooperative worker's housing. This type, which occurs only occasionally, would have probably met Geddes' expectations completely.

46. Patrick Geddes, "Palestine in Renewal," *The Contemporary Review*, CXX. (July 1921): 477.

47 & 48. Ami Shinar, "From Urbanism to Anti-Urbanism and Back," *UIA, International Architect* 9 (London, 1985): 22.

49. The "free plan" was another of Le Corbusier's five points. Briefly, such an arrangement relied on columns for support rather than bearing walls. This allowed for flexible room arrangements, or large, loosely defined living areas.

50. Michael Levin, "1930's" in Natan Harpaz and Michael Levin, "20th-Century Architecture in Palestine and Israel: 1920-80," *UIA International Architect* 9 (London, 1985): 17.

51. Marvin Lowenthal, "A City of Sand and Grit," *Israel: Life and Letters* (Feb-April 1950), Vol. VI, Nos. 1 & 2: 22. He begins: "Because no other place has quite such an array of it or has received such wide photographic publicity, the style is often considered peculiar to Tel Aviv. But the same sort of thing can be found in the newer quarters of cities all the way from Rabat to Cairo: It might be called Neo-Mediterranean. It is a style which compels attention.... Drab, monotonous, jerry-built—the unfriendly critics deem it. But other eyes...delight in the plain lines and find the massed shadows and the white or tawny walls cool and sedative against the blank horizons, intense blue skies and blinding sun."—"Daytime in the Near East can be stimulating to the point of either irritation or fatigue. And the nights are exhilarating to the point that renders sleep only the last degree of intoxication–one goes to bed drunk with the moon, the stars, and the orange-scented air. To this climactic stimulus must be added the tempo of Tel Aviv's characteristic life. Amid such a bombardment from nature and man, any architecture which did not succeed in looking dull would be intolerable."

52. See the Charter of the New Urbanism in this book and Peter Katz, *The New Urbanism, Toward an Architecture of Community* (Mc Graw Hill: New York: 1993).

Top left:
Left on the picture: House
Cytak-Zeitig (1935). Architect:
Philip Hütt.
Photo Allan Shulman.

Top right:
House Pelzmann (1934-35).
Architects: Eliyahu Friedman &
Emanuel Friedman.
Photo Allan Shulman.

Bottom left:
Right on the picture: House
Polishuk (1934-36). Architects:
Salomon Liaskowski & Jacob
Ornstein.
In the background: House
Gottgold (1936). Architects
Raphael & Iehuda Megidovitch.
Photo Jean-François Lejeune.

Bottom right:
Unidentified house.
Photo Allan Shulman.

Andres Duany

Top:
Green spaces in Tel Aviv.
Ben Gourion Boulevard.
Photo Kenneth Treister.

Bottom:
Rothschild Boulevard.
Photo Kenneth Treister.

STREETSCAPES

1.1 The City shall be structured on a set of linear streetscapes composed of vehicular thoroughfares, pedestrian frontages and fronting buildings.

1.2 The Streetscapes shall be disposed along on orthogonal network oriented to the cardinal points. The extend of the network shall be interrupted by shorelines and excessive slopes. The network shall be permanently curtailed when the resident population first reaches 200,000 inhabitants.

THOROUGHFARES

2.1 The network shall generally consist of small thoroughfares of one moving and two parking lanes spaced at 300 ft. on-center. These small thoroughfares shall be no more than 1,500 ft. in length before a hiatus of 300 ft.

2.2 Every third one of the small thoroughfares shall be superseded by a medium thoroughfare of two moving and two parking lanes. These medium thoroughfares shall be continuous.

2.3 The center of the network on both axes shall consist of a large thoroughfare of four moving and two parking lanes. This thoroughfare shall have a continuous central parkway of 65-foot width which shall periodically widen at distances less than 3,000 ft. to form rectangular sites reserved for civic uses such as educational, religious and government buildings.

FRONTAGES

3.1 There shall be a set of frontages lining both sides of the thoroughfares. Their width shall be uniformly 9 meters or 30 feet.

3.2 Along small and medium thoroughfares, the frontages shall consist of (in sequence from thoroughfare to building) a continuous tree planter of 3 ft., a concrete sidewalk of 7 ft., a continuous garden wall, fence, or hedge between 3 & 7 ft., and a private yard of 20 ft. to be paved or landscaped.

3.3 At the intersections of small and medium thoroughfares, the frontage shall consist of individual tree planters of 1x3 ft., a concrete sidewalk of 7 ft., and the extension of the ground level of a building encroaching 20 ft.

3.4 Along the large thoroughfare, the frontage shall consist of individual tree planters of 1x3 ft., and a concrete sidewalk of 25 ft.

BUILDINGS

4.1 At small thoroughfares, buildings shall be confined to residential uses at all levels, except the ground level which shall be raised on pilotis and may be used for parking. At the intersections of small and medium thoroughfares, buildings shall be confined to residential uses at all levels, except the ground level which may be assigned to commercial uses. At the large thoroughfares, buildings shall be confined to commercial uses at the ground level with either commercial or residential uses assigned to all levels above. Parking shall be behind the buildings.

4.2 The height of private buildings shall be no more than 4 levels. The ground level shall not be less than 13 ft. and other levels shall not exceed 13 ft. floor-to-floor. Public buildings shall have no height limit.

4.3 The width of private buildings on small and medium thoroughfares shall not exceed 70 ft. with a separation between buildings of 15 ft. at all levels. At the large thoroughfares, buildings shall not be wider than 160 ft. with a separation between buildings of 30 ft. above the ground level. Public buildings may be any width.

4.4 The roofs of private buildings shall be flat. Public buildings shall have roofs with parapets, or vaulted or pitched roofs.

4.5 The proportion of private buildings shall be horizontal at intercolumniation, fenestration, and balconies. Public buildings shall show vertical proportions throughout.

4.6 The exterior finish of private buildings shall be smooth stucco painted in the white-to-sand range. Public buildings may be finished in brick or smooth stucco colored in the ochre-to-red range.

Side center:
Entrance on pilotis near
Dizengoff Circle.
Photo Jean-François Lejeune.

Three examples of pilotis in
mixed-use and residential build-
ings. Photo (bottom left) Allan
Shulman; Photos (top, bottom
right) Kenneth Treister.

MIAMI BEACH AS URBAN ASSEMBLAGE

A UNIQUE CULTURE OF HOUSING

Allan T. Shulman

There is indeed a charm and sacredness in street architecture which must be wanting to even that of the temple: it is a little thing for men to unite in the forms of a religious service, but it is much more for them to unite, like true brethren, in the arts and offices of their daily lives.[1]

Like many American new towns of the Progressive era Miami Beach was colonized as a speculative venture, and like many Florida cities it was invested with romantic qualities and a special emphasis on health, relaxation, and leisure. Begun in 1912, the city was conceived as a leisure suburb extension to Greater Miami as well as a playground for wealthy northern industrialists. Miami Beach was soon influenced by the tremendous 20th century expansion of wealth in America and advancements in transportation that made it a virtual resort satellite of industrial urban centers like New York City. By the 1930s the romance of a tropical vacation had been appropriated by the rising middle class. Between 1920 and 1945, hundreds of modest hotels and apartment buildings were built in South Beach, an area of approximately one square mile at the southern tip of the peninsula of Miami Beach. Highly stylized and built in an intensely compact fashion, these 'ordinary' buildings produced a coherent urban resort neighborhood that replaced the once glamorous leisure hotels as the symbol and icon of the city.

Many studies have highlighted the role of style in establishing a sense of place in South Beach, particularly the local streams of Art Deco, *Moderne*, and Streamlining used extensively after 1935. This emphasis ignores the contributions of earlier buildings in the formulation of the city's urban character. In the early years, most buildings followed the Southern vernacular tradition. During the 1920s and the early 1930s, the Mediterranean revival dominated the landscape.[2] Even in the modern era, styles were used eclectically and interchangeably by local architects. Style was certainly significant to Miami Beach's hoteliers. It was used as a wrapper to identify the public faces of residential build-

ings. Conversely, the service alleys and the non-public facades remained informal and undecorated. Style was also used to create scenography, vistas, and perspectives as the backdrop to the theatrical movements of the tourists. Tourists were made actors in the public realm, whether sitting in front of buildings, moving through lobby and patio spaces, or promenading in the street.

Within the spatially restrictive and competitive urban context of South Beach, style was also a form of advertising, allowing apartment-hotels to distinguish themselves from their neighbors. The uniqueness of individual structures within the grid was highlighted in the pastel-tinted linen postcards that are an important record of the architecture of Miami Beach. These images showed buildings as isolated objects, juxtaposed against a landscape that is flat but ornamented with features more emblematic of Miami Beach and the tropics than realistic: used as advertisements, they were inherently idealistic, a vision of landscape removed from spatial dimensions. In fact, stylistic devices were fashioned in much the same way as postcard scenery: to effect a lyricism befitting resort architecture.

The recurrence of stylistic themes in the streetscape of Miami Beach was in fact alternating and unsystematic, reflective of its piecemeal development. Most buildings incorporated style for visual effect, while in fact the building forms remained inherently tradition bound. Thus one must affirm that the extraordinary urban cohesion of South Beach's districts resulted from forces that transcended these stylistic variations. In particular, it was a product of the configuration of its urban spaces, as determined by issues of building typology and a clearly defined street hierarchy. Within the parameters of a zoning code that aimed at creating a suburban environment, apartment-hotels instead performed as infill buildings, responding to their restrictive context by using strategies that evolved empirically. These strategies comprised the articulation of building masses to form public spaces, and the relationship of buildings to spaces.

South Beach is actually an assemblage of distinct building types that define public and semi-public spaces in ways that are unique to Miami Beach,

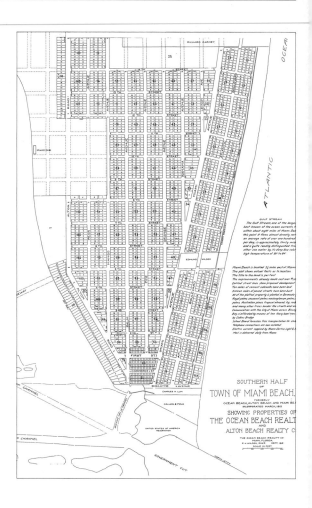

although somewhat similar but less typologically rich conditions can be found, for instance in Tel Aviv. Building placement is controlled by the reticular structure of the American grid, and modulated by the regularity of building forms—setbacks, height, width—which produced a unified streetscape of closely spaced buildings and tight urban spaces. The extremely tight proximity between buildings (the mandatory interval between buildings is normally 10 or 20 feet) allows them, not only to establish well defined street spaces, almost equivalent to a traditional party-wall condition, but also to create significant spaces between each other. The regular rhythms and thematic harmonies contribute to a feeling of overall aesthetic cohesion, congruity, and accord.

The urban environment of South Beach is thus a product of incremental infill, the result of natural accretions and the evolution of design idioms. The American grid structure is the point of departure, but also the stabilizing factor, for this complex urbanism. It is the framework that has allowed contingencies to develop naturally and chronologically. This landscape is inherently decentralized and flexible, allowing for multiplicities of meaning and form. The pattern of the street grid and the rules governing the relationship of buildings to the street are offset by the almost irrational, spontaneous, and organic secondary spaces which develop on corners, between buildings, and in court-yards. An informal network of semi-private spaces weaves through the district and around the buildings in a direction running from ocean to bay. The Miami Beach block is like a gridiron of passages permitting labyrinthine circulation. The proximity and horizontal continuity of facades integrates the whole.

Within this pattern, hotels are both monuments and fabric, creating an alternation between urban and suburban morphologies. Buildings types may be read as detached objects in a continuous system of such pieces. On the other hand, they may be viewed as the texture which defines a continuity of voids. The relationship of mass and open space in South Beach is not that of a traditional space-oriented urbanism, but neither is it really modern. The street, with its horizontal continuity of building masses, approximates the closed and defined outdoor spaces of traditional urban patterns. The spaces between buildings, pieces of continuous courtyards linking street and alley, belong conceptually to the open and flowing space of the modern movement.

Strategies of type usage reinforce the overall hierarchy of streets. Larger and more complex building types are found primarily on corner sites, while simpler bar-shaped types are more common on interior lots. Nevertheless, there is a random quality to the interrelationship of hotel and apartment building types in Miami Beach. The combinations of type and the possibilities for complex urbanism are almost without limits. In spite of a lack of explicit coordination (there were in fact few

real controls in its first decades), South Beach is one of the most typologically consistent districts in the United States. Notwithstanding its ambiguities, and perhaps because of them, its urbanism works.

The American Tradition

The first act of city foundation occurred in 1912, when two Miami bankers, J. N. Lummus and J. E. Lummus, formed the Ocean Beach Improvement Company and platted a small ocean-facing portion of South Beach. A gridiron of streets and avenues, aligned with the Atlantic, was laid out on the south end of the peninsula near an old ferry terminal. The blocks were generally 400 feet by 300 feet, bisected by alleys and parceled into 50-foot wide lots. Wide avenues went north and south while the narrower streets and interstitial spaces between buildings flowed in the direction of the breezes: southeast to and from the beach, where a boardwalk and bathing casinos were built. In *The Miracle of Miami Beach*, J.N. Lummus mentioned the influence of the seaside resort of Atlantic City, N.J., begun about forty years earlier, especially in regard to the relationship of the city to the sea.[3]

The remainder of South Beach was developed through successive subdivisions, which were designed and built by separate developers, including John Collins, Carl Fisher, the Lummus brothers, and the syndicates they formed. These subdivisions followed a repetitive pattern, yet produced discontinuities and

Top two photos:
Typical early house (residence of Smiley M. Tatum, 1914) and first hotel of Miami Beach (Hotel of W.J. Brown). From Ocean Beach Realty Map, 1914. © Historic Museum of Southern Florida.

Bottom:
Courtyard of the Leonard Hotel, 54 Ocean Drive (demolished). © Romer Collection, Miami Dade Public Library.

irregularities reflecting their piecemeal planning. The most notable discontinuity was the shift in the street grid between ocean-facing parcels and the purely north-south grid behind the oceanfront. The areas closest to the ocean, originally the highest and driest, were preferred for development and are today the realm of many seasonal hotels of more than fifty rooms. The areas behind the oceanfront, formerly a watery swamp, eventually became populated with smaller apartment-hotels (four to twenty units) incorporating domestic amenities such as kitchens. No areas were initially set aside for civic functions or public spaces; these were left to develop after the fact on Washington Avenue and later along Lincoln Road.

Planning was accompanied by a major transformation of the land. In the hostile, almost aquatic terrain of Miami Beach, land had to be cleared and elevated in order to be used. Dredges and other specialized machinery were used in the first large-scale creation of fresh land in Florida.[4] The mangrove jungles were shredded and filled in an industrial fashion, creating a tabula rasa of bleached sand. Tropical flora and fauna extrinsic to South Florida were introduced onto the fresh land creating a horticultural metamorphosis. The 'idealist' transformation of the native environment into a romantic leisure suburb made possible what developer Carl Fisher described as "America's Winter Playground." Fisher, a well connected tycoon of the auto industry, saw Miami Beach's potential as a resort and residential city. He accelerated and financed the development of aquatic lands and elaborated his romantic resort suburb, which consisted of grand hotels and private villas designed around major recreational amenities like golf courses and polo fields. Capital earned in the automotive industry was thrust into the creation of land and infrastructure in Miami Beach, making this progressive venture one of the first benefactors of automotive wealth and production.

As early as 1914, the enhanced landscape of South Beach was the suburban setting for many small homes. Some were modest wood structures in the informal bungalow style that were a direct response to the South Florida environment, with large windows, deep porches, and wide eaves, often faced with local oolitic limestone.[5] Others houses, influenced by the Mediterranean Revival style, were faced in masonry and stucco. The scale and character of these homes helped establish the pattern of an Anglo-American suburb. Functional zoning maintained the residential integrity and character of most of Miami Beach, while uniform setbacks and the general regularity of height reinforced the suburban scale.

Nevertheless, during the 1920s, the character of the southernmost section, South Beach, began to shift from houses to apartments, and a new culture of housing began to appear. The dichotomy between the reticular grid of South Beach and the residential development with a more picturesque and contemporary curvilinear pattern on freshly created land immediately to the north may have destined the southern area for a more urban development. Limitations on multi-unit dwellings in other parts of Miami Beach and exclusive (as well as racially restrictive) purchasing privileges, forced less luxurious lodgings to unrestricted areas like South Beach, where they became the dominant building type: Small apartment-hotel buildings were built among the scattered homes of the area. These multi-unit dwellings provided modest hotel amenities for middle class tourists, often in the informal lifestyle of an apartment.

The first hotel on Miami Beach was Brown's Hotel (1914), a two-story wood structure in a plain wood-clad vernacular style. As a housing type, it was a vernacular Florida multi-unit dwelling, a freestanding tenement. Its deep rectangular structure with apartments arrayed into the depth of the lot and facing sideways largely filled the site, although it was maintained freestanding by the provision of five-foot setbacks that kept the sides free. Its facade articulated a narrow townhouse-like street frontage while the frontyard or front porch, as the main public focus of the building and as an area for seating, maintained the primacy of the avenue as an urban space. Consequently, the straight bar shape occupying the depth of a single 50-foot lot, with its central-corridor organization, became the archetype for the housing buildings that subsequently urbanized the area.

The Mediterranean Revival
The Mediterranean Revival corresponded to a less modest and more romantic vision of South Florida development, and coincided with the intensive urbanization of South Beach that followed the Florida land boom of the mid-1920s. It introduced a more urban paradigm that included formal frontages and courtyard-type buildings. If its masonry walls and closed courts were less climatically sensitive, scenographically this architecture began to exploit the potential that tropical Miami Beach could provide.[6] Used first in the grand hotels and villas built in the wealthiest areas, the Mediterranean Revival was soon assimilated into the new apartment buildings sprouting in South Beach. The scale and proportioning of the facades became grander frontally, with tall, urban, palace-like facades facing the street. Mostly three-story tall, the stucco-faced walls were adorned with elaborate door surrounds, arches, decorative grillwork, and parapets. Many buildings featured an asymmetrically juxtaposed facade massing, some with watchtower motifs.

But the most significant impact of the Mediterranean Revival was the introduction of new urban forms and spaces, especially the courtyard patio. Although most buildings were still corridor types built in the space of one lot, many expanded to two lots in order to incorporate courtyards. The court of the U-shaped

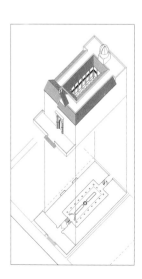

Everglades Apartments is a typical example, creating a symbolic and marketable interior focus. Architecturally the courtyards emulated Mediterranean and Caribbean models with an ornamental mixture of paving, landscaping, and fountains. The Casa Casuarina (1930) was built like an urban palace, with a courtyard modeled on Spanish-American buildings. The Parkway (1936), slightly larger, was organized around a genuine Caribbean court bordered by a two-story wooden arcade in the vernacular tradition of the hacienda. Other buildings adopted similar configurations, such as C-, L-, and O-shaped forms. In contrast, the formal articulation of freestanding building mass to make courtyards hardly affected the design of the units. Furthermore, courtyard spaces supplemented, but did not replace, the importance of the avenue-facing frontyard.

Although the Caribbean or Latin American references are undeniable, another source may explain the emergence of the courtyard type as an urban strategy: the 'garden apartment.' Garden apartments originated as improved workers' housing around the turn of the century on the periphery of New York.[7] They were significant for the presence of a garden within the lot as a feature of the building. The garden decreased lot coverage while increasing access to light and air, and became synonymous with social reform. It also served to reinforce notions of collective living. In New York, social cooperatives built housing with internal courts which became the focus of communal identity. Typical was the Worker's Cooperative Colony, one of a number of housing projects created by Jewish collective organizations. Designed by Andrew Thomas and built in 1927, it had a large U-shaped structure around a raised garden.

The introduction of Mediterranean urban traditions and garden apartment buildings signified an acceptance of density, but it also contributed to mediate its impact. The phenomenon of increasingly dense housing development, even in a resort, ran against the grain of mainstream American middle class culture, which was better represented by contemporary suburban developments.[8] The predisposition towards density and "urbanism as a way of life"[9] can be partially attributed to issues of class and ethnicity, and to the importation of housing models from other urban areas of the country. In particular South Beach served a first generation of Jewish people who migrated from urban slums or garden apartments in New York and elsewhere and sought to retain the sense of proximity which defined that area, albeit in a greener setting. From the 1930s onward, the urban structure of some of New York's outer boroughs was 'stamped' on the peninsula of South Beach.

Miami Beach *Moderne*

Between the Great Depression and the tenancy by the military during World War Two, while much of the nation suffered the lingering effects of the crisis, more than four hundred modestly sized apartment-hotels (a rate of one hundred per year at peak levels of construction) were built.[10] In the post-war boom hundreds more

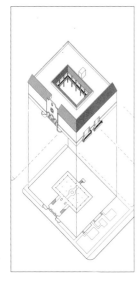

completed the urban fabric of the district. Most of these buildings incorporated two important ideas of the Modern Movement: a functional approach to housing design and a new aesthetic for the Machine Age. In both cases, the prototypical languages of modernism were adapted to the climate and layout of South Beach, producing a truly regional version of the international trends. As elsewhere in the United States, the term *Moderne* was used to describe the particular hybrid of modernist design found in the city.[11]

Miami Beach in the mid-1930s was an ideal setting for the modern aesthetic. The new middle class, who by that time comprised the most important tourist group in Miami Beach, was ready to accept an architecture free from representation of the status quo. Modernism was then widely regarded as a metaphor for progress.[12]

Machines were transforming all aspects of American life, as well as reducing the time of travel. Streamlined trains such as the Silver Meteor and airplanes such as the McDonnell Douglas DC-3, both sheathed in polished lightweight metal, made travel to Miami Beach relatively inexpensive, efficient, and exciting.

Miami Beach *Moderne* became the visual symbol of the sleek and functional nature of the modern city and the sensuous and casual possibilities of a vacation in the tropics. *Moderne* housing integrated architecture and courtyard spaces and while it maintained the traditional masonry and wood frame construction it also explored the plastic possibilities of new architectural types, forms, and materials. New architectonic motifs were invented that lyrically fit into a theatrical decorum of street architecture already typical in Miami Beach.

The mixing of traditional residential types and modern aesthetics was foreshadowed in the earlier development of apartment buildings on the Grand Concourse in the Bronx.[13] But a more influential modernizing trend in housing design, emphasizing efficient domestic plan arrangements, began to influence the area in the mid 1930s. The housing elements of German *Siedlungen* became an important source of inspiration for the new housing types, and they were probably introduced through the active discussion of urban housing issues in American architectural periodicals. Ignited by a national housing shortage and Roosevelt's reform programs, much of the progress of European housing was translated for Americans by writers and architects such as Catherine Bauer and Henry Wright. In an article of 1929 titled "The Modern Apartment House," Henry Wright lamented that fifteen to thirty per cent of floor area built in 1928 was wasted on halls, corridors, and lobbies. He articulated a set of basic requirements for apartment plans which included space-saving walk-up apartment access, two-room deep units with multiple exposures, and formal articulation of the building mass in relationship to open areas in order to define a public realm.[14] The ideas were further elaborated by the Housing Division of the Public Works Administration, which built low-cost housing after the Depression: in 1935 it codified and published model plans and type configurations.[15] These Unit Plans provided a kit of parts from which the designer could arrange spatial compositions.

In South Beach, hotel and apartment building types evolved toward contemporary models of low-cost worker housing. A hybrid structure called the 'apartment-hotel' accommodated the more modest seasonal tourists. Although many of these structures retained the traditional corridor organization of earlier housing, new types appeared, providing access to units through walk-up stairwells or exterior catwalks. Thus lobbies and corridors were eliminated, removing most circulation from the interior of the building. The transverse building thickness was reduced from forty feet to about thirty-five feet, allowing enough space for two-room deep units and a sideyard garden court with entryways, balconies or galleries in the space of a single lot. The reduced building coverage, from about 70% to 55%, improved standards of space, light, and air. The additional open space was important, because the increasing density made courtyards an important amenity.

Walk-up types based on the German *Siedlung* model can be linked to a rowhouse organization. A limited number of units were served by a common entry stair. Homelikeness was emphasized by arriving directly at one's apartment door. A series of staircases connected the units to the garden court as a vertical extension of the semi-public passageway. Within the garden court, the entry to each stair hall was set upon a stoop and articulated as the main feature of the facade. The

practicality and amenity of the typical unit were also improved. More closets and beds folding into walls or sliding under shelves enhanced livability. Every living room faced the courtyard. Corner windows, often located in small articulations of the building facade, allowed more light and air circulation.

Gallery access buildings provided a continuous exterior terrace or catwalk that linked all units. Their origins in the German *Laubengang* models such as at Dammerstock Siedlung (1929) by Walter Gropius revealed the most functionalist aspect of modernism. All interior passageways disappeared. The gallery became both a circulation element, linked to the garden court by stairs at either end, and a continuous terrace facing the passage. With all units opening directly on the court, gallery-access models progressively reinforced the connection and orientation of the building to the garden. Ornamental concrete or metal screens, such as perforated block, tempered the sense of transparency desired by modernists and created features, such as stairs and exterior galleries, completely open to public areas and the street.

Following the already established patterns, and restricted by site constraints, *Moderne* buildings adopted preexistent massing configurations like single-bars, U-, L-, C- and O-shaped courtyard buildings. Yet their thinner massing and reduced circulation spaces transformed those types, and allowed new types—such as double-bars, triple-bars and J-shaped buildings—to evolve. Letter-shaped buildings benefited from larger courtyards, but the transformation of single-bars was most significant. New walk-up and catwalk type single-bars were made narrower and could thus be reorganized asymmetrically to face and activate one sideyard, providing a public entry frontage in the long direction. The other side of the building, always secondary to the main facade, was devoted to services. Double-bars, formed by the mirroring of two single-bars, maximized the potential to define the resulting passageways.

Thus the tight green zones between parallel rows of the older linear bars expanded to form passage-like garden courts that bisected the traditional street structure of Miami Beach in a perpendicular fashion. The passageways formed an informal space toward which most units were oriented. This orientation improved the closeness and accessibility of each unit to open space.[16] The quality of the passages emphasized their continuity with the street and their spatial qualities. The edges joining one space and another often swept seamlessly in a curve, or stepped out toward the street. The entry corner was often chamfered or designed as a curve, usually with wrap-around windows. In most locations the courts became virtual streets, continuous from the avenue to the alley. The rear apartment generally projected into the garden sideyard in order to visually terminate the space. In concept, orienting bar-shaped buildings towards semi-private passages would allow all

Top:
The rounded entry corner of a typical South Beach sideyard building. Photo Jean-François Lejeune.

units to receive the same orientation. In reality, the location and continuities of the passages were never rationalized or systematized. Arbitrary or contextual spatial approaches were preferred to the technical concerns of orientation demonstrated by Ernst May and Walter Gropius in their *Standarte Zeilenbauweise*.

Tropical landscape was integrated carefully into the overall architectural expression. Planters were always attached to the building, allowing the architecture to mold the landscape, or the landscape to serve as architectural ornament. The integration also accommodated spatial constraints, especially in the passageways, which were sometimes no wider than ten feet. The design of the ground plane included pathways, patios, and sometimes elaborate dance platforms, often paved in terrazzo, as places for activity and movement. In spite of the emphasis on semi-private passageways and courtyards, the traditional frontyard space and avenue-facing facade were strictly maintained and highly articulated with regard to the street. The frontyard often included low walls or hedges that defined a small seating patio, provided screening and incremental privacy from the avenue. This freestanding garden-style configuration, coupled with the scale of the buildings and open spaces, brings to mind Tony Garnier's *Cité Industrielle* (1918). The congruity and arrangement of building groupings to form common spaces, particularly the U-shaped court, was also reminiscent of Unwin's cul-de-sac squares at Welwyn Garden City, though definitely more compressed and urban.

Moderne building types quickly lost their association with housing reform and were imbued by local developers and architects with the language of a vacation resort architecture. The sources were diverse, including Art Deco, Streamlining, and the International Style. The synthesis of these in the Chicago Century of Progress Exposition of 1933—with its emphasis on visual effects orchestrated by industrial and set designer Norman Bel Geddes, and scenographic use of color and light designed by Austrian-born architect and set designer Joseph Urban—was particularly influential in South Beach.[17] The interplay of flat and curved surfaces and very texturing fit into a new pattern that outlined volumes, while de-emphasizing ornament and mass.[18]

The sleek and functional nature of the modern city, its "horizontal mobility and flexibility," were accentuated in the more horizontal structure of modern building types and in the architectonics of streamlining.[19] The tall and formal, palace-like facades of Mediterranean Revival architecture of the 1920s gave way to the tension-free horizontalism espoused by Bel Geddes. The simple white cubic forms of the International Style also exerted a reductive and abstracting influence. Planes, volumes, forms, spaces, and colors were assembled and composed. Intersecting geometries of precise, smooth, volumetric masses were flattened and abstracted into shallow setbacks with variations in relief, materials and colors.[20] Horizontal windows cut the building corners, resulting in a cantilever appearance that seemed to suppress mass.

At the same time, the ornamental extravagance of Art Deco reflected the aspirations of local owners toward sophistication. Structural or planar articulations of the building facades allowed for the interplay of sensuous colors and materials. Modernistic materials included keystone (a dyed limestone), Vitrolite (an integrally colored glass product), and glass block. Fresh colors, such as the green and orange of Leon Bakst's designs for the Russian Ballets, highlighted expressive elements of the buildings, such as projecting eyebrows. Ornament was applied in a rhythmic fashion to accent volumes and planes with color and sculptural relief. The thematic and often episodic use of motifs highlighting the tropical verdure and fauna unique to South Florida elevated Art Deco to a regional expression. The design program was picked up in murals, etched glass, abstract patterns of terrazzo, and ornate stainless steel and tubular steel metalwork. The new design affected everything, and it was common for architects to design the lighting fixtures, tableware and terrazzo floor patterns, select the furnishings, match covers and employee uniforms, as well as coordinate with other artisans. Architects were conscious of the cumulative effect their buildings had on the neighborhood, and thus converged toward a similar aesthetic.

Art Deco's vertical emphasis—the smokestack-like stair towers of the Claire Apartments or the signage pylons and marquis of the Albion—was realized in elements that peaked above the parapets. Pylons, fins, fluted pilasters, lanterns, and flag masts were common. Spires, such as the one on the Tiffany Hotel, frequently marked the corners of South Beach. Within the flat plane of a facade, many buildings developed the fiction of multiple setbacks in imitation of Hugh Ferriss' Skyscraper Style. The skyline of Miami Beach was punctuated by these features, an effect that helped counterbalance the tight horizontal continuity of the urban fabric.[21]

In fact, by the late 1930s, high-rise hotels were built, demonstrating the financial feasibility of larger structures. The Tides and the Victor Hotels towered eight stories over Ocean Drive and provided increased amenities, including larger lobbies and dining facilities. Yet these buildings adequately fit into the weave of lower-scaled buildings by incorporating larger setbacks, often associated with a stepped terrace, and by providing entrances scaled to the neighboring buildings. The tower massing provided more room for gardens and terraces on the ground level, while a narrow or tapered silhouette reduced their massiveness above. Towers built along the oceanfront incorporated important sequences of spaces designed to mediate between the avenue and the beach.

The lessons of Miami Beach

The over eight hundred multiple-dwelling structures of South Beach represent not only "the largest concentration of 1920s and 1930s era resort architecture in the United States"[22] but a humanistic alternative to the disjointed urbanism of many American cities. Types brought together the logic of successive architectural traditions, distant urban morphologies and vernacular traditions that respected Miami Beach's unique climate and environment. It was the recourse, both intelligent and haphazard, to established models that gave the district its cohesion. In South Beach, the interfusion of building types was independent of any comprehensive plan, thus achieving great complexity and inventiveness in an informal manner. The lessons of Miami Beach are particularly applicable to contemporary American cities, where individual initiative is more common than public intervention. Development by subdivision and lot remains the most common model of urban development today.

The experience of Miami Beach in the inter-war years and the early post-war period proves that typology is a tool which allows for rational and incremental adaptation of building form and function, for urban continuity, and for contextual responsibility. As an example, the modernist worker's Siedlung and even tower-in-the-park archetypes were synthesized into the type pattern and lot structure of South Beach to make effective and even somewhat traditional street and courtyard spaces. In dense, low-scaled areas, even the motel type—which replaced the apartment-hotel model after the war—was subverted to the scale of the surrounding urbanism, and in fact partially lost its connection with the automobile.

This intimately scaled urban environment has survived several transformations, including a serious decline in value from the 1950s to the 1970s. During this period the area metamorphosed into a retirement community for many of the same patrons who earlier made it a holiday destination. The communal qualities of the buildings, especially the garden courts, were ideal for interdependent seniors, and modest apartment sizes made agreeable retirement housing. Small synagogues that mimic the characteristics of adjacent residential buildings nestled into the urban fabric to serve a mainly Jewish population. Over the years, and in spite of these important demographic shifts, the typological consistency of South Beach reinforced a stable urban form and density.

Nevertheless, important changes occurred that challenged the existing urban texture; these mainly addressed the critical contemporary issues of parking and increased density. Post-1960s buildings contended with parking requirements ill suited to the small lots of the district, resulting in buildings pushed up into the air. The provision of grade level parking (underground parking is impossible due to the high water table) created some unattractive street frontages as well as new discontinuities in the existing network of ground level spaces.

By the 1970s the district was considered 'common' and in disrepair, and plans for its progressive demolition were well advanced. Yet by the latter part of that decade, the unique architectural and urban significance of the area was brought to the public's attention through the advocacy of citizens who admired its underlying design ideals. In what was to be the first dating of a twentieth century architectural community, this group, which became known as the Miami Design Preservation League, achieved the critical success of having the first twentieth century district placed on the National Register of Historic Places in 1979. The designation and its widespread recognition by the public and scholars alike have since attracted an enormous influx of new tourists and residents, reviving a declining economy and setting off a new wave of development.

In other areas of Miami Beach, towers seem destined to replace low-rise buildings based on the current marketability of both security and views, and their inherent suitability to contemporary zoning. However, where controls have been established in the designated area, modifications intended to provide more generous units, often with private outdoor spaces, have been largely successful. Courtyards have been created over parking garages screened from the street. Another adaptation uses a double-bar type in which the court has been widened to provide a well detailed automobile court. Existing buildings are being renovated toward the same ends, with mixed results. Small apartments are being grouped to create larger units, sometimes with rooftop additions. One adaptation of existing typologies joins spaces vertically, creating maisonettes. In spite of their restricted size and lack of many contemporary amenities, the low-scaled types of South Beach continue to attract because of the quality of their common spaces and features. However, emphasis on facade restoration often obscures changes that undermine the function and texture of existing buildings.

Bottom:
The space between these two mirrored buildings is treated as a green passageway. Photo Jean-François Lejeune.

L-shaped apartment building, L. Murray Dixon, architect, 1930s. L. Murray Dixon Collection, Bass Museum of Art, Miami Beach. Photo Gottscho-Schleisner.

1. John Ruskin, quoted in Werner Hegemann and Elbert Peets, *An American Vitruvius: an architects' handbook of civic art* (Braunschweig: Friedr. Vieweg & Sohn, 1922): 151.

2. See Andres Duany & Elizabeth Plater-Zyberk's analysis in "The Three Traditions of Miami," *Miami: Architecture of the Tropics* (New York: Princeton Architectural Press, 1992): 79-89.

3. John Newton Lummus, *The Miracle of Miami Beach* (Miami: The Teacher Publishing Co., 1940).

4. John Rothchild, *Up for Grabs* (New York: Viking Books, 1985): 39. John Rothchild refers to Miami Beach as "the founding example of what happened along both Florida coasts. Once the dredges corrected the basic defect, developers were left with a tabula rasa of dried silt, as empty and devoid of precedent as an atoll after a nuclear strike."

5. Ivan A. Rodriguez, et. al, *From Wilderness to Metropolis: the history and architecture of Dade County 1825-1940* (Miami: Metropolitan Dade County Community Development, Historic Preservation Division, 1982): 79.

6. For the Mediterranean Revival in Florida, see for instance Donald W. Curl, *Mizner's Florida: American resort architecture* (New York: Architectural History Foundation/Cambridge: MIT Press, 1984) and Jean-François Lejeune, "The Grid, the Park, and the Model-T," *Garden City: a Century of Theories, Models, Experiences* (Roma: Gangemi, 1994): 220-265.

7. Richard Plunz, *A History of Housing in New York City* (New York: Columbia University Press, 1990): 122-163.

8. Richard Plunz, op.cit.: 132.

9. Louis Wirth quoted in Richard Plunz, op.cit.:132.

10. Laura Cerwinske, *Tropical Deco* (New York: Rizzoli, 1981): 12.

11. Jennifer Frehling, *Henry Hohauser: Miami Beach Moderne 1935-48*, Master Thesis, School of Architecture, University of Virginia, 1994.

12. Klaus-Jurgen Sembach, *Style 1930* (New York: Universe Books, 1986): 7-24.

13. About the Bronx, see Donald G. Sullivan and Brian J. Danforth, *Bronx Art Deco Architecture* (New York: Hunter College, 1976).

14. Henry Wright, "The Modern Apartment House," *The Architectural Record* (March 1929).

15. Unit Types of Plans for Low-Rent Housing Projects were published by the Housing Division of the Public Works Administration in the March 1935 issue of *The Architectural Record*.

16. The strategy of urbanizing the centers of urban blocks, with buildings composed around cul-de-sac passageways treated as something between a street and courtyard, recalls the Rue Mallet-Stevens of 1927 and other Parisian Squares. See for instance Jean-François Pinchon, *Robert Mallet-Stevens: Architecture, Furniture, Interior Design* (Cambridge: The MIT Press, 1986): 114.

17. Barbara Capitman, Michael D. Kinerk and Dennis W. Wilhelm, *Rediscovering Art Deco U.S.A* (New York: Viking Studio Books, 1994): 63.

18. Jennifer Frehling, op.cit.: 22-23.

19. Peter G. Rowe, *Modernity and Housing* (Cambridge, Mass: The MIT Press, 1993): 172.

20. Klaus-Jurgen Sembach, op.cit.: 10.

21. Laura Cerwinske, op.cit.: 20.

22. National Register of Historic Places Designation Report, 1979.

The Albion Hotel, Igor Polevitzky & Trip Russell architects. © Polevitzky Collection, Historic Association of Southern Florida. Photo Gottscho-Schleisner.

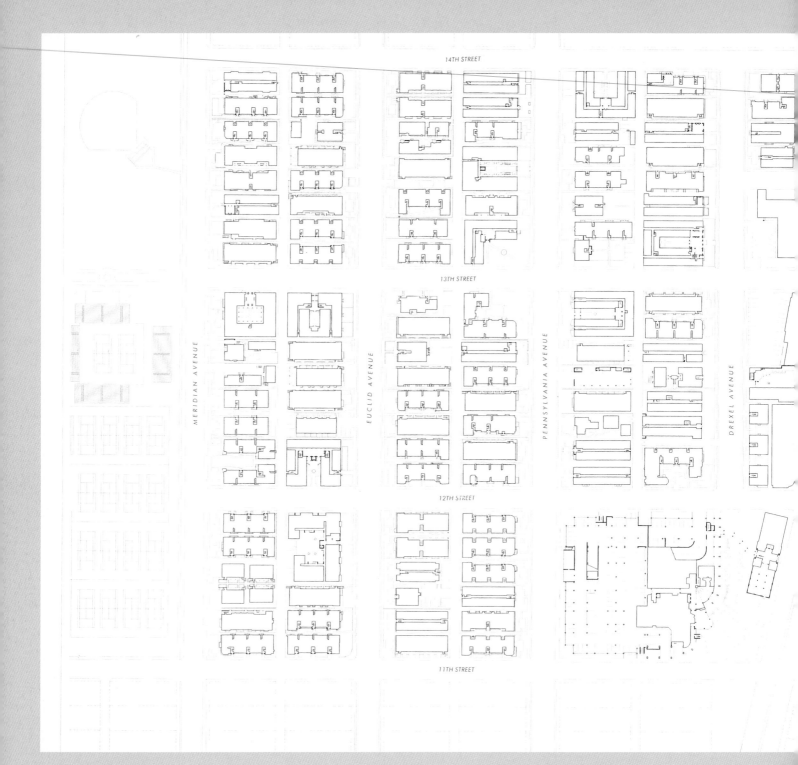

14TH STREET

13TH STREET

12TH STREET

11TH STREET

MERIDIAN AVENUE

EUCLID AVENUE

PENNSYLVANIA AVENUE

DREXEL AVENUE

"Nolli Plan" of South Beach
between 11th street and 13th
street, from the Atlantic Ocean
to Meridian Avenue. Research
and drawing Allan Shulman.

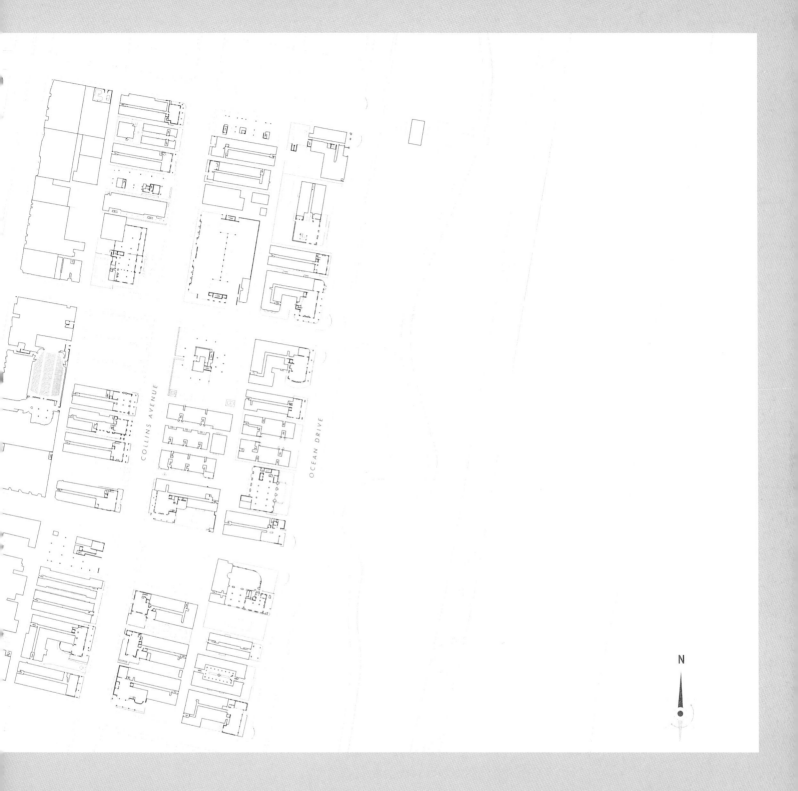

TYPOLOGY OF MODERN SOUTH BEACH HOUSING

A catalog of local buildings types can be gathered from the most common variations of buildings style, form, and organization found in South Beach. The intersection of organizational types and form types produces almost every possible variation. Part of what is characteristic about South Beach is the repetition of typologies and their variation and integration on any single block. Each building represents a random fragment in an unpredictable but strictly ordered whole. Three main organizational prototypes can be noted in pre-1960s residential buildings in South Beach: the double-loaded corridor type, the walk-up type, and the catwalk type. Most frequent forms include single, double and triple bars, U-, C-, L-, O-, and J-shaped building forms.

Single-Bar Corridor:

The single-bar corridor type is the most basic and primitive type of high density housing in South Beach. It is a simple rectangular mass on one lot (generally fifty-foot wide) with a narrow but decorative front. It has an axially symmetrical organization around an internal corridor with stairs at both ends. Miami's hot and humid climate forced corridors and sideyards, which were in line with the cooling breezes, to remain open at each termination to permit ventilation. The freestanding apartment building, with its provision of a front porch or frontyard and unblocked sideyards, maintains an open feel in the district.

The Single-Bar Sideyard:

The sideyard type is the most common type. It is the product of narrower bar-shaped building masses with two-room deep apartment units, popular from the 1930s. The reduced building width allows a higher proportion of open space on the lot, which is given to a larger sideyard on one side. From the sideyard court, the units are accessible via stair halls or catwalks located on one long facade. This facade is articulated in a vocabulary continuous with the avenue-facing facade. The "wrapping" of the avenue and garden facades ties street space and court space together. The other corresponding long facade becomes the backside, and the five-foot setback there is analogous to the alley space. This type is significant for expanding the network of articulated public spaces into the depth of the block.

The Twin:

The twin is a four-unit apartment type that resembles a home. It contains two apartments per floor symmetrically distributed around front and back stairs, and sharing a wall. The combined entrance of these units serves as a unifying feature. The building faces a frontyard but also has a backyard, relating it to the early residential character of the neighborhood. Each unit crosses the depth of the building and thus has three frontages.

Opposite page:

Top:
Single bar sideyard. Hotel Philan, L. Murray Dixon architect, 1938-9. © L. Murray Dixon Collection, Bass Museum of Art, Miami Beach. Photo Moser & Son.

Center:
Single bar sideyard, walk-up type. The Castle Apartments, Henry Hohauser architect, 1935. © Romer Collection, Miami Dade Public Library.

Bottom left:
Single bar corridor apartment. The Oleander Apartments, Henry Hohauser architect, 1937. © Romer Collection, Miami Dade Public Library.

Bottom right:
Single bar corridor hotel. The Kent Hotel, L. Murray Dixon architect, 1939. © L. Murray Dixon Collection, Bass Museum of Art, Miami Beach. Photo Moser & Son.

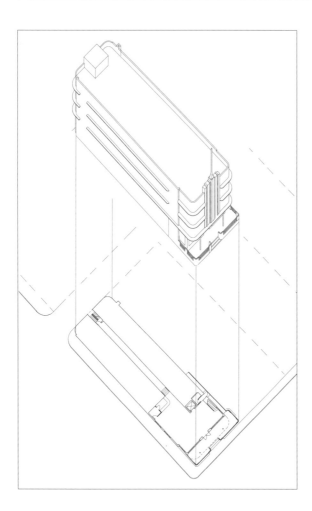

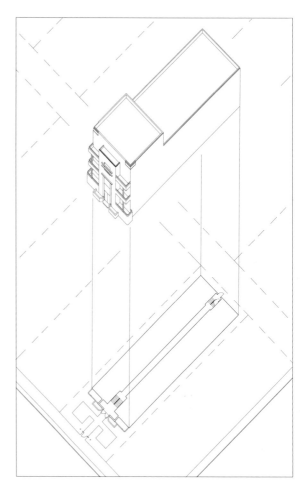

Top left:
Single bar corridor hotel. Lot size: 50'x140', 5' front setback. The Marlin Hotel, plan and axonometric. © Drawing Allan Shulman.

Top right:
Single bar corridor apartment. Lot size: 50'x140', 25' front setback. The Roystan Apartments, plan and axonometric. © Drawing Allan Shulman.

Bottom left:
Single bar sideyard. Lot size: 50'x140', 25' front setback. JBH Apartments, plan and axonometric. © Drawing Allan Shulman.

Bottom right:
Twin type. Lot size: 50'x150', 25' front setback. 1507-1509 Meridian Avenue, plan and axonometric. © Drawing Allan Shulman.

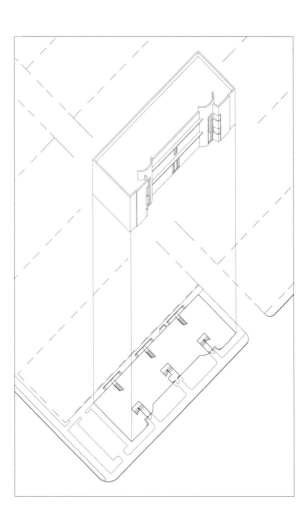

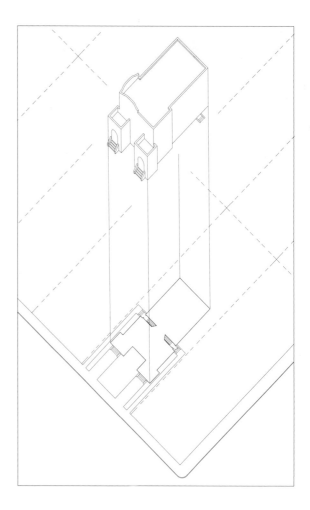

The Double-Bar:

The double-bar is the aggregate of two single-bar sideyard buildings so that in combination they define a larger and more coherent patio court. The Arcadia, plan and axonometric. © Drawing Allan Shulman.

The Bungalow Court:

Built as a double-bar or U-shaped, the Bungalow Court features one story bungalows around a courtyard garden. This type normally features an entry gate facing the street and a larger house or other terminal focus at its interior end.
The Twin Harbour Apartments, plan and axonometric. © Drawing Allan Shulman.

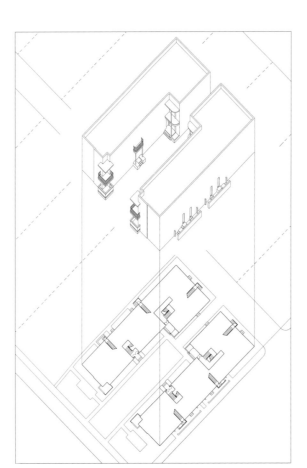

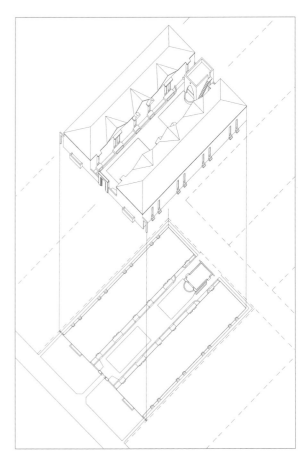

The Triple-Bar:

The triple-bar is rare. It is similar to the double-bar, except that one additional bar terminates the rear end of the courtyard, leaving one end open to the street. The third leg re-establishes a frontal relationship with the avenue which does not exist in other sideyard facing schemes. The Serena Apartments, Henry Hohauser architect, 1936, plan and axonometric. © Drawing Allan Shulman.

The C-Shape:

C-shaped buildings are located on corners but face the narrower street instead of the more important avenue. The practical reason is that it allows the building frontage to take advantage of the 140' lot depth. The Rapsodi Apartments, L. Murray Dixon architect, 1939, plan and axonometric. © Drawing Allan Shulman.

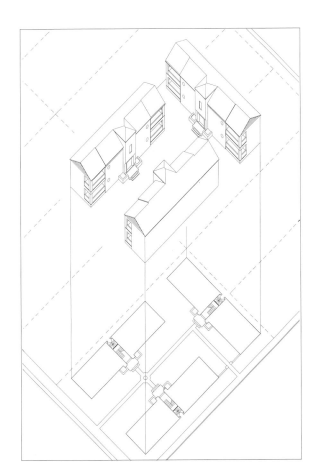

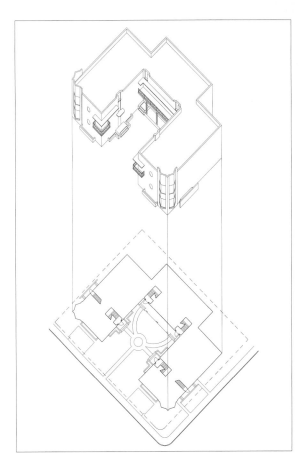

The J-Shape:

J-shaped buildings are similar to L-shaped ones, but one leg is articulated to frontally address the court. J-shaped buildings form either open or closed sideyards.

Top:
The Joy Apartments, L. Murray Dixon architect, 1940.
© L. Murray Dixon Collection, Bass Museum of Art, Miami Beach. Photo Moser & Son.

Right:
The J-Shape. Lot size: 100'x140'. The Joy Apartments, plan and axonometric. © Drawing Allan Shulman.

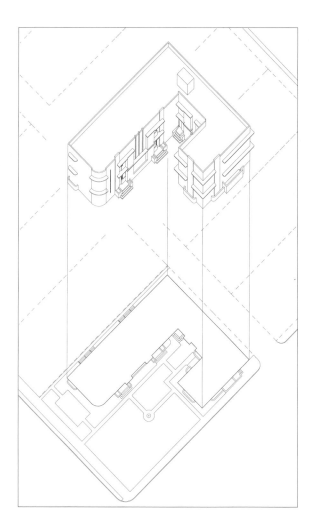

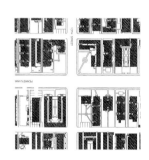

The L-Shape:

The most basic garden court is L-shaped. The two wings of the building create an open frontyard, or shelter a secluded backyard. Invariably located on end lots, they mark the corners with their articulated mass and often with added height. An inversion of the L-shape is found repetitively and almost uniquely on the northeast corners of Collins Avenue. One leg of the "L" projects to the corner while an open east-facing court is formed behind. The projecting corner provides the lobby spaces with multiple exposures on the corner, while the court faces the ocean.

Top:
The Norma-Lee, L. Murray Dixon architect, 1939.
© L. Murray Dixon Collection, Bass Museum of Art, Miami Beach. Photo Moser & Son.

Center left:
Nolli plan of Block 64, between Meridian Avenue, Euclid Avenues, 12th Street and 13th Street. The mirror reflection of the two L-shaped structures creates a localized urban space.
© Drawing Allan Shulman.

Bottom right:
The L-Shape open courtyard type. Lot size: 100'x140'. The Collins Park, Henry Hohauser architect, 1939, plan and axonometric. © Drawing Allan Shulman, Angelica Rohznova.

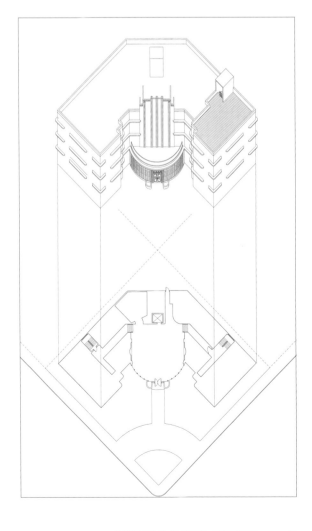

Top left:
The Plymouth Hotel, Anton Skislewicz architect, 1940. Rendering. © Romer Collection, Miami Dade Public Library.

Top right:
The Senator Hotel, L. Murray Dixon architect, 1939. © L. Murray Dixon Collection, Bass Museum of Art, Miami Beach. Photo Moser & Son.

Bottom left:
The L-Shape closed courtyard. Lot size: 100'x140'. The Plymouth Hotel, plan and axonometric. © Drawing Allan Shulman, Angelica Rohznova.

Bottom right:
Inverted L-Shape. Lot size: 100'x140'. The Senator Hotel, plan and axonometric. © Drawing Allan Shulman.

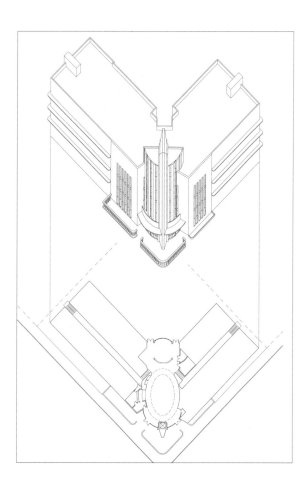

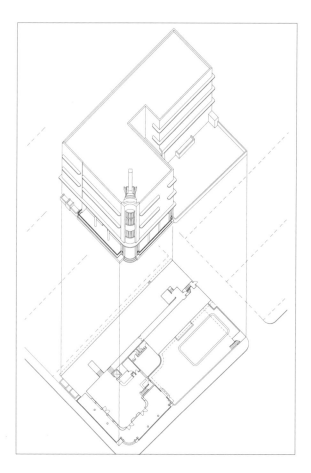

The Tower:

Within the grid, most of the early towers were about eight stories tall. If perpendicular to the avenue, the tower is narrow and deep, simply a vertical extrusion of a typical single-bar type. The building follows the setback of its neighbors and uses the lots on either side to buffer their lower scaled neighbors. If parallel to the avenue, the tower is set further back, providing a generous forecourt with an elaborate entry feature. On ocean facing lots, towers often have an articulated form to maximize ocean front rooms. The larger size of most towers permits a more elaborate development of the sequence and quality of public spaces. Two-story lobbies were typical, usually incorporating a mezzanine permitting both views and a grand entry into the lower lobby.

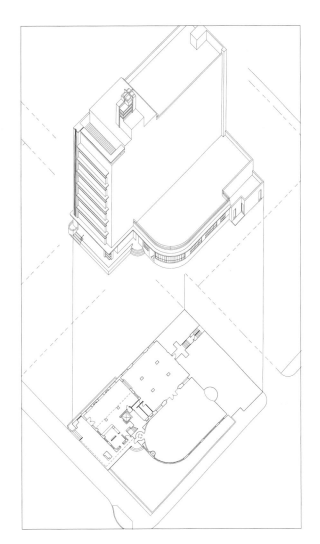

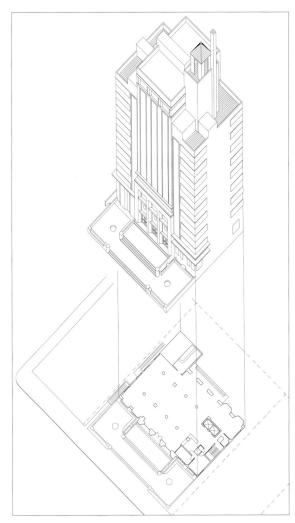

Top left:
The Victor Hotel, plan and axonometric. Lot size: 100'x130'. © Drawing Allan Shulman

Top right:
The Tides Hotel, plan and axonometric. Lot size: 100'x130'. © Drawing Allan Shulman.

Bottom left:
The Victor Hotel, L. Murray Dixon architect. © L. Murray Dixon Collection, Bass Museum of Art, Miami Beach. Photo Moser & Son.

Bottom right:
The Tides Hotel, L. Murray Dixon architect. © L. Murray Dixon Collection, Bass Museum of Art, Miami Beach. Photo Gottscho-Schleisner.

The O-Shape:

O-shaped buildings have completely enclosed courtyards. The fact that they are rare may relate to the disadvantages of this solution in the hot and humid climate. Most O-shaped buildings are in fact open on the ground level, allowing some visual transparency and cross ventilation.

Top:
The 1567-1577 Meridian Avenue Apartments, L. Murray Dixon architect, 1939.
© L. Murray Dixon Collection, Bass Museum of Art, Miami Beach. Photo Moser & Son.

Bottom left:
The O-Shape type. Lot size: 100'x150'. The 1567-1577 Meridian Avenue Apartments, plan and axonometric.
© Drawing Allan Shulman.

Bottom right:
The mixed-use Hybrid type. Lot size: 150'x200'. The Lincoln Center Hotel on Lincoln Road, Igor Polevitzky architect, 1937.
© Drawing Allan Shulman, Hao Shan, Fabrice Kordus.

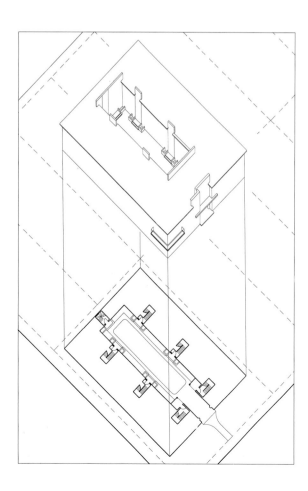

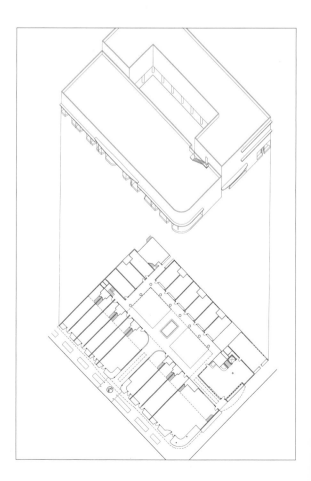

Top & center:
The Lincoln Center Hotel, Igor Polevitzky & Trip Russell, architects, 1937. © Polevitzky Collection, Historic Association of Southern Florida. Photo Gottscho-Schleisner.

Bottom right:
The Albion Hotel, Igor Polevitzky & Trip Russell architects. 1939. © Polevitzky Collection, Historic Association of Southern Florida.

The mixed-use Hybrid:

The intersection of Lincoln Road, a main east-west commercial axis, and of some residential streets produces a hybrid type incorporating hotel and commercial functions around a courtyard-patio. The hardscaped courtyard may serve both as a retail arcade and as an amenity to the hotel. The inclusion of the patio in these mixed-use buildings emphasizes its importance in the urban morphology of Miami Beach.

FROM HELLERAU TO THE BAUHAUS

MEMORY & MODERNITY OF THE GERMAN GARDEN CITY

Jean-François Lejeune

Opposite page:
Aerial photograph of the Hohe Lache Siedlung in Dessau. The Bauhaus building is at the bottom center, facing the residential square, now Bauhausplatz, completed in the 1930s with elegant "Heimat-style" housing bars. The Hohe Lache Siedlung and its octagon square (see plan p. 69) is visible in the upper part of the picture. Photo Archiv Industrieller Gartenreich, 1991. Courtesy Stiftung Bauhaus Dessau.

Top:
Aerial photograph of the Bauhausplatz with the housing bars built in the 1930s. Photo Barthold, 1992. Courtesy Stiftung Bauhaus Dessau.

"Modern buildings—Oswell Blakeston wrote in 1932—call for modern artistic photographs to do them justice." The critic's appeal underscored the necessary condition for the diffusion of the ideology of the new architecture, for "the directness of instrumental realism was as inadequate to the acclaimed new aesthetic of modernist architecture as the blurred mists and shifting foci of pictorialism."[1] Among the many techniques used by the "new photography," the surprising viewpoints, the equal intensity of attention irrespective of the subject, the emphasis on material surface and abstract structure, and more importantly the exclusion of context, were the most effective in conveying the principles of the new architecture. Thus "the machine for seeing" met "the machine for living."[2] Along with Bertolt Brecht who outlined a more political criticism, Walter Benjamin denounced the universalization of this uncritical formalism—his reflection was not specifically addressed to architecture—and argued with premonition against the "creative" principle in photography "which raises every tin can into the realm of the All but cannot grasp any of the human connections that it enters into."[3]

Repeatedly reproduced since the 1920s, the exhilarating photographs of the Bauhaus-Dessau by Lucia and László Moholy-Nagy—to name their most famous authors—were instrumental in establishing the mythical image of the white complex rising, splendidly isolated, out of the countryside. For generations of architects, the urban reality of Gropius' masterpiece was thus ideologically obscured. Its distorted representation—particularly after the 1930s, the dramatic changes brought to the building due to material failure, and its partial destruction in the allied raids—made the analysis of its context a secondary affair, unworthy of attention and scholarship. Hence it is to many visitors' surprise that the reconstructed Bauhaus appears today as a major public building, a truly monumental presence at the heart of a tree-lined residential neighborhood of the 1920-30s; more unexpectedly its workshop wing faces a residential square, now named Bauhausplatz. New research led by scholars at the Stiftung Bauhaus during the early 1990s has shown that this highly contextual relation was not the effect of

chance but of very deliberate urban design decisions that, for the most part, preceded the construction of Gropius' project. Thus the celebrated "open fields" have been hiding a momentous urban history whose traces can be read on contemporary aerial photographs.[4]

Karl Henrici's competition entry of 1890 for the plan of extension of Dessau did not carry the first prize, but it was a foundation stone in German city planning. It was indeed the first urban plan directly inspired by Camillo Sitte's *Der Städtebau nach seinen künstlerichen Grundsätzen*, published one year earlier.[5] Through this competition for a new district to the west of its historic center, the city was eager to recover part of the prestige that it had gained at the end of the 18th century under Prince Friedrich Franz von Anhalt-Dessau (1740-1817)—a prime actor of the *Aufklärung* and sponsor of the first "English landscape" in Germany, the Dessau-Wörlitzer Gartenreich—and that had been damaged by industrialization and the expansion of the workers' quarters. Henrici's project for "an elegant district" was a genuine urban proposal that included a sophisticated network of streets, squares, parks, and public buildings, all arranged according to Sitte's principles of terminated axes, controlled viewpoints, and planned irregularities.[6] Its gridded, picturesque, and multicentered pattern contrasted strongly with most other entries, and among them Joseph Brix's first prize, a "beaux arts" composition focused on a large square straddling the main avenue.

Top:
View of the Bauhaus square from the Bauhaus studios. Photo Jean-François Lejeune, 1995.

Bottom:
Karl Henrici. Projected plan of extension for the city of Dessau, 1890. From Georges Collins & Christiane Craseman Collins, Camillo Sitte: The Birth of Modern City Planning (New York: Rizzoli, 1986). Originally from L'art de Bâtir les Villes. Notes et Réflexions d'un Architecte traduites et complétées par Camille Martin (Genève: Ch. Eggiman & Cie/Paris: H. Laurens, 1902).

No development materialized in the next twenty years and it is eventually in 1924 that Dessau city planner Theodor Overhoff laid out a definitive version of the plan for a middle-class neighborhood. At the center of the new district and at the intersection of the street connecting to the train station, the masterplan included the square proposed by Henrici, Brix, and other competitors. Yet, in the new socio-political context, the city was not eager to see the proposed church as an appropriate catalyst for construction around the square. At the outset of 1925, renewed hopes of development emerged with the end of the economic crisis; at the same time, negotiations were going on for the transfer of the Bauhaus from Weimar—what Schlemmer called "the dance of German cities around the golden Bauhaus."[7] In March Dessau Mayor Hess proposed the affiliation of the Bauhaus to the State Arts and Crafts School, and Gropius' institution was offered the site originally reserved for the church.

Analyzed in relation to this planned environment the siting and design of the building by Gropius, Neufert, and Fieger can be interpreted as a highly contextual response to the particular conditions of the site. In the words of Harald Kegler, "[the Bauhaus building] oddly appeared like a fragment of Henrici's plan. It is not a solitary complex in open land, but a part of a potential new center, which turned away from the old city and oriented itself toward new development."[8]

For the visitors or residents coming from the train station, its bridge-like structure marked the entrance of a new district and brought to mind the memory of the *Torhaus* or gate house, a centuries-old traditional sight of the German city, and a building type that was favored by the Garden City Movement for its picturesque effects. Winfried Nerdinger has shown that Gropius had envisioned a similar concept for an administrative building planned in Berlin for the Sommerfeld group (1920). Facing Asternplatz, the U-shaped complex—to be built in wood and supported by pillars located on the sidewalks—bridged the street as a large expressionist, Frank Lloyd Wright-inspired gatehouse; typologically and urbanistically, this project was an obvious precursor of the Bauhaus.

Another plan, sketched at the Bauhaus-Büro by Carl Fieger in 1928, reveals how strongly the Bauhaus of the early Dessau period remained connected to the urban tradition: it showed a large cultural and sport complex, planned between the Bauhaus and the train station, that recalled both Baroque planning and contemporary urban proposals by Mendelsohn and Poelzig.[9] The fact that Gropius did not emphasize the urban context of his works should not forbid us to underscore the cultural and educational background—the "collective memory"—of the architect and most of its collaborators: the Expressionism, the Werkbund, the theories of Camillo Sitte, and the Garden City. In this context, it is important to recall the extraordinary figure of Theodor Fischer (1862-1938), the architect and urbanist who best synthesized these movements at the outset of the 20th century. He was, as Gabriele Schickel wrote, "the teacher of the avant-garde:" Fred Forbat, Bruno Taut, Eric Mendelsohn, Hugo Häring—to name a few—either worked in his office or were his students in Stuttgart and in Munchen. His influence can be discerned both in the Bauhaus and the other currents of modernity based upon "reform and tradition."[10]

The DGG, the Werkbund, and Camillo Sitte

Although "the union of the Garden City theory with Sittesque street layouts was a natural one for Germany," most writings about Camillo Sitte and his book, including the fundamental work of George and Christiane Collins, have remained silent about the achievements of this timely convergence.[11] Critical figures like Georg Metzendorf, Richard Riemerschmid, Paul Schmitthenner, Heinrich Tessenow, Paul Wolf and many others artisans of the garden city as modern "re-creation" of the German medieval or Baroque town, have generally been ignored whereas Sitte's influence on the metropolitan condition—such as his debate with Otto Wagner and Josef Stübben, Theodor Fischer's plan for Munich, the competition for Groß-Berlin of 1910, etc.—has been studied extensively.[12] Among the few authors to deal with the "suburban" issue, Anthony Sutcliffe has put in parallel the fates of Camillo Sitte's and Ebenezer Howard's books and discussed how their distorted theories eventually merged in the debate on the metropolis. For Sutcliffe, both Sitte and Howard understood that their influence depended on public debate and they did nothing to discourage changes made to their ideas by their followers. Sitte's anti-Haussmanian, "modest, historic, national, moral, and organic" approach could not but encounter the aspirations of the German bourgeoisie

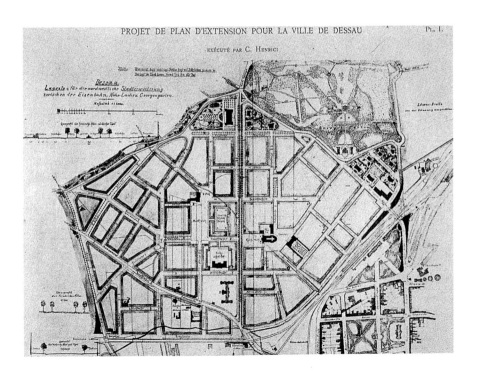

PROJET DE PLAN D'EXTENSION POUR LA VILLE DE DESSAU   Pl. I.

·EXÉCUTÉ PAR C. HENRICI·

for whom "with the economic crisis now behind them…, the obliged model is the medieval city that comforts the bourgeoisie which affirmed its rights during that period." Yet, Sitte's potential as urbanist and theoretician was to be restricted by its own individualism: "Reluctant to restrain, inside the city, the individual freedom and interests, he looked for a structure where attention to particular interests would enable an acceptable level of urban planning. In practice, this strategy would only be possible at the level of the single lot, of the small residential settlement, or of the urban village."[13]

From its foundation in 1902, the Deutsche Gartenstadtbewegung or DGG (German Garden City Movement), the first of its kind outside of England, was marked by a profound dichotomy that made it at once more utopian and more realistic than its English original source. It was not only a breeding ground for socialist, cooperative, and reformist ideals, but also for nationalist, capitalist, and idealized vernacular values.[14]

On the utopian side, the DGG became the point of crystallization of the ideas and ambitions of the *Lebensreform* movement that had developed in Germany since the end of the 19th century. Its center was in Berlin where *Der Neue Gemeinschaft* had been founded in 1880 as a community movement which emphasized the role of the free individual, the rejection of bourgeois values, the pursuit of physical health, and the flight from the city. Among its members was Hans Kampffmeyer (1880-1932), poet and writer, social reformist, economist, but also a student of gardening and landscape architecture who was to become secretary of the DGG in 1907 and its first theoretician. The critic and author Julius Posener, whose exile to England made very familiar with the English context, wrote about the Kampffmeyers: "they were looking for the meaning of life…, they attacked the industrial expansion of Kaiser Wilhelm which was strongly connected to a patriotic vision, and carried through the writings of Naumann and Rohrbach. Thus they were at once more careful and more exalted than their English counterparts: more cautious in facts, more radical in spirit."[15] Another important influence was the utopian socialism of Petr Kropotkin (1842-1921), whose main supporter was Franz Oppenheimer (1864-1943), a strict opponent of Marx's collective socialism, but a passionate advocate of cooperative thinking and production, the Garden City movement, and the "regeneration in the countryside."[16]

All these German movements stressed the need for administrative autonomy, decentralized organization, and an economic model that was alien to profit. Kropotkin's theories included in particular the restoration of craftsmanship as a production system. As an alternative to the metropolis or as a healing solution to it, this ideology of community embodied the *Gesellschaft* against the *Gemeinschaft* in the definition given by Ferdinand Tönnies. In this context, it is bare-

ly surprising that some members of the DGG emphasized the sociological importance of Camillo Sitte's theories of perception of space, as can be witnessed, for instance, in this excerpt from the manifesto written by Hans Kampffmeyer in 1911:

If individual houses in garden cities are placed together in homogeneous groups and road perspectives are created, this is not at all accidental or arbitrary but it is the perceptible expression, become logic, of the existence of a social community…. As in society, the individual has to subordinate his desires to the general will of the group to a certain extent,… just as his house does not wish to detach itself from his neighbor's house but joins with it to form a whole.[17]

On the pragmatic side, the objectives of the German Garden City association were adapted briskly to the national reality and oriented towards the concept of environmental reform rather than Howard's new socio-economic foundations. From the start the Germans included the possibility of expanding the field of application of garden city principles to the improvement of the suburban conditions. In 1909 Hans Kampffmeyer already mentioned in *Die Gartenstadtbewegung* a list of settlement types vaguely inspired from Howard and that could be developed throughout the country: the garden suburb, the garden village, workers' villages near industrial plants, etc. Ebenezer Howard's praise for, and his association with, the industrial new town of Bournville was certainly a factor in the confusion—or more accurately, the pragmatic response—that characterized the German vision. Raymond Unwin, whose book of 1909 *Town Planning in Practice* promoted similar concepts, was another paramount influence.[18]

The immanent contradictions of the movement were clearly reflected in Hellerau, a new urban foundation established from 1906, in the periphery of Dresden, to the plans of Richard Riemerschmid and under the auspices of Carl Schmidt (1856-1934), director of the Deutscher Werkstätten. Extolled as the first German garden city it was in fact a capitalistic enterprise, an improved and civic version of the worker's settlements that had appeared in the late 1800s. Before 1914, more than two thousand workers, many employed in Schmidt's factory, had taken residence in the small town. At the same time Hellerau was being transformed into an intellectual hub that far transcended the urban reality of the place. During the first decade, Dresden was indeed a strategic carrefour of social and urban reforms: it is there that Georg Simmel delivered his lecture *Die Großstädte und das Geistesleben* (1903), that Richard Avenarius created the Dürerbund (1902), and Paul Schultze-Naumburg founded the Deutscher Bund Heimatschutz (1904). In a few years, Hellerau became the home of the Jacques Dalcroze Institute, built by Tessenow in 1910-12, the meeting ground of the *Lebensreform* movement, and the headquarters of the DGG and of the Deutscher Werkbund. Together these

Top:
Richard Riemerschmid. Plan of the garden city of Hellerau (1910-1913). The large building at the bottom right is the factory of the Deutschen Werkstätten; next to the right, the market square; in the upper left area, the Dalcroze Institute. © Kristiana Hartmann. From Julius Posener, Berlin: auf dem Wege zu einer neuen Architektur (München-New York: Prestel, 1979).

Below:
Heinrich Tessenow. Dalcroze Institut, Hellerau (1910-12). Photo Marburg. From Moderne Architektur in Deutschland, 1900-1950. Reform und Tradition (Stuttgart: Hatje, 1992).

Right:
Richard Riemerschmid. Shops on Market square, Hellerau, ca. 1910. Architektur Museum, Technische Universität München, inv. n° 2188. From La Ville (Paris: Editions Centre Pompidou, 1994).

associations "concurred in defining a new culture of the industrial age that aimed at creating a new Heimat for the uprooted masses of the modern society."[19]

Created in 1907 under the impulse of Hermann Muthesius (1861-1927) and Friedrich Naumann (1860-1919), the Werkbund was specifically dedicated to "the ennobling of productive work through the collaboration of art, industry, and handicraft in education, propaganda, and united positions on issues of concern."[20] The history of the German Garden City is in fact inseparable from the Werkbund, as the latter gathered the most important garden city protagonists: Richard Riemerschmid, Theodor Fischer, Fritz Schumacher, Carl Schmidt, Heinrich Tessenow, and Georg Metzendorf were among the founders or members. It is also through the Werkbund and the Deutscher Heimatschutz that Sitte's ideas were to be put into use: Muthesius' endorsement of the Viennese was very influential as were Fischer's and Henrici's, his first followers.

A comparable artistic convergence took place in England between the Garden City and the Arts & Crafts movements. Yet, paradoxically, Raymond Unwin's, Barry Parker's, and Edwin Lutyens' designs for Letchworth, Welwyn and Hampstead Gardens owed more to Christopher Wren and to French classical and Haussmanian urbanism than to the vernacular English village, venerated by the Arts & Crafts. Similarly, Howard's urban image of the Garden City and Camillo Sitte's theories gave way, in Unwin's writings and projects, to a more romantic interpretation that strongly mediated their potent urban connotations through an intensive use of landscape. To the contrary, in Germany, the particular cultural conditions of encounter between Howard's theories, the rampant nationalism, the Werkbund's ideology, and the lessons of Sitte produced a particular type of urban foundation, a genuine revival of the traditional German city as esthetic and sociological archetype. Thus it was in Germany that the Garden City acquired its most urban character.

A detailed spatial analysis reveals that, in spite of their stylistic differences, all German garden cities—from Hellerau to Bruno Taut's Großsiedlungen in Berlin—shared a clear and unique set of urban principles that can be synthesized as follows:

•The spatial definition of the streets relied primarily on buildings, their architecture and height, the repetition and rhythm of elements such as gables, chimneys, staircases, entrance doors, etc. In contrast and in accordance with Sitte, street trees were rare and used only in specific circumstances and for specific spatial effects—in some cases, like at Berlin Britz, an overgrown landscape has actually significantly altered the spatial experience. Most streets were narrow with no or very small setbacks (often paved or defined as courts) even within entirely residential areas. Asymmetrical street sections were usual.

•Housing types were few and strongly standardized, both dimensionally and materially; most houses formed long rows, were attached in groups of two or more, or organized around courtyards. These typologies were directly linked to the German tradition described by Paul Mebes in his best-seller Um 1800 and in Paul Schultze-Naumburg's ten documentary volumes titled Kulturarbeiten.[21]

•Market squares and other public spaces followed the medieval repertory, while some—for instance, of circular form—borrowed to the Baroque models. Main entrances were treated as urban gates, while town walls were often simulated with long, uninterrupted rows of houses along the edges of the district.

•Narrow and deep allotment gardens at the back of houses created a strong rural image and provided substantial support to the family; thus blocks were not continuously built and frequent openings allowed a varied and always changing perception of both worlds: town and countryside.

Georg Metzendorf and Margarethenhöhe

In spite of its "mythical" status, Riemerschmid's Hellerau was neither the first manifestation of garden city principles nor its genuine archetype. On the one hand, the pioneer at reforming industrial workers' housing along the lines of Sitte and the garden suburb was Theodor Fischer, who in 1903 designed the textile

Top right:
Georg Metzendorf. Passage
through the gatehouses leading
to Steiler strasse. From
Brinckmann, A. E., & Georg
Metzendorf, Margarethe Krupp-
Stiftung für Wohnungsfürsorge:
Margarethen-Höhe bei Essen
(Darmstadt: Verlagsansalt
Alexander Koch, 1913).

Bottom left:
Georg Metzendorf. Plan of
Garden City Margarethenhöhe,
Essen, October 1912. In black,
the completed phase in 1912.
From Brinckmann, A. E., &
Georg Metzendorf, op. cit.

Column:
Georg Metzendorf. View of
Steilestraße with house plans
(three attached single-family).
From Brinckmann, A. E., &
Georg Metzendorf, op. cit.

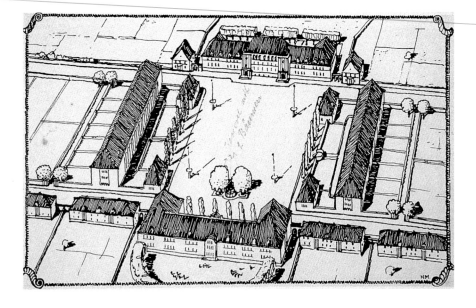

workers' village of Gmindersdorf, Reutlingen in Baden-
Württtenberg. For the first time in Germany, this small
settlement was thought of as a traditional community:
structured along a central axis, it was marked by a market square that led to a semi-circular square with the
village hall in its center *(see p. 63)*. On the other hand,
Hellerau lacked a strong image in plan and its most
idiosyncratic spaces appeared more powerful as parts
than as an urban whole.[22]

It is actually in the Ruhr region that a fundamental step forward was taken in defining the urban model
of an independent and clearly defined garden city.
Initiated as early as 1906, the new district of
Margarethenhöhe was due to the reformist vision of
Margarethe Krupp, window of Friedrich A. Krupp. The
project for the 260-acre site, put in the hands of a
strongly capitalized non-profit foundation, was eventually planned from 1909 and built in phases until the 1934
by a single man: architect, planner, sociologist, and
Werkbund member Georg Metzendorf (1874-1934).[23]

On top of a wooded plateau in the outskirts of
Essen, Metzendorf laid out an organic, distorted grid
whose streets closely followed the contours of the site.
Conceived as a full-fledged town for a socially balanced
population of sixteen thousands, Margarethenhöhe was
circled by a 160-acre natural greenbelt, donated by city
planning director Robert Schmidt, as part of the extensive park system that he established for Essen in collaboration with landscape architect Otto Linne.[24] The
sequence of entrance arriving from Essen brought back
the memory of Bern: A 500-ft long bridge, built in
stone, crossed the greenbelt; on the opposite side,
flights of steps led to a group of houses straddling the
passage like an archway gate toward Steilestraße, a long
winding street of gabled houses leading to the market
square and the church; car and streetcar traffic was
diverted along a 90-ft ring road, whose asymmetrical
section offered simultaneous urban views toward the
town and open perspectives toward the gardens and the

surrounding landscape. In his enthusiastic description
of the Marktplatz—a genuine Baroque arrangement
integrating an inn, rowhouses, a Krupp cooperative
retail building, and freestanding market stalls with
granite columns and curved copper roofs—Albert
Brinckmann showed how Sitte's thesis had permeated
the urbanistic culture: "the square was given such a
dominant composition axis that the streets that pass
alongside it cannot destroy its spatial impression to be
an urban room."[25]

In his own words, Metzendorf had no "intention
to reform the big city." His goals were more modest but
no less critical for the future: "I have not attempted to
experiment with new forms. The modern in the construction of small houses must be grounded in practical
solutions, in specificity, and in simplicity."[26] Behind
the picturesque image Metzendorf concealed a truly
experimental urbanism and typological research. The
whole town was based upon a basic module, a compact
housing unit whose main rooms were organized like a
windmill around a sanitary interior block. Through various methods of rotation, inversion, and assemblage, the
units could be combined to create single or duplex
houses, rows of two or more, with one or two floors indif-
ferently. In addition, doors, windows, and staircases
were also modulated and prefabricated in series. In the
post-war phases of construction, the architect developed a structure of large, organically shaped
superblocks within which he inserted linear groupings
of rowhouses. This system permitted smaller street sections, better traffic control, and complex picturesque
effects, while responding sensitively to the increased
demand for economic standardization.

From Staaken to the Trabantenstadt
Like Margarethenhöhe, Gartenstadt Staaken, a 100-
acre new town west of Spandau was another *gesamtkunstwerk*, built from 1914 to 1917 by a single man,
Paul Schmitthenner (1884-1972). The young architect
and planner had been urbanist of the city of Colmar,
collaborator of Riemerschmid in Hellerau, and designer of the garden city of Carlowitz near Breslau; he was
then commissioned to design three garden cities built in
the 1910s by the Reichminister to support the war
effort: Plaue in Brandenburg, Forstfeld near Kassel and
the largest, Staaken, a cooperative company town for a
armament factory near Berlin.

Often viewed as a 'romantic' medieval plan,
Staaken was in fact more 'modern' than Margarethenhöhe, more rational than Hellerau. Recent scholarship
has shown that the State wanted to build a "model-
Siedlung" that would help establish guidelines for
future projects, not only architecturally and urbanistically but also "from the point of view of the housing
construction standards, the types of financing and types
of organization."[27] The result of a strong geometric diagram and parti, Staaken's plan was somewhat abstract

Right:
Georg Metzendorf. Fountain at
the Market Square,
Margarethenhöhe (1909-1913).
From Brinckmann, A. E., &
Georg Metzendorf, op. cit.

Column:
Georg Metzendorf. Housing
typologies, Margarethenhöhe.
From Brinckmann, A. E., &
Georg Metzendorf, op. cit.

in its collage of juxtaposed urban elements sacrificing the organic quality of the traditional medieval plan to a more functional approach. "The art of building cities was for Schmitthenner an issue of organization": first the natural conditions of the site like creeks, vistas, etc.; then the design of the streets precisely derived from the rationalized selection of typologies and groupings of buildings, the dimension of lots and gardens.[28]

At the heart of the town, Schmitthenner designed a scenographic grouping of squares. The arcaded Marktplatz (market square) was seen as the world of the 'grown-ups' with the administration building, the central stores, the inn, and apartments: a busy and active environment in contrast to the adjacent Kirchplatz (church square), separated from the market by the school's buildings, and dedicated to tranquillity, contemplation, and childrens' play. This highly symbolic organization was to be reinforced by the church, planned on the main axis crossing both plazas but unfortunately never built. Also noteworthy were the multiple *allées* of trees that simulated a greenbelt, the

square-like entrances punctuating the walls of row-houses defining the edges, the interior park integrating a natural pond, and the Sitte-inspired terminated vistas, asymmetrical sections, and 'turbine' squares. The open system of blocks created controlled viewpoints which emphasized the grouping of houses as genuine fragments of medieval cities while always reminding of the rural character of the site and the importance of subsistence gardens for the workers' families.

Schmitthenner single-handedly built more than eight hundred houses, one department store, shops, and two schools—an impressive account that represented eighty per cent of the original plans. Inspired by Tessenow for his careful study of proportions and the progressive level of simplification and abstraction that he applied to his designs, he developed five building types whose geometric combinations, variations in facades and roofs, and sophisticated use of prefabricated parts such as doors and windows made the construction very economical and gave the impression of an even richer variety than at Hellerau. In Staaken like in

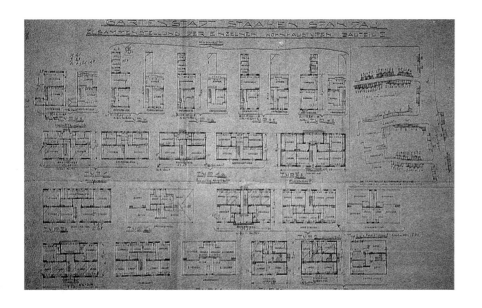

Margarethenhöhe, the handling of grouped houses was particularly inventive and followed a method of composition that Karl Kiem compared to "the writing of Baroque music:"

The house types are the notes and the groups of houses are the chords. The organization of the groups form the motifs and the specific zones of houses become the different movements.[29]

One typical solution was the 'four-house group.' such a group displayed one double street entrance in the center, whereas the two endhouses were accessed on the side or at the back through a garden gate opening on the street. This made for an elegant composition directly inspired from the 18th century baroque architecture, a villa-like yet truly proletarian type of house popularized through the above-mentioned books by

Mebes and Schultze-Naumburg. As for the rows of gabled houses facing the Marktplatz and other streets and squares, their effect was spectacularly urban and recalled both the traditional medieval city and the nearby Dutch district in Potsdam.

Staaken's military origin has long tarnished its reputation, while Schmitthenner's ambiguous stand for a traditionalist modernity at the outset of the Third Reich unjustly curtailed an exceptional career. Yet, at the time, the lessons of Staaken were not lost. Not only did it directly influence important realizations such as Tempelhofer Feld by Fritz Bräuning (1919-28), and Martin Wagner's first Siedlung of Lindenhof also in Berlin (1919-21), but it also helped, along with other similar experiments, to re-ignite the debate about the post-war metropolis. In 1918 Franz Oppenheimer

apologetically described Staaken as "a home for the returned warrior,... the big solution to calm down shattered nerves, to heal the sick lungs, to procure help and occupation to the crippled, to give hope and happiness to the disabled, the wounded, the widows, and the orphans."[30] Oppenheimer's exalted style was but one particular expression of the German defeat and of the deep crisis that shook the intellectual classes and their industrial vision of progress: "let us build small houses with gardens in ownership. But not only for the invalids, for the whole German people."[31]

A key spokesman of this 'heroic' period, Heinrich Tessenow saw the first world war as a direct consequence of the industrial urbanization; in *Handwerk und Kleinstadt*, he developed the themes of the artisanal community and of the small town "as points of equilibrium between the ills of the metropolis and the nostalgia of the rural village."[32] At the same time, Muthesius discussed the benefits of the "small house and Siedlung" (*Kleinhaus und Kleinsiedlung*), while Bruno Taut published his utopian visions of *Die Stadtkrone* (1916-8) and *Die Auflösung der Städte* (1920). In these books Taut "saw the planning of the whole earth itself as a purely artistic task" and imagined a network of new

urban communities, designed as garden cities, self-governed, and disseminated all across the land.[33]

Less utopian, more operational, but equally critical of the metropolis of unlimited growth was the concept of the Trabantenstadt—city of cities—that Paul Wolf theorized in 1919 and that had been prefigured by Arminius in 1874 and by Schmitthenner & Langen's competition entry (1916) for the extension of Soest. Perfected by Ernst May in Frankfurt, this global planning strategy for the creation of a polycentric metropolitan structure, based upon the small town or independent urban entity, was empirically adopted by Fritz Schumacher in Hamburg and Köln and by Martin Wagner (1885-1957) in Berlin.[34]

Bruno Taut, Ernst May, Fritz Schumacher

Bruno Taut (1880-1938) was the most important link between the pre-war garden city movement and its postwar revival during the Weimar Republic: Julius Posener rightly saw in his Berlin Siedlungen the apotheosis of the movement. Taut's flair for streets and squares layouts, his admiration for Sitte, his talent to comprehend both the "whole" and the "parts," his attention to building types and to the expression of materials went straight

Top:
Martin Wagner. Aerial view of Siedlung Lindenhof, Berlin-Schöneberg, ca. 1918. From Manfredo Tafuri, The Sphere and the Labyrinth (Cambridge-London: MIT Press, 1987; original edition Torino: Einaudi Editore, 1980.

Bottom:
Paul Schmitthenner. Plan of the garden city of Staaken. From Oppenheimer, Franz, & Fritz Stahl, op. cit.

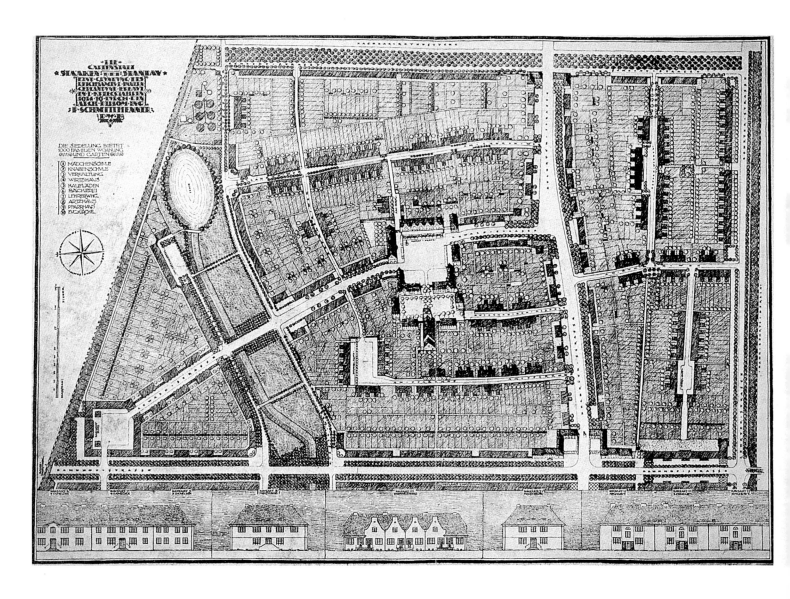

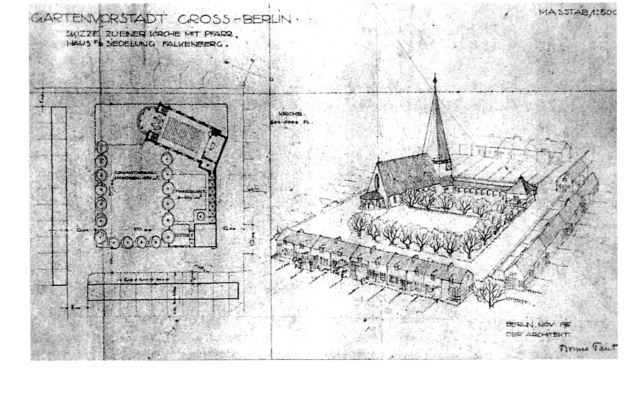

back to Fischer for whom he worked from 1904 to 1908.[35] The master's unrelenting belief in the reconciliation of tradition and modernity profoundly influenced Taut who, as late as 1938, declared in Istanbul that:

All my works…can be traced back to my first two commissions, which I obtained through the recommendation of my highly esteemed master Theodor Fischer: the renovation of the gothic church in Württemberg and the turbine hall for the iron works of Harkort in Wetter an der Ruhr. That is to say, on the one hand, adaptation to the old building traditions, and on the other hand, architectonic solutions to the modern industrial functions…What we must look for is the synthesis between the old tradition and the modern civilization.[36]

It is clearly this aspiration to synthesis that explained the very strong continuity in the vision—and in the formal vocabulary—of the new cities that Taut developed from 1910 to 1930. From his first garden city at Falkenberg in Berlin-Grünau—a genuine cooperative enterprise commissioned in 1913 by the Gemeinnützige Baugenossenschaft Gartenvorstadt Gross-Berlin—to the Berlin Großsiedlungen built in collaboration with Martin Wagner, Taut's "analogous German cities" powerfully married the traditional elements of town design with the resources of the landscape.[37] In the first project for Falkenberg, a long Baroque *allée* was to structure the main public elements of the community, whereas at the Hufeisensied-lung (Horseshoe-Siedlung) these fragments of the 'urban and the rural' were tied together through Leberecht Migge's garden design. The unbuilt Ledigenheim (1915) recalled the Baroque squares of Nancy, but Taut used shifts of axis and distorted symmetries to create genuine public spaces like the Akazienhof at Falkenberg (1913-14),

the enclosed square at Freie Scholle (1924-32), or the housing groups at Onkel-Toms-Hütte Wald Siedlung (1926-32) that he modeled on Mebes' and Emmerick's nearby Gartenstadt Zehlendorf (1912 onward). It is also in Falkenberg that Taut first applied his idiosyncratic use of colors in order to personify the standardized houses and to 'modernize' their vernacular-inspired typological traits.[38] At the heart of Britz, the horseshoe illustrated his love of community-related symbolic forms displayed in *Die Stadtkrone* but it also echoed the crescent that he helped design in Fischer's office for the Siedlung Gmindersdorf; similarly the fascinating but unbuilt expansion project Britz III (1927) would have demonstrated his talent at creating a genuine urban center, with an elegantly long market square terminated at both ends by a school and a *Volkshaus* (People House).

Taut came dangerously close to the dissolution of urban space, for instance in the latest phase of Britz (1931), but it is in Ernst May's *Neues Frankfurt* that the model of the garden city was further recast, and ultimately destroyed, through a series of "dialectic experiments." These aimed at demonstrating that, in Tafuri's words, "no contradiction existed among the rationalization of production, the full assumption of technical reproducibility and the enhancement of the characteristics of the site." Influenced by Sitte, Fischer, and Unwin with whom he worked at Letchworth, May (1886-1970) used "controlled surprises" to show that "the infinite capacity of the 'type' to vary while remaining itself."[39] This intellectual game quickly degenerated, from the spatial inventions of the Siedlungen Bornheimer Hang (first plan, 1926), Römerstadt (1927-29), and Bruchfeld-straße (1926-27) to the inhuman rigidity of Praunheim (1926-30) and Westhausen (1929-31).

In tragic contrast to Taut's, Wagner's and May's, Fritz Schumacher's fame—Lewis Mumford mentioned him in *The Culture of Cities* (1938) as one of the grand "innovators" of the century on a par with Berlage, Behrens, etc.—hardly survived the ideological turmoil of the post-war era and his 'rehabilitation' has been relatively recent. In the context of this essay, it is sufficient to outline how Schumacher, strongly influenced by Georg Simmel, succeeded in reconciling Sitte's objectives with the reality of the metropolis. In the words of historian Hartmut Frank:

Schumacher made a definitive step forward when he defined and based the design of his public spaces, still very artistically defined, on precise typological studies of housing. Common to him and to Sitte was the hope to lift the heterogeneity of the modern city to a new level of harmony. Whereas the Viennese architect intended to salvage the manageable, Biedermeyer-like city, Schumacher advocated and demonstrated that it was possible to equally rescue the Moloch, torn by social conflicts, that was the metropolis.[40]

It is in Hamburg, where he was director of building and planning from 1909 to 1933, that he implemented his theory. In opposition to Henrici and others who wanted to "break" the metropolis apart and reorganize it in small villages, Schumacher adopted Simmel's positive interpretation of the metropolis and advocated a coherent vision, both at the large and the small scale. The hundreds of public buildings, schools, monuments, Siedlungen, and parks that he planned, built, or helped to build, literally transformed Hamburg into "a social and esthetic total work of art" or *sozial gesamtkunstwerk*.[41] During these years Schumacher was able to culturally control the process of metropolitan growth and to give it a specific identity. The use of brick—that he recommended since 1901 as a response to the aspirations of the Heimatschutz—was responsible for a genuine regional and metropolitan architecture. Based upon the Hanseatic tradition but liberated from its gothic association, the brick became the unifier of all architectural expressions. Schumacher's, Gerson's, and Ostermeyer's works in Jarrestadt (1927-30) or the

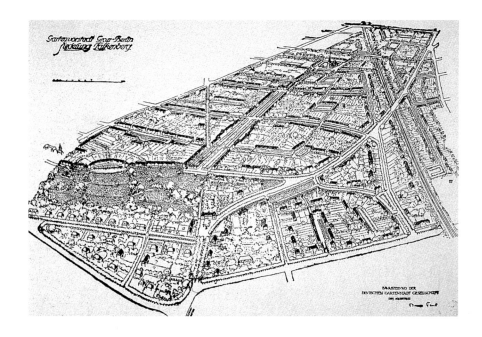

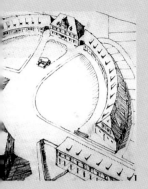

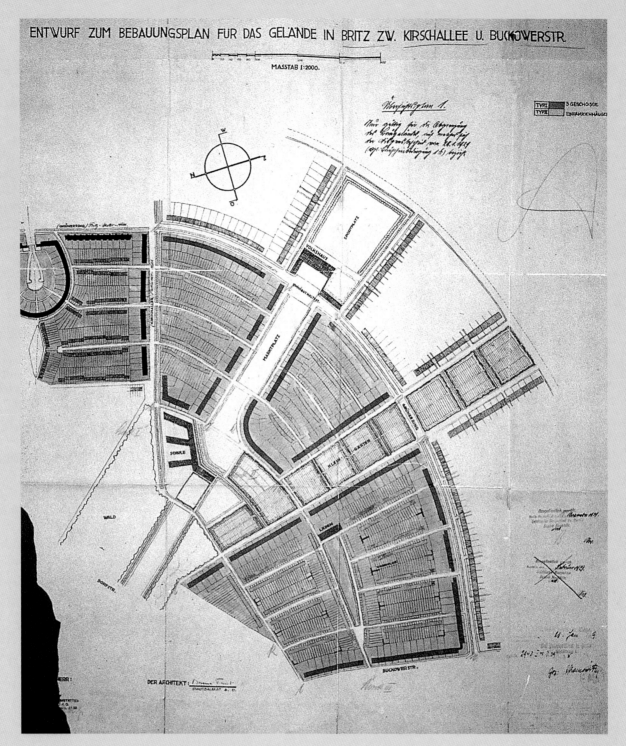

Top right:
Bruno Taut. Project "Britz III"
for the extension of the
Hufeisensiedlung, 1926.
© Akademie der Künste. From
Vier Berliner Siedlungen der
Weimarer Republik: Britz-Onkel
Toms Hütte-Siemenstadt-
Weiße Stadt (Berlin: Argon
Verlag, 1984).

Top left:
Theodor Fisher. Siedlung
Gmindersdorf in Reutlingen
(1903-1915): aerial view of the
Altenhof. From Moderne
Architektur in Deutschland,
1900-1950. Reform und
Tradition, op. cit.

Bottom left:
Bruno Taut (with Leberecht
Migge, landscape architect).
Britz (Hufeisensiedlung), play-
ground park at Minningstraße.
© Photo Köster, Akademie der
Künste. From Vier Berliner
Siedlungen, op. cit.

Bottom right:
Bruno Taut. Schollenhof at
Siedlung Freie Scholle, Berlin-
Tegel, 1924-32. © Photo
Köster, Akademie der Künste,
Berlin. From Vier Berliner
Siedlungen, op. cit.

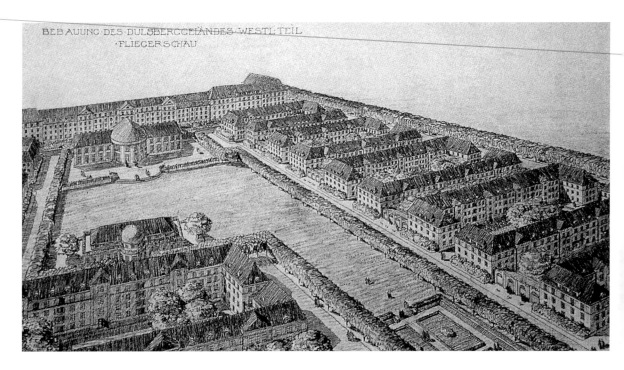

BEBAUUNG·DES·DULSBERGGELÄNDES·WESTL·TEIL
·FLIEGERSCHAU·

Dulsberg-Siedlung (1919-31) were often typologically identical to Gropius' or Taut's; but built in brick, their housing bars were incompatible with the Zeitgeist and the "Red Hamburg" was ostracized by the "orthodox" historians.[42] As shown here, Schumacher's revised project for Siedlung Dulsberg was a surprising encounter between a very rational, quasi-modernistic urban layout, and a strongly traditional architecture. Interestingly, the changes in architecture styles that took place along the twelve years of construction barely impacted the spatial quality of the place.

Walther Rathenau, & the *Industrielles Gartenreich*

Until recently, historians have erroneously associated Dessau's entry into modernity with the arrival of the Bauhaus and its protagonists. In fact, from the end of the 19th century onward the region played a pioneering role in the construction of modern industry, economy, and urbanism in Central Germany. Among the key figures were the industrialist, philosopher and statesman Walter Rathenau (1867-1922), the aviation industry founder Hugo Junkers (1859-1935), city planners Gustav Langen and Stephan Prager, landscape architect Leberecht Migge (1881-1935), industrial architects Werner Issel and Georg Klingenberg, Adolf Loos' disciple Leopold Fischer, and the "other Modern" Swiss-born architect and urbanist Otto Rudolf Salvisberg (1882-1940). It is in the periphery of Wittenberg, that the latter designed one of the most accomplished garden cities of the period (1916-18).[43] Built like Staaken by and for the State to house workers of a war-time factory, the Piesteritz Siedlung was the brainchild of Walther Rathenau, son of Emil Rathenau the founder of AEG, and one of the few German industry leaders who realized that governmental direction of the nation's economic resources would be crucial for victory in the

first World War.[44] Walther Rathenau's role at the head of the War Department was a spin-off—a paradoxical one in light of his anti-militarist philosophy—of his advocating, from around 1910, plans for a collective economy (*Gemeinwirtschaft*) based upon state-regulated private enterprises. His experience of ruthless capitalist competition lived in Bitterfeld led him in *Zur Kritik der Zeit* (1912), and in his other books *Mechanisierung des Geistes* (1913) and *Von kommenden Dingen* (1917), to denounce the negative consequences of industrialization on society and culture, and to attempt at resolving that contradiction without abandoning capitalist principles.[45]

Georg Haberland—a businessman and owner of several housing companies in and around Berlin, who had also supervised the construction of Staaken—and Friedrich Gerlach, former planning director of Berlin Schöneberg, planned the Siedlung at its outset. The model for Piesteritz was the *Randbebauung* or superblock, i.e., a large block designed like a Sittesque little town, complete with its streets, public buildings and squares, and fully surrounded by a continuous wall of apartment houses, accessible through limited entries. This urban alternative to the *Mietkaserne* had been defined by Unwin and Stübben, and seductively drawn by Bruno Möhring, Rudolf Eberstadt, and Richard Petersen in their entry to the Competition for Groß-Berlin of 1910. It was first successfully applied by Paul Wolf (1879-1957) for the Ceciliengärten neighborhood (planned in 1912 and built in the 1920s) and in the same years by Haberland himself for the Rheinische Viertel.[46] Piesteritz's suburban adaptation of this concept was a masterpiece: the 470 houses, town hall, school, churches, and gatehouses were designed and built by Salvisberg as a small town surrounded by a quasi-continuous row of houses. Its plan blent both

Fritz Schumacher. Siedlung Dulsberg-Gelände, Hamburg-Barmbek. Street view. Photo Paolo Rosselli. From Abitare 289 (July-August 1991).

From top to bottom:
Fritz Schumacher. Approved masterplan for Siedlung Dulsberg-Gelände, Hamburg-Barmbek (1916-1919). From Moderne Architektur in Deutschland, 1900-1950. Reform und Tradition, op. cit.

Fritz Schumacher. Redesigned masterplan for Siedlung Dulsberg-Gelände, Hamburg-Barmbek (1916-1919, as built 1919-1931). From: Ibidem.

medieval and Baroque features. The three interconnected squares and the entry sequence from the main gate houses formed the most remarkable spaces of this "small town utopia" where, through a sophisticated use of types and historical references, "all parts tell, in a certain way, a social story."[47] Salvisberg's most distinctive project after Piesteritz-Wittenberg was the Weiße Stadt Siedlung (Berlin, 1929-31). Its plan for thirteen hundred apartments distributed in three- and four-story bars was determinedly metropolitan in character; a long and thin housing block bridging over Schiller Promenade marked the district's entrance as a modernist gateway that cannot but recall the Bauhaus Dessau.

Piesteritz was but one of a score of Siedlungen developed in the triangle Wittenberg-Bitterfeld-Dessau by Gardern City associations and industry giants such as AEG, Bitterfeld Elektro-Chemie, and film manufacturer AGFA. The most suggestive of the industrial villages was undoubtedly Zschornewitz (1919-20), built in the awesome shadow of the largest AEG powerhouse in Central Germany. Its garden city layout and "heimatschutz" square and streets were the works of Georg von Mayenburg.[48] Located in Dessau, bordering on the Bauhaus-platz, the Siedlung Hohe Lache was another astonishing Siedlung, a genuine and abstract encounter between the "urban" and the "rural," between pure urban forms as fragments and the cultivated garden as potent symbol of the self-sufficiency goals of the workers' housing movement. Designed by Theodor Overhoff from 1919, it was completed around 1926 in collaboration with Leberecht Migge for the layout of collective and private gardens.[49] Its plan was based upon a series of urban moments: the U-shaped entrance plaza, the Lindenplatz defined by four long buildings with arcaded ground floors, the "street of gables," the elliptical square (unfortunately unbuilt), and the spectacular *Achteck*, a totally enclosed octagon with two symmetrical gates, whose "metaphysical" quality was best observed from a Junkers plane or along the "medieval" sequence of access from the adjacent streets to its center.

Not surprisingly it was also in Dessau that Leberecht Migge associated with Leopold Fischer reinterpreted the tradition of garden design and realized his project of "Selbstversorgung-Siedlung" (self-sufficient Siedlung). The ninety-one double houses and large subsistence gardens of Dessau-Ziebigk, built far from the city like a modern *castrum* on a grid of parallel streets, were part of Migge's vision of "German inner colonization." In construction at the same time than Gropius' Törten, Leopold Fischer's starkly Loosian but traditionally built volumes were, like all "non-Bauhaus" experiments in the region, the victims of the exclusive modernist propaganda and its bias for mechanization.[50]

Following the German reunification of 1989-90, the *Industriell Gartenreich* and its many communities struggle for survival, amidst a lunar landscape of abandoned powerhouses and factories, coal mines craters,

and lakes of contaminated dust. Irony of history, the Bauhaus has now become—under its third director Rolf Kuhn—an avant-garde center for environmental reform. It devotes most of its forces to the unprejudiced preservation of the pre-war industrial and housing heritage of the region while attempting to construct the "third landscape" of Prince Franz's Gartenreich.

Handwerk und Kleinstadt in Weimar

Gropius' first experience with urban planning was in Weimar, immediately after his nomination at the head of the Bauhaus. In the manifesto of April 1919, he demanded a new cooperative living arrangement for teachers and students, coupled with opportunities for theater and music buildings. He envisioned the concept of a Bauhaussiedlung where, along the argument of Tessenow in *Handwerk und Kleinstadt*, the students would "learn how to build…learn it concretely, with the hands, executing carpentry and other types of work." The first but failed project designed in 1920 by Bauhaus student Walter Determann resembled a large campus whose colorful wood houses were symmetrically organized along an axis: its beaux arts reminiscences were tempered by an expressionistic use of the ground and a Taut-inspired glass-pyramid.[51]

It was Fred Forbat, a former student of Theodor Fischer, who was put in charge of the new project. At Am Horn, a hilly site overlooking the Park an der Ill, Forbat and Gropius planned a small village whose plan combined both the principles of standardization and a typical Sittesque design. The heart of the Siedlung, laid out for about four hundreds residents, was a triangular plaza bordered on two sides by eighty students houses in the form of three- to five-story bars; a tower marked the entrance of the square whose third side, occupied by nineteen detached houses, opened to the landscape and the slopy terrain reserved for cultivation. A bridge-gate connected the plaza to a L-shape structure made up of two streets lined with fifty-three rowhouses carefully laid out in the spirit of the garden city tradition. On the eastern edge the plan included an area dedicated to workshops that Farkas Molnár rendered as Bruno Taut's "crown of the city" over Weimar. One prototype of detached house, built by Georg Muche and financed by Adolf Sommerfeld on the basis of Forbat's sketches for the Bauhaus exhibition of 1923, was the lone reminder of this *gesamtkunstwerk*: its plan showed a Palladian inspired U-structure around a central, barrel-vaulted square living area.[52]

In comparison with Am Horn, the four master houses built in Dessau on the edge of the Siedlung Hohe Lache formed a pale and urbanistically uninspired grouping—a suburban anomaly. Their luxurious and spacious setting, that was criticized by both students and young faculty, formed a striking contrast with the tight and problematic domestic spaces of the Siedlung Törten (1926-28). In actuality, the interest

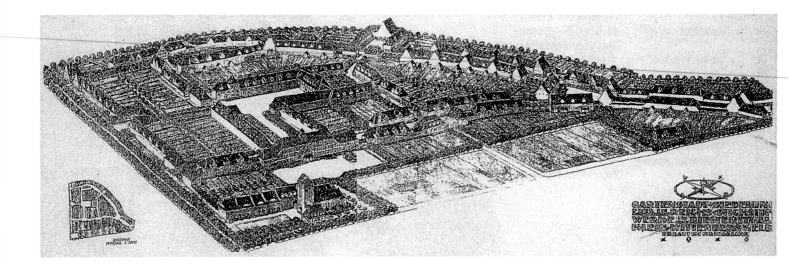

Top:
*Otto Rudolf Salvisberg.
Isometric view of Piesteritz
(1916). © Archiv Piesteritzer
Stickstoffwerke AG. From
Harald Kegler,* Die Piesteritzer
Werkssiedlung *(Dessau, 1992).*

*Otto Salvisberg. Square in
Piesteritz. From* Otto Rudolph
Salvisberg (1882-1940): Die
andere Moderne *(Zürich, gta
Verlag, 1985).*

Bottom:
*Bruno Möhring, with Rudolf
Eberstadt, Richard Petersen.
Competition entry for Groß-
Berlin (1910), Et in terra pax."
View of a superblock. From*
Deutsches Bauzeitung 29, *1910.*

and quality of the Törten Siedlung resided in its ingenious urban design. Noteworthy were its concentric, fan-shaped network of streets, the pedestrian paths meandering through the blocks, the Sittesque method of setting back or pushing forward houses to mark street entrances and other spatial moments, and especially, the four-story mixed-use cooperative building, another reminder of Taut's drawings in *Die Stadtkrone*.

Back from Törten and at the end of this long journey, we turn once again the corner of Bauhausplatz to discover the "reef gently lapped by a placid tide."[53] What is most extraordinary about the Bauhaus is how urban the building is. Consider, for instance, how the short section of street created by the two parts of the building—now transformed into a small piazza—and the two entrances and glass-enclosed staircases facing each other bring to mind Vasari's Uffizi in Florence; the sophisticated use of setbacks along the streets; the bridge that offers protection from the sun and the rain; the transparent studios, illuminated at night, facing the square across the avenue; or the steep outdoors staircase that provides entry to the housing tower, magnifying its height and forcing the visitor to look up. In such a context, "the importance of the diagonal views of the Bauhaus" mentioned by Colin Rowe and emphasized by the "new photography" discussed at the outset of this essay, can even be construed as a final expressionist move, the ultimate demonstration of the collective memory of *Die Gestalt der deutschen Stadt* before the advent of the "New Man" and the surrender to the Taylorist dreams of urban mechanization *(see pp. 126-127)*.[54] At the time of the competition for Dammerstock Siedlung in Karlsruhe (1929), Taut and Martin Wagner accused Gropius of avoiding the main issue: "The agenda is not to enlarge windows and save space, but to increase the buying power of families by lifting their income and reducing the price of housing.... Moreover the lowering of rents depends more of the interest rates than of the costs of construction."[55] The "modernist" critic Adolf Behne echoed these comments and added: "The whole district seems to be on railroad tracks;...to put men mechanically in boxes is not urbanism."[56]

1. Quoted by Terry Smith, "Pure Modernism and Co," *Making the Modern: Industry, Art, and Design in America* (Chicago-London: The University of Chicago Press, 1993): 402. Oswell Blakeston's quote is in "Still Camera Today," *Architectural Review* 71 (April 1932):154.

2. Terry Smith, op. cit.: 402. For another vision of modernity, see Andrew Higgott, "Reflecting the New, the Architectural Photography of Frank Yerbury 1920-1935," *Composición Arquitectonica* 3 (June 1989): 5-38.

3. Walter Benjamin, "A Short History of Photography," translation by Phil Patton of "Kleine Geschichte der Photographie," *Litterarische Welt*, Sept. 18, 25, and Oct. 2, 1931.

4. I am indebted to Rolf Kuhn, Harald Kegler, and their collaborators at the Stiftung Bauhaus Dessau for their help during my stays at the Bauhaus in November 1992 and May-June 1995. See also Harald Kegler, "Ort und Auftrag," *Bauhaus Dessau: Dimensionen 1925-1932* (Dessau: Bauhaus Dessau, 1993): 22-31; on the reconstruction of the Bauhaus, see Ralf Koerner, *The Bauhaus building at Dessau. Architecture-Symbol-Myth-Architecture,.* Master of Art Thesis, University of Miami, 1994.

5. George R. Collins & Christiane Crasemann Collins, *Camillo Sitte: The Birth of Modern City Planning* (New York: Rizzoli, 1986): chapter 8.

6. On Dessau and the Gartenreich, see *Weltbild Worlitz: Entwurf einer Kulturlandschaft* (Stuttgart : G. Hatje, 1996); and Regina Bittner, Heike Brückner, Harald Kegler, et. al., *Bauhaus Dessau: Industrielles Gartenreich Dessau-Bitterfeld-Wittenberg* (Berlin-Dessau: Stiftung Bauhaus Dessau, 1996). On the competition, see Gehrard Fehl, "Sitte ed Henrici: il principio dell'individualità," *Camillo Sitte e i suoi interpreti* (Milano: Franco Angeli, 1992): 73; Karl Henrici, *Konkurrenzentwurf der nordwestlichen Stadterweiterung von Dessau* (Aachen, 1890).

7. Oskar Schlemmer, in C. Kutschke, *Bauhausbauten der Dessauer Zeit* (Weimar, 1981): 19. Quoted by Harald Kegler, op. cit., p. 24.

8. Kegler, op. cit., 24.

9. Winfried Nerdinger, *Walter Gropius: Opera Completa* (Milano: Electa, 1988; Bauhaus-Archiv & Harvard University, 1985): 69-71. For Fieger's urban plan, see Kegler, op. cit., 24-25. In contrast, later projects by Hilbersheimer and Fieger (1930) proposed the destruction of the center of Dessau.

10. Gabriele Schickel, "Theodor Fischer als Lehrer der Avantgarde," *Moderne Architektur in Deutschland, 1900-1950. Reform und Tradition* (Stuttgart: Verlag Gert Hatje, 1992): 55-68. On these influences on Gropius, see Julius Posener, *From Schinkel to the Bauhaus: Five Lectures on the Growth of Modern German Architecture* (New York: Wittenborg, 1972). On page 44, he recalls how he found, in the Berlin Senate Library, a book on the English Garden City whose first owner was Gropius (1911).

Below:
Paul Wolf. Housing development Ceciliengärten, Berlin (project, 1912; built in 1925 in a different style). Originally published in In der Ceciliengärten (Berlin). From 750 Jahre Architektur und Städtebau in Berlin (Stuttgart: Hatje, 1987).

From top right to bottom:

Otto Rudolf Salvisberg. Weiße Stadt, Berlin: bridgehouses over Aroser Allee, view from the north and the south, 1930. © Bauwelt 1930, H. 48. From Vier Berliner Siedlungen der Weimarer Republik, op. cit.

Otto Rudolf Salvisberg, with Friedrich Gerlach, architects. Siedlung of the Nitrate Company Piesteritz, near Wittenberg (1916-1919). Photo Volker Bartholdt.

Walter Gropius & Fred Forbat. Masterplan of the Bauhaussiedlung at Weimar "Am Horn," 1922. © Busch-Reisinger Museum, Harvard University, Gropius Archives.

11. Georges Collins & Christiane Crasemann Collins, op. cit., p. 110.

12. These names did not appear in George & Christiane Collins most extensive reference bibliography and index to date. At the international conference, held at the University of Venice on the 100th anniversary of Sitte's book in 1990, Gerhard Fehl, Guido Zucconi, Anthony Sutcliffe mentioned Sitte's impact on the garden city, but no complete essay was dedicated to it. See the proceedings by Guido Zucconi, *Camillo Sitte e i suoi interpreti*, op. cit. For more, see the new generation of monographs by Marco De Michelis, *Heinrich Tessenow, 1876-1950* (Milano: Electa, 1991); Winfried Nerdinger, *Theodor Fisher: architetto e urbanista, 1862-1938* (Milano: Electa, 1990); Winfried Nerdinger, *Richard Riemerschmid: vom Jugendstil zum Werkbund* (Munchen: Prestel, 1982). The more complete compilation on the garden city is by Gabriele Tagliaventi (editor), *Garden City: a century of theories, models, experiences* (Roma: Gangemi Editore, 1994); see also in this book Gabriele Tagliaventi's essay, "The romantic tradition in XXth century urbanism," 35-64.

13. Anthony Sutcliffe, "La diffusione delle teorie sittiane: un'ipotesi per definirne lo sfondo," *Camillo Sitte e i suoi interpreti*, op. cit., 99-108.

14. The reference for the DGG is Kristina Hartmann's dissertation *Die städtebauliche Konzeption der Deutschen Gartenstadtbewegung* (Berlin, 1977). I have used Julius Posener's synthesis in *Berlin: auf dem Wege zu einer neuen Architektur* (München: Prestel, 1979): 264-288.

15. Julius Posener, op. cit., 265-6.

16. Julius Posener, op. cit., 265-6. See also Emanuel Tal, "The Garden City Idea as Adopted by the Zionist Establishment," *Social utopias of the Twenties: Bauhaus, Kibbutz and the Dream of the New Man* (Dessau: Stiftung Bauhaus, 1995): 64-71. Oppenheimer was one of the instigators of the garden city as model for the new settlements in Palestine in the 1920-30s.

17. Hans Kampffmeyer, "Die Bedeutung der wirtschaflichen und sozialen Grundlagen der Gartenstadt für den Städtebau," in Keller, Wagner, Osthaus, Kampffmeyer, *Bauordnung und Bebauungsplan, ihre Bedeutung für die Gartenstadtbewegung* (Berlin: report of the DGG conference, 1911), quoted by Kristiana Hartman in: "Garden Cities' Experiences in Germany," *Garden City:...*, op. cit.: 270. Ferdinand Tönnies' book (1855-1936) was titled *Gesellschaft und Gemeinschaft: Abhandlung des Communismus und des Socialismus als empirischer Kulturformen* (Leipzig: Fues's Verlag,1887).

18. Hans Kampffmeyer, *Die Gartenstadtbewegung* (Leipzig, 1909): 13-14. From Julius Posener, op. cit.: 266.

19. From Hartmut Frank, "La metropoli come opera d'arte totale e sociale. Il caso di Schumacher ad Amburgo e Colonia," *Camillo Sitte e i suoi interpreti*, op. cit: 213-220. The word *Heimat* is hard to translate: "Home" or "genius loci" in the large sense is probably the closest. Hartmut Frank gives the etymology of the word in Indo-European root *khei* that means a place where one makes its camp, settles. In its contemporary sense it means a place where one lives but it also involves more than the human, such as the environment, the landscape. It also indicates the sentimental qualities of the place (*genius loci*) and the concept of melancholy contained in the word nostalgia (*nostos*: return to home, *algos*: pain, sorrow). In the 1930s it acquired a negative resonance from Nazi abuse of the concept.

20. From the Satzung des DWB 1908, Deutscher Werkbund, *Die Veredlung der gewerblichen Arbeit in Zusammenwirken von Kunst, Industrie und Handwerk* (Leipzig: R. Voigtländer, [1908]). The founders included twelve firms and twelve artists and architects who were: Peter Behrens, Theodor Fischer, Josef Hoffmann, Wilhelm Kreis, Max Laüger, Adelbert Niemeyer, Josef Olbrich, Bruno Paul, Richard Riemerschmid, J.J. Scharvogel, Paul Schultze-Naumburg, Fritz Schumacher. For a succinct presentation, see Stanford Anderson, "Peter Behrens, Friedrich Naumann, and the Werkbund: Ideology in Industriekultur," *The Architecture of Politics: 1910-1940* (Miami-Genova: The Wolfsonian, 1995): 8-21.

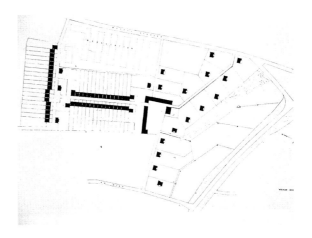

Leopold Fischer and Leberecht Migge. Landscape housing Siedlung Dessau-Ziebigk (1926-28). Photo Junkers-Luftbild-Zentrale, 1921. From Social utopias of the Twenties: Bauhaus, Kibbutz and the Dream of the New Man (Dessau: Stiftung Bauhaus, 1995).

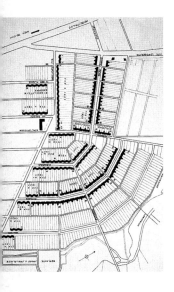

Top:
Walter Gropius. Plan of Törten Siedlung in Dessau (1926-28). From Social utopias of the Twenties, op. cit.

Bottom:
Walter Gropius. Consumer's Club (Konsumverein), Törten Siedlung, Dessau, 1928-29. Photo Archiv Bauhaus Dessau.

21. Paul Mebes (1872-1938), *Um 1800. Architektur und Handwerk im letzten Jahrhundert ihrer traditionellen Entwicklung* (Munchen: F. Bruckmann, 1908); Paul Schultze-Naumburg (1869-1949), *Kulturarbeiten* (Munchen: G.D.W. Callwey, 1904/1917).

22. Fischer was an adviser for the plan of Hellerau and an architect as well. For brief references on projects mentioned in this essay, see the rich catalog *La ville: art et architecture en Europe 1870-1993* (Paris: CCI, 1994).

23. A. E. Brinckmann & Georg Metzendorf, *Margarethe Krupp-Stiftung für Wohnungsfürsorge: Margarethen-Höhe bei Essen* (Darmstadt: Verlags-ansalt Alexander Koch, 1913). See also Rainer Metzendorf, *Georg Metzendorf, 1874-1934 : Siedlungen und Bauten* (Darmstadt/Marburg : Selbstverlag der Hessischen Historischen Kommission Darmstadt, 1994). Like Fischer, Metzendorf played a critical educational role in these years: for instance, Hannes Mayer and Richard Kaufmann, responsible for the first garden city projects and kibbutzim on the radial model in Israel, worked in his office.

24. Renate Kastorff-Viehmann, "Robert Schmidt and the changing role of landscape, parks, and gardens in the pre-1914 industrial town," *Open Spaces for Tomorrow (Robert Schmidt Prize 1993)* (IBA Emscher Park/Kommunalverband Ruhrgebiet, 1993): 81-95.

25. A. Brinckmann, op. cit.: 9

26. G. Metzendorf, "Vorwort," op. cit.: 1. About the superblock, see p. 65.

27. Karl Kiem, "Die Gartenstadt Staaken als Prototyp," *Moderne Architektur in Deutschland, 1900-1950. Reform und Tradition*, op. cit., 133-150 (quote in page 133). Also see Franz Oppenheimer & Fritz Stahl, *Die Gartenstadt Staaken von Paul Schmitthenner* (Berlin: Ernst Wasmuth A. G. , 1917).

28 & 29. Kiem, op. cit., 134 & 140.

30. Franz Oppenheimer, op. cit.

31. Quoted by Marco De Michelis ("Tessenow riformatore: Siedlung e piccola città," *Casabella* 54, February 1990: 44-58) from E. Högg, *Kriergergrab und Kriegerdenkmal* (Wittenberg, 1915): 55-56.

32. From Marco De Michelis, op. cit.: 55.

33. G. Collins & C. Crasemann Collins, op. cit., p. 114. Herman Muthesius, *Kleinhaus und Kleinsiedlung* (München: Verlag A. Bruckmann, 1918).

34. On the Trabantenstadt, see Manfredo Tafuri, "Sozialpolitik and the City in Weimar Germany," *The Sphere and the Labyrinth: Avant-Gardes and Architecture from Piranesi to the 1970s* (Cambridge: The MIT Press, 1987): 197-233. The reference to Soest comes from Gabriele Tagliaventi, "The Romantic tradition," op. cit., 48-49: Theodor Goecke, "Die Wettbewerbsentwürfe für die Stadterweiterung von Soest," *Der Städtebau* n°12, 1916.

35. Iain Boyd Whyte, *Bruno Taut: Baumeister einer neuen Welt* (Stuttgart, 1981); I. B. Whyte "Bruno Taut," in *La ville*, op. cit.: 339-341; Kristiana Hartmann, "Garden-Cities' experiences in Germany," *Garden City: a century*, op. cit.: 267-284.

36. *Bruno Taut 1880-1938* (Ausstellung Katalog, Berlin 1980): 260. Quoted by Schickel, op. cit.: 61.

37. I have used the word "analogous" in the sense discussed by Aldo Rossi in *The Architecture of the City*.

38. From Kristiana Hartmann, "Garden-Cities' experiences in Germany," op. cit.

39. Tafuri, op. cit.: 207-8.

40. Hartmut Frank, "La metropoli come opera d'arte totale…," op. cit.: 220.

41. For a synthesis of Schumacher's considerable works and writings, see Hartmut Frank (editor), *Fritz Schumacher: Reformkultur und Moderne* (Stuttgart: Hatje, 1994).

42. In truth, Taut's works were often ignored as in the International Style Exhibition in New York of 1932: his sloped roofs at Britz and brick facades at Schillerpark must have been serious reasons for anathema.

43. Claude Lichtenstein (editor), *Otto Rudolph Salvisberg (1882-1940): Die andere Moderne* (Zürich: gta Verlag, 1985). On the Industrial Gartenreich, Rathenau, etc., see Regina Bittner, Heike Brückner, et. al., *Bauhaus Dessau: Industrielles Gartenreich Dessau-Bitterfeld-Wittenberg* op. cit.

44. Harald Kegler, *Die Piesteritzer Werksiedlung* (Dessau: Bauhaus Dessau, Werkssiedlung GmbH, Stadtverwaltung Wittenberg, 1992)

45. The backbone of Rathenau's *Gemeinswirtschaft* was to be the electrification of the entire country, a theory that was to directly influence both Henry Ford's capitalist projects and revolutionary Soviet Union. On his life, see Graf Harry Kessler, *Rathenau and his life* (New York: Harcourt, Brace & Co, 1930). Walter Rathenau was murdered in 1922.

46. From J. Posener, "1888-1918: Die Zeit Wilhelms des Zweiten," *750 Jahre Architektur und Städtebau in Berlin* (Stuttgart: Verlag G. Hatje, 1987). Also see in this book the discussion by Neal Payton in Tel Aviv.

47. Kegler, op. cit.,: 26.

48. See Herlind Reiß, *Kraftwerk und Kolonie Zschornewitz* (Dessau: Bauhaus-Dessau, 1995).

49. From Torsten Blume, *Die Siedlung "Hohe Lache,"* (Dessau: Stiftung Bauhaus Dessau, 1994) and Theodor Overhoff, *Die Siedelung Hohe Lache bei Dessau* (Dessau, 1921) reprinted by Arbeitskreis Siedlungen im Verein Industrielles Gartenreich e. V., 1994.

50. Torsten Blume, "Gartenstädte: Reform und Industrialisierung," *Bauhaus Dessau: Industrielles Gartenreich*, op. cit.: 116-121; on Migge, see also Harald Kegler, "Die 'Selbstversorger-Siedlung' in Dessau Ziebigk," *Bauhaus Dessau: Industrielles Gartenreich*, op. cit.: 130-131.

51. Michael Siebenbrodt, "Toward a New Working and Living Community: Plans for a Housing Development in Weimar (1920-1923)," *Social utopias of the Twenties: Bauhaus, Kibbutz and the Dream of the New Man* (Dessau: Stiftung Bauhaus Dessau, 1995): 47, note 2 and 4.

52. See Walter Gropius, "Wohnhaus-Industrie," *Ein Versuchhaus des Bauhauses in Weimar* (München, 1925): 5-14.

53. From Colin Rowe (with Robert Slutzky), "Transparency: Literal and Phenomenal," *The Mathematics of the Ideal Villa* (Cambridge: MIT Press, 1982): 160-176. In this essay, first published in *Perspecta* (1962), Rowe does not discuss the transparency of the building in relation to its context or to its function.

54. Colin Rowe, ibidem. From Karl Gruber, *Die Gestalt der deutschen Stadt ihr Wandel aus der geistigen Ordnung der Zeiten* (Munchen: Callwey, 1937).

55. Quoted by W. Nerdinger, Walter Gropius, op. cit., p. 34, from M. Steinmann, *CIAM. Dokumente 1928-1939* (Basel & Stuttgart, 1979), p. 70.

56. Quoted by W. Nerdinger, Walter Gropius, op. cit., p. 34, from Adolf Behne, "Dammerstock," in *Die Form*, 1930: 163-166. *Die Form* was the magazine of the Werkbund.

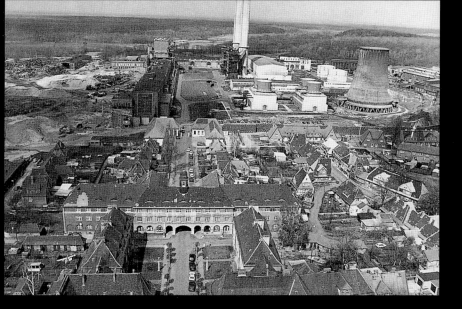

Top left:
Walter Klingenberg, Werner Issel, Georg von Mayenburg, architects.
Powerhouse and Zschornewitz Colony (1915-1922). Aerial photograph.
© Photo Schrader, MC Medien & Communikation Leipzig.

Center left:
View of Wörlitz Park in the Gartenreich near Dessau. Photo Jean-
François Lejeune, 1995.

Bottom left:
Walter Gropius & Fred Forbat. Aerial sketch of the Bauhaussiedlung at
Weimar "Am Horn," 1922 (corresponds to plan at bottom right page 67).
Drawing Farkas Mólnar. © Bauhaus Archiv Berlin.

Bottom right:
Theodor Overhoff. Plan of Siedlung Hohe Lache (1919-21). From Die
Siedelung Hohe Lache bei Dessau (Dessau, 1921; reedition of
Arbeitskreis Siedlungen im Verein industrielles Gartenreich, 1994).

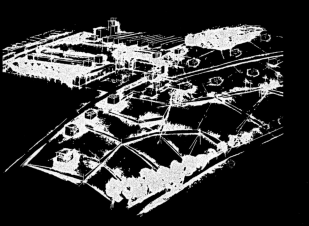

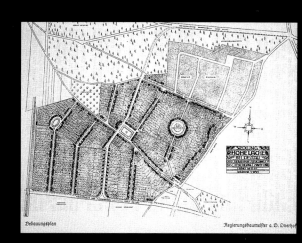

FERNAND POUILLON (1912-1986)

NEW FOUNDATION OF THE CITY
NEW FOUNDATION OF A DISCIPLINE

Alberto Ferlenga

Beneath the many skies that looked over Fernand Pouillon's frenetic life and saw his adventure as architect flow and unfold, the buildings to which he gave birth are slowly aging, and their stones tarnish with the stains of time.

He probably never imagined such a rapid historicizing of his own works, while he flew nightly from building site to building site, from studio to studio, between Paris, Marseilles, Algiers, and Teheran. Then, as we can read in his beautiful autobiography *Mémoires d'un architecte*, there was no time to stop. The projects were born anywhere and everywhere, during the journeys, the short pauses, or directly on the construction sites, where he played, as on a musical score, all the variations on his use of stone.[1]

Now we can inspect his buildings either in the pages of the handful of publications which have recently discussed them, or discover them in situ and marvel about the type of beauty and importance that emanate from them. Indeed, there are always reasons to wonder when terms such as "monumentality" or "massiveness"—of which modern architecture is normally critical—appear to be perfectly suited to these works, who do not shy at affirming their distance from the most celebrated realizations of the last fifty years. For the use of stone, the complicated life without restrain, the prison, the evasion, the exile, the rehabilitation and the return to France, the fortune and the disgrace which alternated quickly, the power games and the love affairs, cannot but permeate the architecture. On the one hand, we are faced with the impression that his is a story of the past, in part because the opportunities that he had and the quantity of works he produced have few parallel nowadays. On the other hand, Pouillon wisely built his career of architect, in complete indifference to the Zeitgeist and the architectural fashions, yet in total immersion in the ebb and flow of his time.

In the introduction he wrote to the only monograph dedicated to Pouillon and published at the time of his death in 1986, Bernard Huet recalls how his first encounter with the architect's works had revealed to him—he was then studying architecture—that another way to make architecture existed, different from the ones in fashion, yet not really marginal. He also explains how, amidst the controversy with the *Ordre des Architectes*, he took the side of Pouillon, the misunderstood and controversial figure who "represented the honor of architecture," against the technocrats who merely aimed at "satisfying the exigencies of the grand industrial conglomerates."[2]

Great artists are only discovered, when their time has come. Moreover, in the field of architecture, it can be even more difficult to extract the truly significant works from the confusion of the built environment. But soon comes the moment when the recognition of a specific body of work cannot be further delayed, and when appears the "objective necessity" to know it, study it, and use it. This phenomenon already occurred years ago with Adolf Loos, Heinrich Tessenow, Joze Plecnik. It is now time for Fernand Pouillon, Dimitris Pikionis, and for a couple of others.

To go back to the origin of Pouillon's career would oblige us to confront important historic events and actors of French and European architecture. One would easily realize that the suspicion and the obscurity of which he is still a victim cannot be explained by the mere vicissitudes of his private life and judiciary entanglement. For, starting with Auguste Perret whose critical contribution to architecture seems to be relegated to the defeated fringes of history, there is an important side of French modern architecture that has been put aside or deliberately forgotten. Pouillon's lifework did not follow a linear path; he never flirted with the academic world and its internal battles; he always chose his masters by "elective affinities" and only practiced them at work. He was never a direct disciple of Eugène Beaudouin or of Auguste Perret, whom he often met during the reconstruction of the Vieux-Port in Marseilles, but he felt deeply indebted to both. His acquisition, at his wealthier, of Auguste Perret's mythical studio, located Rue Raynouard in Paris, had the taste of a illegally seized heritage. But it is precisely the character of this heritage, harvested by Pouillon and intensified within his own work, that makes it so fundamental in relation to contemporary problems of architecture. Or better, one should say that throughout its

Opposite page:
Algiers, "Climat de France" (1955-1957). Contemporary aerial view of the central square and entrance portico. Photo Jacques Lucan.

Top right:
Sidi Ferruch, tourist village (Algeria), detail of a loggia. From Bernard Félix Dubor (editor), Fernand Pouillon (Milano-Paris: Electa-Moniteur, 1988).

Top:
Marseilles, reconstruction of
the Vieux-Port (1948-1953).
The stone loggias in construction. From Dubor, op. cit.

Center:
Meudon la Forêt, Paris (1959-
1961). Buildings in construction
with load bearing stone pillars.
From Dubor, op. cit.

Bottom:
Algiers, "Climat de France"
(1955-1957): stone construction of the central square. From
Dubor, op. cit.

Opposite page:
Marseilles, reconstruction of
the Vieux-Port. View of the new
waterfront arcade. Photo
Marcela Gallotta.

development, Pouillon's work responded to problems that had not yet manifested themselves with the intensity of our time. When he started his career in the immediate postwar era, the types of destruction with which he had to measure up did not presuppose, like it might today, the disappearance of the very idea of the city. Moreover, the urban peripheries still resembled those that constituted the background in the best French films of the period or in Ferdinand Céline's novels: landscapes in the process of disintegration but still understandable as disarticulated reflections of the urban image.

In a very short time Pouillon was engaged in the huge task of reconstruction and obliged to control large-scale operations, while simultaneously rejuvenating the traditional organization of the architectural studio, experimenting with new construction techniques, and dealing with geographically dispersed projects. In spite of his intense activity, he was able to spend a lot of time on the construction sites, at the heart of things.

Almost ten years after his death, his words about the history of architecture and how to use it remain regrettably absent from the contemporary architectural panorama. In the interview of 1988, published by the Editions Connivences, he talked, among others, of the decadence of contemporary architecture, of his own method of work, and of "fashionable" architecture.[3] Reading these lines, one cannot but instinctively sense that his arguments came from afar, that they were grounded in many lands and traditions, and that they concurrently prefigured a desirable future.

There was the force of his reflection: to demonstrate that the references to history, the widespread use of stone as main building material, the continuity and the links with an antique culture could painlessly fuse with the modernity of the large building projects, of the multiplicity of architectural languages, and with the development of advanced technologies.

The continuity with the constructive tradition
In 1962, from a French jail where he was detained following a financial scandal, he wrote his book, *Les Pierres Sauvages*.[4] Pouillon, the author, provocatively identified himself with the master builder of the Cistercian abbey at Le Thoronet and his struggle with an inappropriate stone material. Pouillon, the architect did not always build in stone, although it was his favorite material. In his works he used concrete, metal, wood, and employed equally traditional techniques and nascent prefabricated systems. Yet it was undoubtedly the use of stone which marked the most successful period of his career and was responsible for the little notoriety that his works carry nowadays. It is important to remember that, during his short teaching career from 1948 to 1953, Pouillon intensively traveled throughout his native Provence and studied it in depth with his students: the results were compiled in

his first book *Ordonnances* that included detailed studies of the monuments of Aix-en-Provence, and in following publications dealing with the Cistercian abbeys of Provence, the city of Les Baux, and the rural constructions of 18th-century Provence.[5] Hence the use of stone must have been for him like following his destiny. The blond stone, strong and easy to work, of which he measured the aging process on the monuments and the houses of his native region, was indissolubly equated with his concept of building. Such was his attachment to stone that he would use it even when the conditions seemed to impose other materials.

Building in stone was neither an eccentric decision or the arrogant demonstration of the favorable environment in which his activities took place for some time. In the large projects of Paris and Algiers, stone was indiscriminately employed as formwork or as load bearing masonry; yet it was also hewn with the newest and most modern methods in the quarries of Fontvielle. The architecture itself required the stone: as its most logic component, as a way to express the desire to find its place within history and to stand up to, equal to equal, the works of the past. Pouillon also studied how to best use it, inexpensively and rapidly.

For he did not resort to stone to build villas and palaces, but to erect large housing complexes for people of small means. Although these projects quite often recalled villas and palaces, they formed somewhat understated ensembles, built more rapidly, more economically, more beautifully, and more durably than their contemporary counterparts, which, based on similar programs, succeeded only in increasing the spatial vacuum of the most remote peripheries. Besides its competitiveness in price and construction time—made possible through the perfectioning of the hewing techniques and the very abundance of material—the real advantage of stone construction was more directly architectural: a good example can be seen at the housing complex of Meudon-la-Forêt, where the organization of exterior spaces, suggesting a "popular" Versailles, contributes to expand the elementary architectural language, which uses stone pilasters to give order to the different buildings. Evidently, this type of order, enriched by time along with the very stone surfaces, sets up a quasi-parental link with the history of architecture, even though no explicit "imitation" of the forms of the past can be found.

In Pouillon's works, stone became the primary means of mediation and communication, as in the Roman cities of North Africa, in the Muslim monuments, or in the architecture of Provence. His extreme attention to constructive methods led him to study thousand of examples around the Mediterranean, and to emulate them. Africa, Provence, and the Orient have fecundated his architecture, and particularly the buildings of Algiers and the caravansaries and hotels, dispersed between Timimoun and the coast. In the latter

Bottom top:
Marseilles, "La Tourette"
(1948-1953). Model of the
reconstruction of the old quarters. To the left the St-Laurent
church, the complex of the
"Tourette" by Fernand Pouillon;
to the right, the sector designed
by André Devin. Photo Renzis.

Bottom:
Marseilles, "La Tourette." The
stairs leading up to the interior
square. Photo Giulio Barazzetta.

also, the materiality of the houses, the use of wood, the colors, the cupolas, evoke the lost traditions, integrate them, and ascertain that architecture is also the encounter of many itineraries. Above all they make clear that the architect uncovered the antique paths along which the architectural forms have moved and settled for hundreds of years.

In Pouillon's works it is the mode of construction, more than the architectonic forms, that mediates and confuses the epoch; through the recuperation of antique knowledge, it aims at reconnecting with the human vicissitudes, and thus at becoming their "scenario."

History as material

If construction appears to be the principal vehicle by which the tradition of images and forms was transferred to his buildings, Pouillon's attitude toward history seems much more complex. The collector of rare books and invaluable houses which he bought and sold repeatedly to pay off his debts, the publisher who reprinted and displayed precious drawings in his boutique on the Place des Vosges, and the architect who freely restored palaces and castles, considered history as the most valuable of his materials. Yet his vision of history was far from academic; to the contrary, his nomadic life seems to have repeatedly crossed and slowly absorbed the secret of the complex migrations that affect the life of architectonic forms, make them disappear to the west and blossom to the east and vice versa, and leave traces of their passage that can be understood only by those who want to follow their most secret paths. This is probably why his personal research always avoided the traps of historicism, even when, like in his last works in Algeria, he came dangerously close to them.

Fernand Pouillon used history with surprising intuitiveness; he strove at length to reproduce, in his contemporary practice, both its linearity and its thousand contradictions. To this, he did not put any limits; he knew quite well how little temporal and spatial limitations can do to control the inner life of architectonic forms. Walking in the footsteps of the antique masters, Pouillon traveled through the territories of his labor like an erudite and uprooted artisan. Like Marco Polo or other travelers of the past, to whom he often alluded, he stubbornly insisted to bring back from his journeys "the feeling of wonder," and "to transform knowledge into wonder" in an epoch during which, as he admitted himself, "knowledge has almost nothing of wonder because it belongs to all and all are equally illuminated by culture."[6]

Paradoxically it is his uprooted condition that allowed him to enter so profoundly in contact with the sites he visited. His architecture is foreign to the question of style, although one could define as style the coherence of the elements of his architectural language. Style and coherence relate primarily to his expressing,

throughout all projects, the genius loci, the spirit of the place and the many stories with which they have intertwined. Even when his work could be confused with others', whether of antique or modern tradition, it is this "style from the heart," this "style from the soul" which makes them instantly recognizable.

The interventions of "foundation"

In Aix-en-Provence, in Marseilles, in the Parisian suburbs, and in Algiers, the large residential complexes built by Pouillon go well beyond their own functional structure and the urban areas that they directly relate to. They measure up with the city as a whole. The forms that this influence takes, either at some distance or in the immediate proximity, are always perceptible; they are independent of the location of the interventions and of their present condition. In fact they are even more perceptible today as the city seems to decompose around them.

In his indefatigable fight against urban desolation, Pouillon demonstrates that the instruments of urban architecture cannot always coincide with those of "regular" architecture, and that some degree of architectural "exaltation" may be indispensable to redress or salvage the quality of the place. The very mode of "exaltation" that he attempts to create is, at once, extremely contained and developed at the urban scale. Thus it is not about volumetric deformations of pure geometries in the manner of illuminist architects, or about excessive decoration of baroque or neo-eclectic type. His experience of architecture is prone to a complete "reversal of its normality."

Whether lower-class or middle-class, whether isolated or already inserted in urbanized areas, Pouillon's new housing districts stand out in the landscape as "citadels of foundation." More specifically, their architecture reaches "epic" proportions. It seems that, through recurrent means, these *quartiers* aim at reaching up to an ancestral "myth of foundation," which in itself explains the tight relationship they establish with the city, and, along with their very dimensions, distinguish them from the works of similar program by other architects. Among the many factors converging to make this operation possible, the most potent are the free and evocative use of the forms of urban history, as well as the enchantment of natural stone. Here and there—and this historicist indulgence is emphasized also at the planimetric level—the *quartiers* recall the acropolis, the Ottoman fortresses, the walls and historic squares, the cashba, or even some baroque interventions. More often they constitute the synthesis of many urban forms, and stand out as genuine "analogous cities."[7] In the example of Algiers' housing district called "Climat de France," the primary elements of the city (walls, streets, squares), the traditional relation between monuments and urban fabric, and the pluralism that always results from the passage

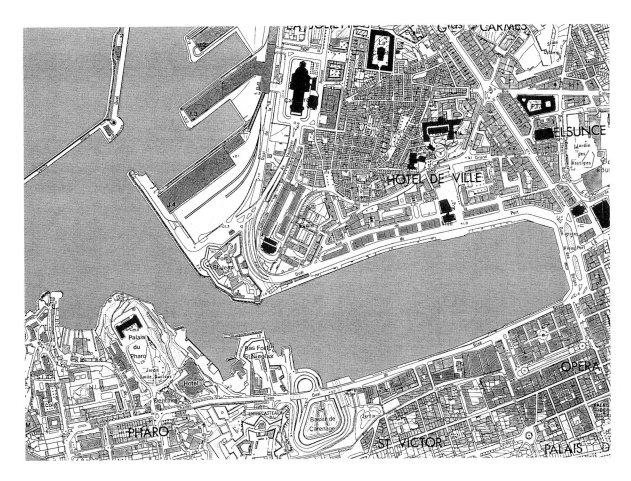

Top:
Fernand Pouillon. Elevations for the reconstruction of La Tourette (above) and the reconstruction of the Vieux-Port. From Mémoires d'un architecte (Paris: Editions du Seuil, 1968).

Bottom left:
View of the city and the port of Marseilles. Jacques de Maretz, 1664. From Marseille: la passion des contrastes (Liège: Mardaga, Collection Villes, 1991).

Bottom right:
Modern plan of the port of Marseilles. One can see in dark the architectural interventions of Fernand Pouillon along the harbor, and the complex of La Tourette between the entrance of the harbor and the cathedral. Drawing by Stefania Celli.

The reconstructed Vieux-Port with Pouillon's buildings on both sides of the old City Hall. In the background, Pouillon's tower and complex of La Tourette. © Photo Dominique Delaunay, 1990. From Marseille: la passion des contrastes (Liège: Mardaga, Collection Villes, 1991).

of time and the changes of uses, can be seen, reinterpreted, in the variations of the residential blocks.

Without a doubt, the life and memoirs of the architect who walked and described, day by day, the steps and doings of the builders of medieval abbeys, are not foreign to the construction of his own mythical self; and when this mechanism is applied to the works of architecture—as in the case of the Climat de France district—it becomes an integral part of them and, to some extent, changes their character. So he evoked for us readers of his *Mémoires*, in an Algeria on the eve of the war of liberation, the antique ceremonies of foundation, the selection of the site, the relation with the enlightened sponsor—the liberal mayor of Algiers, Jacques Chevallier—the struggle to domesticate the grounds, the transportation of the blocks of stone across the Mediterranean, the race with time, the creation of a new geography, and even the identification of the construction workers, the real "heroes" of this universe of stone. The towers, the square defined by the two hundred columns, the staircases that march down toward the sea, the suspended garden of palm trees, all of these architectonic elements create precise hierarchies. Rooted in the replication of specific urban images, they essentially result from a process of "dramatization" of the architecture, created by the material circumstances of the operation but also seen by the architect as a "necessary condition" of the work. The postcards, printed in

Algiers at the end of the 1950s, keep intact the memory of the inauguration days: they proudly display the towers, the squares, the markets, and the cable-car that unites the old city with the new housing districts on the hill. There are no traces on these images of the feeling of void, emptiness, and exile that typically emanate from many propagandistic views of other "modern" quarters built during the same period. In contrast the richness of Pouillon's works resides in the quality of the exterior spaces and in their potential to positively impact their surroundings: They act like small historic centers in the periphery and relate strongly to the geography of the place. In fact, Pouillon gives to geography the same treatment than history: on the one hand, he unearths the existing landscapes, underlines their antique patterns, and encloses them within his architectural frames; on the other hand, he reinvents them and evokes a new topography. He transforms the original traces, or their simulation, into a new ground whose major lines escape the confines of the site to reach down to the city and blend with it. In doing so he is able to renew the particular beauty of the city of Algiers, a beauty which finds its strongest expression in its interstices and infrastructures—such as the staircases and the arcades of the port—more than in its monuments.

This capacity to penetrate the language of cities and to renew it had already manifested itself in his first buildings in Provence, and even more so in his

Center:
Marseilles, the Saint-Charles University Library (1956-1958). View of the entrance facade. Photo Giulio Barazzetta.

Bottom:
Marseilles, reconstruction of the Vieux-Port. View of the entire front just after the completion of the works: in the center, the old city hall built by Puget and which survived the demolitions of 1943. From Dubor, op. cit.

extensive interventions in Marseilles, genuine anticipation of his Algerian work. With the reconstructed district of La Tourette, Pouillon changed the profile of the city. It rises on the site of the Greek acropolis like a vast forum whose background is the church of Saint-Laurent. Some new edifices jut out, like the twenty-story tower, and others recall the defensive walls of the Fort Saint-Nicolas and protect from the mistral. On the side that overlooks the old port, the porticoes and the stepped descents tie the city back to the mythical place of its foundation.

His most significant works in the city can be found along the Vieux-Port, in the popular and dense section destroyed by the German occupants who razed 1500 houses in 1943. There, in collaboration with André Devin and under the patronage of Auguste Perret, Pouillon radically "corrected" the official project of reconstruction designed by André Leconte after the war. The high porticoes of stone, juxtaposed to the pseudo-rationalist skeletons of Leconte, echo the nineteenth-century arcades of the port of Algiers built by the engineer Chassériaux on the other side of the Mediterranean. Thus the arcades of Marseilles appear like the metaphorical place of embarkation of those of Climat de France at the port of arrival, a couple of years later. Today, the simplicity and repetitiveness of the stone arcades framing the reconstructed side of the har-

bor give unity to a rich urban sequence, made up of covered streets, small squares, and narrow passages that reveal the streets of the old city.

Finally, to suggest the word "ethical" while talking about such a controversial figure and turbulent life may seem odd at first. Yet, when one examines the works that Pouillon built until his Algerian exile, one cannot but be impressed by the great moral rigor in his relation with the urban context; similarly his profound sense of responsibility can be measured in the capacity that his buildings have to reverberate their intrinsic qualities on the surroundings and to contribute, by a phenomenon of "architectural attraction," to their improvement. Work after work, Pouillon contributed to the reconstruction of a specific discipline, the art of building cities, mixing antique knowledge with new savoir-faire, and applying it to new territories. This intellectual commitment relates to his large residential complexes but also to invaluable public buildings like the Lycée Colbert in Marseilles (1952-54) or the Saint-Charles University Library (1956-58). Both are small masterpieces, which modestly compare with the major works, are built in the same material and with the same methods, and are devoted to equally "take care" of the city albeit in areas of lesser importance.

To illustrate my thesis, I will present four works in more details: the three quarters of Algiers —

Top left:
Algiers, view of the waterfront.
Photo courtesy Alberto
Ferlenga

Bottom left:
Algiers, view of the waterfront
built by the French in the mid-
1800s and of the supporting
arcades that contain the port's
warehouses. Postcard Edition
Jomone, Algiers. Courtesy
Alberto Ferlenga.

Right:
Algiers, location of Pouillon's
quarters (in black) within a sec-
tion of the city plan: Diar es
Saada is in the top right corner
of the map; Diar el Mahçoul is
visible to the left. Drawing by
Stefania Celli.

Top left:
Algiers, view of the city at the
beginning of the 1800s.
Courtesy Alberto Ferlenga

Below:
Diar el Mahçoul. General view
of the complex with the church
in the foreground. From Dubor,
op. cit.

Right:
Algiers, "Climat de France."
Location of Pouillon's district
within a section of the city
plan. Notice the casbash and
the modern quarter along the
harbor. Drawing by Stefania
Celli.

scape into the composition: the landscape merges with the architecture and becomes under its impact, here a terraced stage, there a flight of stairs to watch the spectacle of the old city, the gulf, and the animated harbor.

Diar es Saada and Diar el Mahçoul directly evoke the memory of the compact citadels of the Kasbah, of the Ottoman forts—transported onto high grounds—and of the many villas and gardens—now disappeared—that made the admiration of European visitors of Algiers. All of these influences are simultaneously acknowledged, but they are recomposed into a new whole, open to the urban context and to the landscape in a geographic position that recalls the idea of the acropolis. Seen from the sea each housing project appears as a small acropolis, as a residual point of orientation within the skyline of a city which has now lost all spatial limits.

Each acropolis is accessed along modern "sacral" streets: at Diar el Mahçoul, the route departs from the cable car station designed in the Mediterranean rationalist style, follows an ample terrace which overlooks the sea, before it rises up as "propylaea" into the heart of the district. At Diar es Saada, the route follows the watercourse designed as the generating structure of the quarter to evoke Arab fountains and torrents. Nowadays these places are denuded and sometimes lay in ruins; many fountains and works of arts were eliminated or moved to other locations; as for the works of Pouillon's friend, sculptor Jean Amado—the lumps of colored ceramic attached to the towers and the grand mosaic of Diar es Saada's market square—they are now barely recognizable.

Yet even in these deplorable conditions the fundamental character of the districts continues to transpire with utmost clarity: the aging of the stones reacts positively with the evidence of the historic references, with the simplicity of the architecture, and the absence of maintenance. It is actually difficult to escape the sensation of being in a place whose deterioration has the nobility of the Ksour in the desert or of the extinct Roman cities of the interior, rather than the hopeless nature of the popular neighborhoods of the twentieth century.

Like in Djemila or in other archeological sites whose confines merge into the landscape, the separation between the exterior and the interior of the "settlements" is not clearly defined. The streets and the squares have become accentuation of roads and places that come from afar and belong to the topography. But what is in Djemila the consequence of time and abandonment turns out to be, at Diar es Saada and Diar el Mahçoul, a simple project expedient to solidly link the districts to their surrounding territory. Only thirty years ago their public spaces, today invaded by garbage and automobiles, mirrored those in the villages of the "interior"; the markets took place under the shade of airy terra-cotta vaults, now the receptacle

—Diar es Saada, Diar el Mahçoul, and Climat de France—and the large housing complex of Meudon-la-Forêt in the periphery of Paris.

Diar es Saada, Diar el Mahçoul (1953-55)

Built on the crest line of Algiers' hills, the two housing quarters of Diar es Saada and Diar el Mahçoul stand out as fragments of an urban fabric characterized by powerful public spaces, that are dimensionally and qualitatively comparable. In both cases the various buildings—to which the aged stone has given golden reflections that links them so well to the African land—are grouped around central spaces or in relation to axes. In Diar el Mahçoul, the focus is a square; in Diar es Saada the axis materializes as a fountain/staircase which solidifies in stone the trace of an old torrent. To these places, which do not exhibit the character of monumentality achieved later at the Climat de France district, the architect grafted secondary public spaces, like the Hanging Piazza of the Palms and the market square at Diar es Saada, or the loggia and the grand staircase at Diar el Mahçoul. Yet the list could be longer, for, thanks to the quality of "interstitial" architecture, every void tends to transmute into a small square or alley. Similarly every passage or opening—particularly at Diar el Mahçoul which has conserved intact its relation to the gulf—becomes an opportunity to insert fragments of land-

Top:
Diar el Mahçoul. Main access staircase. From Dubor, op. cit.

Bottom:
Diar el Mahçoul. View of the portico between the piazza and the access staircase, with the sea and the port in the distance. Photo Giulio Barazzetta.

Top left:
Diar el Mahçoul. Inauguration
view of the tower built in the
square with the fountain and
the statues of horses in the
foreground (today removed).
Postcard Edition Jomone,
Algiers, 1950s. Courtesy
Alberto Ferlenga.

Top right:
Diar es Saada. Contemporary
view of the tower and the
hanging garden of palms. Photo
courtesy Alberto Ferlenga.

Center:
Diar el Mahçoul. Detail of the
market. From Dubor, op. cit.

Bottom:
Diar el Mahçoul. The market.
From Dubor, op. cit.

of metallic containers; the basins of water, with their statues of dolphins and horses, embellished the esplanades, shaded by thousand of palm trees which had been transplanted, already fully grown, in an epic journey from the desert oasis to the city, in the hours preceding the inauguration.

On the other hand, the architecture of stone, adorned with many references to the constructive tradition of houses, has barely changed. These citations are true and proper, and never become a repetitive norm: the bracketed balconies with their consoles made of *thuja* wood, the window grills, and the ceramics and bricks, used here and there to indicate specific sections of the buildings. The towers continue to mark the central spaces and to signal the quarters from afar. On the highest one, at Diar es Saada, the names of all the workers and the notation of the incredibly short time of construction, less than one year, were engraved in the stone. The old church of Diar el Mahçoul, transformed by Pouillon into a mosque, also remains on the site, albeit half in ruins: he was well aware that such "mutations" had been frequent in the region across the centuries.

"Climat de France" (1955-57)

The vast housing district containing the Square of the Two Hundred Columns had a painstaking gestation. From the architect's account and the few surviving drawings, we know that, following the exploration of the site and the definition of the program with Mayor Jacques Chevallier, dozens of architects and draftsmen spent weeks and months to draw and develop the buildings and public spaces of this new city of ten thousand residents. The first project, a large district where the subtle hierarchies, characteristic of the late Parisian works, had not yet been shaped, was judged inadequate and rejected by the author, who left to travel in the desert for a time of reflection. In his autobiography Pouillon described this brief journey as a pilgrimage on the traces of the architecture and landscapes of the South. Yet one cannot but think that he took along many other ideas and images of architecture.

The new and built project, elaborated after his return, appears like a sophisticated weaving of urban visions freely reinterpreted through the sober volumes of stone and borrowed from the strata of Mediterranean history. Much of its merit derives from the impressive beauty of the colonnaded square which constitutes its center; but its importance comes even more from the overall composition, its evocative potential, and the impact that it had for the rehabilitation of the marginal area and its inhabitants.

More than any other Pouillon's work, the district was conceived like a genuine urban foundation, and it is probably not by accident that the overscaled central edifice recalls some of Giorgio Vasari il Giovane's sketches for an ideal city—drawings that were more

Top:
Algiers, Diar es Saada. View of the stairs/fountain which structures the district. The basin and and the sculpture in the foreground are now removed. From Dubor, op. cit.

Bottom left:
Diar es Saada. Detail of the terrace/square with the hanging garden of palms. From Dubor, op. cit.

Bottom right:
Diar es Saada. Aerial view of the new district. Postcard 1950s. Courtesy A. Ferlenga.

Top:
Diar es Saada. Contemporary view of the first section of the stairs/fountain.
Photo Giulio Barazzetta

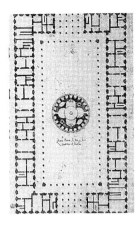

than likely in the bibliophile's library. Through its adaptation to the undulation of the hilly terrain, the typological variety, the use of stone, and the subtle contrasts between built volumes and open spaces, this urban quarter establishes links with the two cities that face each other across the Mediterranean: Marseilles and Algiers. Moreover, the ships that transported the quarried stones from port to port reactivated an antique road of transportation and cultural transfer between the two cities. The geography is in fact what more potently unites them. Along the slopes of the mountains, the ridges, the ravines, and the beds of the torrents were naturally metamorphosed into terraces, paved streets and squares, low walls, and fountains. These spaces resolved the problems of water distribution and site levels in such a manner that they emerged as an architecture of "topographic derivation" that characterizes both cities as eloquently as their main monuments. At the Climat de France, like at La Tourette in Marseilles, the ground imprint conjures up the antique methods of terracing and, along with the stone construction, captures the secret of the fascination of the city.

This state of fusion between the modern conception of housing and the recuperation of an antique know-how makes the Climat de France district one of the architect's masterpieces and a fundamental work in the history of architecture of the twentieth century. The dimensions of the apartments, the solar exposition, the control of ventilation and light, the quality of services and equipment, i.e., all the elements of the habitational comfort, were resolved with an ingenuity that completely underscores the enormous effort of the construction process, and in no way, sacrifices to the "urban" parti of implantation. Eventually the overall impression left by the complex is, even in the extreme force of the architectonic forms, one of an extraordinary testing ground for a subtle balance between the ideology of the modern and the fascination of the past.

Paradoxically it is easier to negatively define the project than to outline its genuine genealogy. The Climat de France is not a lower-class, rationalist neighborhood; it does not belong to the family of the "grands ensembles"; and it certainly cannot be described as a late nineteenth-century neighborhood, even less as an eclectic or historicist one. Trying to analyze it we are confronted with the insufficiency of the critical apparatus used during this century to catalog architecture. This fact may be interpreted as one of the hiatus of a profession, too accustomed to read and understand history in a linear fashion and constantly embarrassed when confronted with complex figures, apparently contradictory or too close in time.

Meudon-la-Forêt (1959-1961)

A long journey through the periphery of Paris represents the genuine cross-section of all the mistakes of the urbanistical and architectural culture in post-war Europe. Yet, to enter nowadays into Pouillon's large

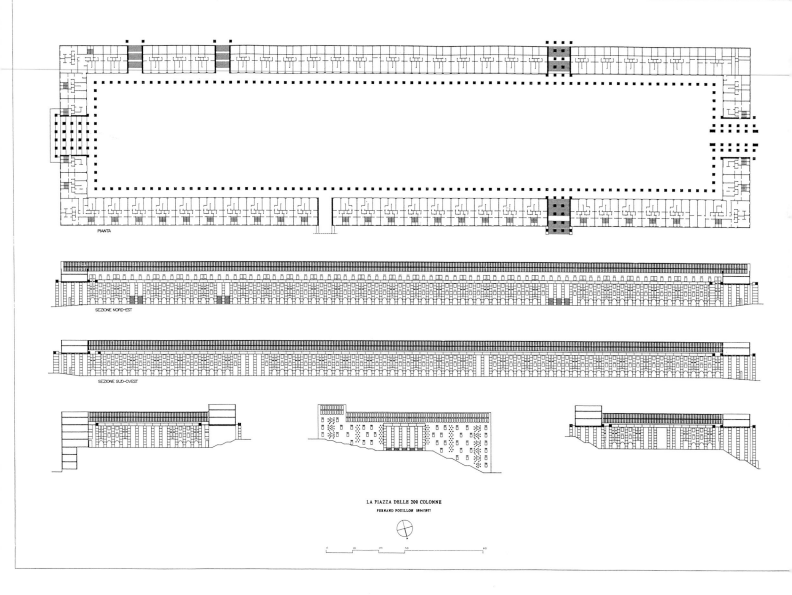

LA PIAZZA DELLE 200 COLONNE
FERNAND POUILLON 1954/1957

Top:
Algiers, "Climat de France."
Plan, elevations, and sections
of the square of Two Hundred
Columns. Drawings by Giulio
Barazzetta, Nicola Braghieri,
Giuseppe Di Simmeo.

Bottom & right:
Algiers, "Climat de France."
Contemporary views of the
square of Two Hundred
Columns. Photos Giulio
Barazzetta.

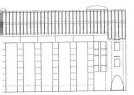

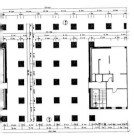

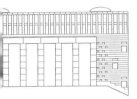

Top:
"Climat de France." Plan, perspective, and section of the "propylaea." Drawings by Giulio Barazzetta, Nicola Braghieri, Giuseppe Di Simmeo.

Previous spread:

"Climat de France." Aerial view of the square before inauguration. Postcard Edition Jomone, 1950s. Courtesy Alberto Ferlenga.

peripheral district of five thousand apartments is an experience full of surprises. The first is the excellent state of conservation of the complex: resulting in great part from the use of stone which has eliminated the problematic peeling of cement and stuccoes, it creates, along with the particular order of the architecture of the facades, a built environment rarely encountered in this type of projects that are barely thirty-five years old. Secondly, the constructive system—protruding stone pilasters defining the openings—is directly responsible for the apparent "double perception" of the edifices. Whereas the frontal vision emphasizes the monumental aspects that the architect systematically looked after, and frames between the pilasters the small and inevitable disorders of the domestic life, the oblique views obliterate any confusion and impose, along gardens and paths of movement, a highly scenographic and unexpected order and unity. Produced by the subtle dislocation of the built masses, this oblique vision projects in fact the district's real character of monumentality. The capacity to elevate the urban image of the place through the repetition of a simple expedient, i.e., the succession of pilasters, is definitely more effective than the impressive central space of the complex, albeit masterfully organized around the enormous basin.

In both examples, the most surprising is to encounter genuine "monumental values," obtained through the synthetic and essential utilization of spatial models belonging to the "great architecture." One penetrates in the working-class neighborhood and one reminisces the royal spaces of French architecture: the grand basin, "larger than the one in the Tuileries or in the Luxembourg Gardens" in Pouillon's words; the green perspectives that develop between the houses; the sophisticated relation between volumes. Then, seen now out of axis, the facade transforms itself into a classical colonnade, whose spatial rhythm seems accelerated. Around the preexisting buildings, one understands the hierarchy and the spatial relations as those of a small center: the oblique perspectives that contract both old and new buildings continuously break the grandiosity of the intervention.

Like in Perret's reconstruction of Le Havre, the undeniable modernity of the architecture does not yield to the formalism of the citations; but, much more than in Le Havre, the architecture of Meudon, though strongly conditioned by the modesty of the program, develops a high capacity of "evocation."[8] And such an evocation—of many distant and detached histories, thus not related to one unique model—is undoubtedly the most fascinating aspect of the small city. If it is true that destiny of cities ties them to the act and the reasons of their foundation, then the district of Meudon-la-Forêt cannot but become richer and richer with the passing of time: like a genuine city, its beauty and present condition confirm this future. Albeit of a smaller scale, Pouillon's interventions in other districts of the

Parisian periphery, in Pantin or at the Cité Buffalo in Montrouge, are equally stimulating examples of his capacity to rationalize construction and to create public spaces of urban quality.

Pauses in the Algerian landscape
"They had confided him a nation; he filled it with his phantasms:" This commentary, captured in the abandoned garden of the Hotel Transatlantique of Bou Saada, colonial residue of an old thermal station not far from one of the best hotels built by Pouillon—the Hotel Le Caïd—can serve as introduction to the analysis of the other side of the architect's activities: a period less often mentioned but in many ways more surprising, which unfolded during almost twenty years on the territory of the new Algerian nation.

In 1965, the year that the French judicial system commuted his three-year prison term for a financial scandal, Pouillon was granted asylum by the new Algerian government.[9] Whereas the years preceding the disgrace and the exile are well documented in Pouillon's own writings (they were initiated during his flight and completed in jail) and by his very built works, the second Algerian adventure remains unexplored and contradictory. Or perhaps it would be better to state that the lack of detailed studies and published documents or testimonies keeps a veil over these later works and the conditions in which they took form. A critical or historical classification of the realizations of this period is overly complicated by their quantity, their extreme variety, and the apparent disappearance of the elements of recognition that had characterized the architect's first career. For instance, the availability of stone from the French quarries became more and more aleatory and thus the particular relationship with history that accompanied its use progressively vanished. During this second career, Pouillon's relations with Algeria changed profoundly: he was not any more the hurried visitor and scholar, but a man who had initiated a new cycle in his life at the same time that the country which was now hosting him. Algeria was to become for him the almost exclusive field of professional intervention.

He studied the country, its history, and the entire history of Islamic architecture which extended his already ample frame of references. He observed Algiers at length from his studio, housed in the villa Les Arcades which dominated the gulf. At the end of a war that had devastated the country, the task of reconstruction was urgent. Its new image could not coincide anymore with the one of an epoch which had ended painfully. It was now critical to "found" the new nation in the architectural sense, and Pouillon once again gave to his architecture a regenerating function.

As architect of the Ministry of Tourism he invented a new hotel structure that had to supersede the exiguous and selective character of the colonial hotels. His hotels, more than forty, form a constellation across

the Algerian territory, from the oases to the Mediterranean. At the end of the 1970s, many travelers, in particular architects, visited Algeria and stayed in the hotels; they admired their beauty and force of expression, but could only speculate about their architect. Along the coast and in the interior of the country, in Tapaza, Sidi Ferruch, Biskra, Ghardaïa, Timimoun, and in dozens of other places, the network of Pouillon's interventions became the obliged point of passage of the modern nomads, from the organized groups of tourists to the off-season and week end excursions of the collaborators and foreign technicians participating in the reconstruction the country. The architect explained how the hotels responded to simple programs:

In Seraidi I impersonated a tourist who comes during the summer to look for fresh air, and during the winter to see the snow in Algiers(...). In Annaba I became a businessman in a hurry who wants to live in a somewhat luxurious hotel where he can work and leave with memories of the gulf of Annaba.[10]

Built in places which had already lost the literary and romantic appeal of "extreme" destinations, the new constructions did not coincide with the century-old nomadic roads. Yet they formed a contemporary chain of caravansaries, dispersed in a modern country in search of its past and its future. On the coast they appear as white constructions, villages, and ports, which reinvent a Mediterranean landscape, midway between the Greek islands and Andalusia, molded by the repetition of architectonic forms, and the constant encounters of distant cultures and places. In the interior of the country the pale yellow of the sand and the red

of the rocks color the tightly built volumes, which protectively hide swimming pools and patios; designed as squares or open-air theaters, they embellish the patios and terraces and serve as sources for the fountains and water channels. Scenography, folklore, and historic reproduction: all these concepts—that a superficial analysis would reproach the architect—are completely under control by Pouillon who uses and avoids them when necessary. He was not afraid, to the contrary of his first period linked to the use of stone and to the process of synthesis adopted by Perret, to quote directly the sources of the projects and of their free forms. Of course the images evoked here—Ksour of the mountains, streets of the Kasbah, fishing villages, forts, souks, etc.—do not correspond to function. He built his

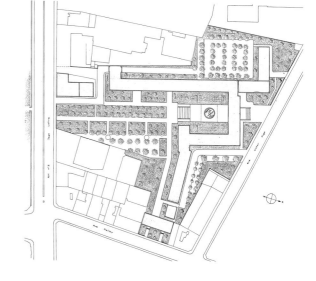

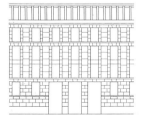

hotels as villages and sites which seem to have always existed along the coasts; in the mountains and in the sand of the deserts he imagined the Hotel el Montazah (Seraidi) or the Hotel Gourah (Timimoun) as castles or touareg villages. Yet the distance between these realizations and similar projects that have destroyed the Spanish and Italian coasts is incommensurable.

Pouillon's hotels borrow from a wide range of constructive traditions. Among the "added values" they display, those of "exhibition" and "museum" are the most daring, for they seem to transform the projects into safeguard operations of architectonic forms and artisanal knowledge. The ambiguous fascination of an exotic colonial period, like the *Pueblo Español* in Barcelona or the *Mostre d'Oltremare* in Naples, comes to mind. The difference lies in the conviction that an architectonic tradition can be reborn from its roots and simultaneously be renewed. There are the reasons for the recuperation of the traditional constructive techniques, intelligently rejuvenated and coupled, if necessary, to new systems. Besides its complete insertion within the context, the capacity of Pouillon's architecture to be totally appropriate, either at the urban or territorial level, is apparent everywhere. It proposes methods of construction and composition that can easily be followed and replicated: they were, in fact, in the cases of many houses and hotels, built in Algeria or in Provence and whose authorship can be difficult to establish. Thus Pouillon was able to attain, consistently and in quantity, that quality that Auguste Perret called *banalité*, the positive banality that he himself had reached with much difficulty.

Sometimes, and this is not a contradiction with the above remarks, the hotels fulfilled a genuine and proper monumental function, particularly when they occupied sites at the city edge, like at Ghardaïa where the Hotel Les Rostémides absorbed the remnants of an old fort and amplified its nature within its own architectonic forms and terraced courtyards. But the hotels were not the only new monuments to emerge from the Algerian soil. At El Oued, again in Gardhaia and in other locations, the architect grouped markets, cinemas, and civic buildings into small complexes, hence giving to the most recent neighborhoods an urban center. In spite of their programs and the period of construction (1960s-1980s), these realizations are miles away from their counterparts of the international movement,

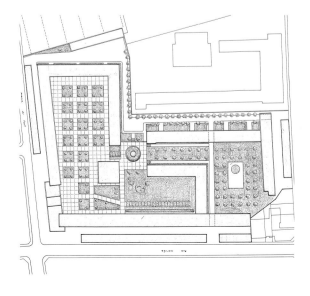

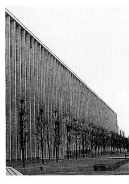

thoughtlessly utilized to transform the territories of the Third World into facsimiles of the limitless and undifferentiated peripheries of Europe and North America.

Pouillon achieved very similar results with the construction of university residences, laid out as small cities (like in Constantine for instance), with residential neighborhoods, and other public buildings that, since the 1960s, constellate the new Algeria. In all of these the eclecticism of the architect's late period was the vehicle of his genial incursion across the past and the present of a discipline. Whereas the first part of his professional itinerary undoubtedly continued a particular French tradition and the style of his masters, the second one, in the African land, brings to mind, in its successes, the grandest Islamic architect of our times, Hassan Fathy. Quite different from Pouillon in many aspects, Fathy was like him obsessingly tied to a material which became in his work a vehicle of history—in Fathy's case, the earth of the bricks baked in the sun—and to the possibility of rescuing an architectonic culture and its forms without renouncement to its renewal.

A history to be written

As for many other protagonists of the architecture of the twentieth century, the history of Fernand Pouillon remains to be written. What exists does not suffice to reveal its complexity and its interest. Yet these writings have allowed us to realize that we remain confronted with the same problems that Pouillon had to resolve, and that our architectural education and instruments of action are less and less adapted to challenge them. Pouillon reminded us of the simplicity and dignity of the discipline known as architecture; he underlined the specific way in which this discipline has always established its own culture and tradition, while adapting them to the new problems and situations that have never stopped to arise. His own words about the approach to the project sound like an evidence and, at the same time, as a conclusion:

Top:
Paris Region, Meudon la Forêt. General plan. From Dubor, op. cit.

Center & bottom:
Paris Region, Meudon la Forêt. Two views of the colonnaded facade in stone. Photos Alberto Ferlenga.

Translated from the Italian by Jean-François Lejeune

I go through the program. And above all I go through the site. The site and the program. Afterwards I must confess to you that I don't do anything more. I let myself go. I let myself go and think, three hours a day, six hours a day, twelve hours a day. I am going from the parts to the whole, from material to form, from the interior structures to the foundations. I think of the quality of materials through a kind of analysis and synthesis, permanent and imaginary. In fact I do not design anything without knowing what I will design. My first drawings have always been small drawings. I make tangible the research of many days, many weeks, along with the experience of fifty years of practice. And then, all of a sudden, in a flash, the project is finished. What is left is to work it out.[11]

1. Fernand Pouillon, *Mémoires d'un architecte* (Paris: Editions du Seuil, 1968).

2. Bernard Huet, "Introduction," *Fernand Pouillon*, edited by Bernard Félix Dubor (Milan-Paris: Electa Moniteur, 1986).

3. Fernand Pouillon, *Indiscutablement les architectes se sont laissés manoeuvrer, mais ils étaient contents*, interview by B. F. Dubor & M. Raynaud (Paris: Editions Connivences, 1988).

4. Fernand Pouillon, *Les pierres sauvages: journal du maitre d'oeuvre du Thoronet* (Paris: Editions du Seuil, 1964). English version: *The stones of the Abbey* (New York: Avon Books,1976).

5. Fernand Pouillon, *Les Baux de Provence* (Paris: Fernand de Nobele, 1960); *Ordonnances, hotels et residences des XVIè, XVIIè et XVIIIè siècles; ordonnances des cours et des places et ensembles harmonieux d'Aix-en-Provence, relevés et dessinés par l'atelier de Fernand Pouillon* (Aix-en-Provence: Cercle d'Etude Architecturale, 1953); and recently the reprint of his *Auguste Choisy* (Paris: Altamira, 1994).

6. Interview by B. F. Dubor & M. Raynaud, op. cit.

7. In the sense of Aldo Rossi in *The Architecture of the City*.

8. See for instance J. Abram, "Auguste Perret and Le Havre, Utopias and Compromises of a Reconstruction," *Lotus International* 64, 1990: 108-127.

9. For this affair which saw Pouillon's figure as "grand monsieur" of French architecture transmuted into the one of an inmate, then an escaper, and finally of an exile, see the *Mémoires d'un architecte*, op. cit.

10 & 11. Interview by B. F. Dubor & M. Raynaud, op. cit.

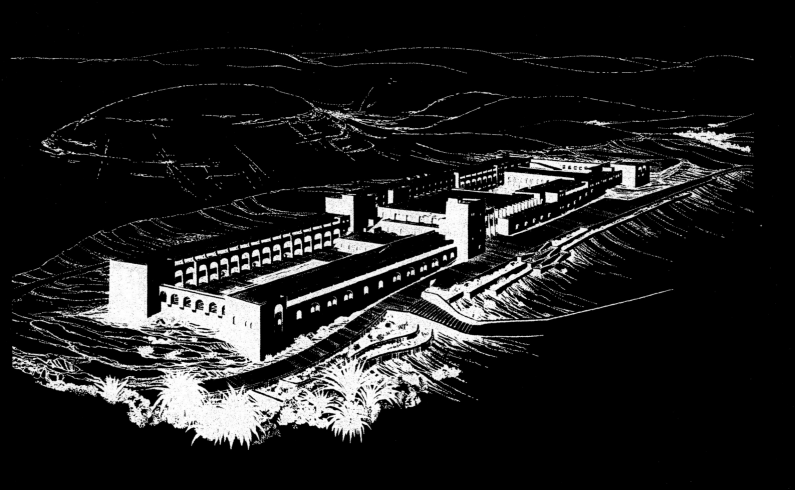

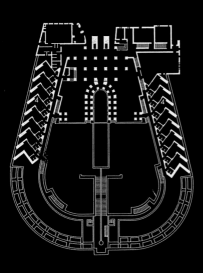

Top:
Ghardaïa, Hotel Les
Rostémides. Axonometric draw-
ing. From Dubor, op. cit

Bottom left:
Ghardaïa, Hotel Les
Rostémides. From Dubor, op.
cit.

Right:
Algeria, Timimoun, Hotel El
Gourara. Plans and elevations.
From Dubor, op. cit.

Algeria, Timimoun, Hotel El
Gourara. The staircase leading
to the swimming pool. Photo
Félix Dubor.

APARTMENT BUILDINGS IN CASABLANCA

TYPES & LIFESTYLES 1930-1950

Monique Eleb

The first architects at work in Casablanca immediately after the first world war imported the doctrines, styles, and know-how from their mother country or from their respective places of education and training: Algiers, Tunis, France, or Italy. The most numerous contingent graduated from the Ecole des Beaux Arts in Paris. In keeping with the time of their arrival and in spite of an evident attempt to integrate some typically Moroccan dimensions, the impact of the contemporary theoretical debates could be observed in the facades and the plans of their buildings. Attentive to local conditions, these architects undertook to take advantage of the peculiarities of the country, without neglecting precise needs and demands. Thus the imported references were transformed by their contact with a different urban culture, just as working teams of variegated disciplinary and ethnic backgrounds were formed, mixing architects and entrepreneurs from Italian origin together with the *m'allemîn*, the Moroccan master artisans. Next to the Protectorate and the large insurance companies, private investors played a determinant role, in a country where the real estate speculation and the needs for housing kept increasing constantly. The rich and *nouveaux riches* Europeans, along with the Jewish North-African bourgeoisie, joined the Moroccan aristocracy in building apartment houses and villas in which they established their residences.

Once the first buildings had been completed, the problem of their inadequacy to the different groups of the population arose. The influx of immigrants — newly arrived French or Moroccan rural families — made the question of housing for single people very critical, while the new and pre-existing habitat ranged from villas and buildings with small apartments to shanty towns. While most of the Europeans were French, Casablanca was populated until 1960 by a highly composite group of Spaniards, Italians, as well as Portuguese, Russians, Poles, Swedes, Englishmen, and Americans, especially after 1945. The French, also from varied regional origins, arrived from the metropolis in total ignorance of the lifestyles of North Africa, Algeria or Tunisia, and in the case of Casablanca, often Jewish. Builders and clients among the latter group were very dynamic and contributed in creating both habits of life and taste that were quickly communicated to the metropolitan population. The contrast between the colonial administration and the poor Muslims, which is the center of most of the studies devoted to the period, appears to be exaggerated: the influence of other European and Moroccan social groups and their direct contribution to the construction of the city is generally not sufficiently taken into account.

At the end of the 1920s, many new quarters were created in Casablanca as a result of the Prost plan. By 1931, the city had 160,000 residents and had set a record in terms of new construction. This was a very prosperous period for the city, in which many quality buildings and houses were erected, most of which were truly for the luxury market, definitely oriented, as the specialized press did not fail to point out, "toward maximum comfort rather than minimum rent."[1] From the stylistic point of view, neo-Moroccan nostalgia continued for some time. Some critics made a subtle distinction between the applied ornamentation derived from foreign cultures and the decoration anchored in local traditions. These positions soon became minority; many architects close to the European modernism attacked the traditionalist attitude of their colleagues.

The facades were now getting barer and barer, and the volumetric composition more and more like a pile of shifted cubes. An aesthetic was born based upon horizontal, vertical, the design of full and void surfaces, free from any decorative tinsel *(fig. 1)*. This was the triumph of the "beautiful quiet nudes,"[2] that the Parisian critics already evoked before the war, the final phase of "the evolution of an architecture which, after a period marked by the large 'rental house' typology and Louis XVI stucco work, moved on to a sort of neo-Arab style...to finally reach a style whose beauty is but the result of a perfect adaptation to local climate and customs."[3] The decorative dimension which dominated the design of facades during the earlier period gave way to a play of volumes, to the rational reflection. The decor stemmed from the new interior distribution: not only did the bow-windows and balconies make the rooms more spacious, or the terraces and bracketed loggias

*Opposite page:
Fig. 1 (see p. 99). Edmond Brion, Bendahan building, square Edmond Doutté, 1935, back facade. Photo Jean-Louis Cohen.*

Top:
Fig. 2. Marius Boyer, Assayag Building, boulevard de la Marine, 1930, general view (origin unknown).

Bottom:
Fig. 3. Marius Boyer, Assayag Building, boulevard de la Marine, 1930, view of the garage ramp. Photo Jean-Louis Cohen.

allow daily outdoors exercises, but they became the structuring elements of the facades. Actually there were observers who expressed the fear that this excessively clean style might incur important risks for "the entire industry of artistic work applied to construction."[4]

As opposed to the pastiche and syncretic vision of the first buildings, the "modern" aesthetic and compositional principles seemed particularly well-suited to Morocco. Some remarked that "the austerity of the principles of a Le Corbusier does not look at all out of context against the background and the simple, harmonious lines of Morocco's horizons."[5] Others went as far as hypothesizing that the sources of inspiration for "modern" architecture had been found in the Maghreb.[6] After a trip to Casablanca, Henri Descamps wrote that "it is curious to notice how well-fit the modern international style is to Morocco: it even creates a happier effect than it does in the countries where it was born."[7] While difficult to acclimate to Paris, the roof terrace was a tradition in Morocco, and it became such a common feature that a pitched roof looked incongruous in the landscape. Jean Gallotti was struck in 1927 by the resemblance between French architecture in Morocco and the houses of Mallet-Stevens in Paris.[8] For European visitors, Casablanca appeared like a huge construction site, a capital of architecture in the making, with a strong influence on new Parisian works.

Around 1930, some new architects entered the Casablanca scene, while the usual references were being transformed through the use of forms more typical of Central Europe than from Paris. Rental houses and low-cost housing were in the vanguard in terms of modernity of design, hygienic facilities, and comfort. The basement floors housed parking garages reserved to the tenants; most of the buildings were equipped with trash incinerators; complete bathrooms were installed in even the smallest units. Washers and dryers, elevators, and service lifts were now indispensable.

Already at the end of the 1920s American skyscrapers, or the ones of Madrid, prompted some architects and developers to imagine modern residential complexes, breaking away with the tradition of the small edifice. The press trumpeted regularly every record height. Marius Boyer, the most original of the local architects, reworked for Moses Assayag in 1930 the "stepped type" or *immeuble à gradins* developed by Henri Sauvage, but in a context more favorable than that of Paris *(fig. 2)*. Besides the strong local demand for terraces, the size of the lots was greater than in Paris, the clients wealthier and strongly determined to exhibit their modernity. The main section of the Assayag building, ten-story high, consisted of three flower-shaped towers. The hexagonal core of each tower housed an elevator and distributed four apartments per floor. A cross-shaped atrium, topped with a glass roof, brought light to the service quarters; an interior street concealed a garage *(fig. 3)*. From the eighth floor up, at the first terraced setback, one found the *garçonnières* or single-men flats, the maid rooms, and duplex apartments who enjoyed a spectacular view on the port and the *zelliges*-covered cupolas of neighboring buildings.[9]

Fig. 4 Marcel Desmet, apartment building, boulevard de la Gare, rue Savorgnan de Brazza, 1931-32, general view. Photo Jean-Louis Cohen.

From then on, high-rise buildings became a true ideal for many architects. With the Assayag building Boyer had the opportunity to demonstrate his perfect understanding of modern Parisian models, and to propose modes of construction yet unknown in Casablanca.[10] Another large-scale operation was that of the "Brazza Complex" which occupied a 45,000 square-foot triangular block (figs. 4, 5). The seven-floor building surrounded a fine central courtyard housing forty stores. One hundred and fifty-six apartments, from one to five rooms, were of the cross-ventilated type, with the main rooms overlooking the street and the secondary ones opening on the central and lateral courtyards.

During the 1930s, luxury apartment buildings blossomed around the most beautiful squares of the city. Across from the gardens of the administrative square, the building by Xavier Rendu and Roger Ponsard borrowed its white and earthly tones from the adjacent city hall built by Boyer, while resembling a typical Parisian corner building with its angle tower and its tripartite composition. The mirador that crowns it made a pleasant addition to the roof terrace. The base housed some stores and apartments; the underground garage was accessed through a ramp and a revolving platform; three main staircases with elevators, two service stairs and two service lifts offered a rare and luxurious quality of service to the six apartments occupying every floor. In addition, the apartments were large and counted many service rooms (figs. 7, 8, 17).

Another highly praised work was the Bendaham building, designed by Edmond Brion, who also lived and worked there. Surrounded by four streets, the main volume rose over an important intersection, and faced one of the busiest squares of the city. Edmond Pauty saw in it a perfect example of French modernity, but insisted on its adaptation to the high standards of the Casablanca population in matter of comfort.[11] The large apartments of three or four rooms had their main rooms aligned on the street facade, while the secondary ones opened on a large courtyard and open-air access corridors distributed by a service stairwell. The architect's studio on the fifth and sixth floor comprised a double-height living room and its upper floor was entirely reserved to the pleasures of body and mind: library/smoking room, mirador, gymnastic room, and garden-terrace (figs. 1, 6, 9, 10).

The "modernization" of the Place de France and the Sidi Belyout district began in 1934 with the construction of the Moretti & Milone building, designed by Pierre Jabin. Its facade expressed clearly its mixed-use organization: the concrete base was arcaded and housed two floors of office; the six lower levels of housing alternated balconies, bow-windows, and brise-soleil windows; the three superior floors had long balconies alternating full and void surfaces; the tenth floor, made up of studios, formed a long loggia with columns, while the last one was reserved to large apartments and studios with a vast terrace overlooking the Place de France, the medina, and the port (fig. 11). The same year, Erwin

Top:
Fig. 5. Marcel Desmet, apartment building, boulevard de la Gare, rue Savorgnan de Brazza, 1931-32, view of the courtyard. Photo Flandrin.

Bottom left:
Fig. 6. Edmond Brion, Bendaham building, square Edmond Doutté, 1935, plan of typical floor.

Top:
Fig. 7. Xavier Rendu & Roger Ponsard, apartment building avenue Mers-Sultan, avenue du Général d'Amade, 1930-31, corner view. Photo Jean-Louis Cohen.

Center:
Fig. 8. Xavier Rendu & Roger Ponsard, apartment building avenue Mers-Sultan, avenue du Général d'Amade, 1930-31, view of the continuity with Marius Boyer's city hall. Photo Jean-Louis Cohen.

Bottom left:
Fig. 9. Edmond Brion, Bendaham building, square Edmond Doutté, 1935, general view. Photo Jean-Louis Cohen.

Bottom right:
Fig. 10. Edmond Brion, Bendaham building, square Edmond Doutté, 1935, view of the courtyard and the open air service corridors. Photo Jean-Louis Cohen.

Top:
Fig. 11. Pierre Jabin, Moretti-Milone building, place de France, 1934-35, general view. Photo Jean-Louis Cohen.

Bottom:
Fig. 12. Erwin Hinnen, Socifrance building, place de France, boulevard de la Gare, 1934-35, general view. Photo Jean-Louis Cohen.

Center:
Fig. 13. Marius Boyer, building Les Studios, avenue d'Amade, 1933, general view. Photo Jean-Louis Cohen.

Top left:
Fig. 14. Marcel Desmet, SIF building, place de la Gare, 1935, general view. Photo Jean-Louis Cohen.

Center left:
Fig. 15. Marcel Desmet, SIF building, place de la Gare, 1935, the claustra wall on the roof. Photo Jean-Louis Cohen.

Top right:
Fig. 16. Marcel Desmet, low-cost housing, boulevard de la Gare, 1935, general view. Photo Jean-Louis Cohen.

Bottom:
Fig. 17. Xavier Rendu & Roger Ponsard, apartment building avenue du Général d'Amade, 1930-31, view from the park. Photo Jean-Louis Cohen.

This text was translated from the French by Jean-François Lejeune and Roselyne Pirson.

Hinnen erected another corner building on the Place de France, which stood out with its rhythmic design of Viennese inspiration, and the usual projecting facades, terraces, and applied decoration (fig. 12).

Generally, the presence of an entrance way and a private laundry room in each apartment put the buildings in the luxury category. In fact, a large square footage area was considered less important than the high level of building equipment and comfort facilities. Even small buildings were often furnished with modern conveniences such as garages, incinerators, elevators, and the laundry room on the roof terrace. All families, even those of clerks in the middle class, had servants: hence the service entrances and separate staircases. One of the main elements of excellence was the large master bedroom, well located with a panoramic view and a terrace. Large families were not supposed to reside in the city center: couples without children or single people were the prime target, as can be seen on the top floors of new buildings which were usually devoted to garçonnières. These single apartments, that until then had been the result of chance or of the need to adjust to the size of the parcel, then became prestigious. In 1932, when the "European" city was already fifteen years in the making, Casablanca was described as a city of bachelors and pioneers who had settled there for a Moroccan adventure.[12]

Marius Boyer had already integrated this theme when he worked on the project "Les Studios" in 1933. Designed for the avant-garde artists and intellectuals, but also for bachelors and couples without children, these small luxury apartments with emphasis on quality of service were an enormous success. Boyer, who was also the owner of the building, reserved for himself an apartment on the top floor, a genuine model of luxury dwelling in a large complex. Consisting of double-height apartments, the building gave on the avenue d'Amade: its windows and loggia grouped four by four under the same brise-soleil was a direct echo to the Studio Building, built in Paris by Henri Sauvage in 1926 on a similar program (fig. 13). Another architect, Marcel Desmet, was seen as one of the best personalities of the avant-garde. His building on Place de la Gare was built above "an arcade imposed by city planning regulations,"[13] and its interior organization adapted to all the criteria of modernity mentioned above (figs. 14, 15). On the roof, the three characteristic elements of habitat in Casablanca could be found: the terrace, the laundry room, and the claustra. The latter had a traditional origin: the moucharabieh, which ornates the traditional houses, allowed to see without being seen, and to ventilate while respecting the privacy.

The problem of providing housing for the functionaries and the low middle class from French or European origin became increasingly urgent with the advent of the economic crisis. But the norms regarding size and comfort of social housing were superior to those applied in France. In spite of the less wealthy clientele, this type of edifice provided the same level of services than the high-level rental complexes (fig. 16). Ferro-concrete, interior partitions in hollow bricks, stuccoed facades, and granito floors to improve acoustic insulation were the materials of choice for all buildings of the period. All entrances, even the modest ones, were treated with great care: pavements integrated mosaic with granito, marble was used in all its variations of texture and color, and the wrought iron doors were often remarkable examples of local craft (figs. 18, 19).

An architect from Rabat also observed that Morocco "is a country where there is much talk about skyscrapers, but where a huge amount of villas are being built."[14] The wealthier and most educated clients often commissioned the architects close to the "modern movement" and renounced the "pastiche" in favor of a new image of the house. "Casablanca—wrote another critic—is without a doubt one of the cities with the finest collection of modern houses in the world."[15] Yet, for many, true luxury remained associated with an image blending architectonic elements from both traditions, the French and the Moroccan (figs. 20, 21). These villas, located in the low-density neighborhoods, in proximity to the central park of the city, were usually mixed with small buildings in Art Deco style.

In contrast, the workers' quarter, designed by Edmond Brion in Aïn Sebaa for the Compagnie Sucrière Marocaine, was inspired by the Habous district which Brion had started, together with Auguste Cadet, ten years earlier. Reserved for Moroccan Muslims, the district was encircled by a wall; two gates allowed passage and access to squares bordered with shops; a mosque, a Koranic school, a fountain, a public oven, and a hammam were also included. The patio houses were protected by a high wall and zigzag entranceways, and their positioning followed strict principles of social hierarchy. During the following years, other industrialists such as Lafarge Cement Works, sponsored other working class districts of this type (figs. 22, 23, 24).

The economic crisis that hit Morocco at the end of the 1930s put a brake to the construction of large buildings. After the war, architects started to experiment with Le Corbusier's theories of collective housing and socio-ethnological research. The systematic study of the lifestyle of the three population groups of the city led to a new conception of housing founded on, in the words of French architect Michel Ecochard, the "secular habits" of the country of origin.[16] Among these experiences, those of ATBAT-Afrique led by Candilis & Bodiansky, became important topics of discussion, particularly among the members of Team X who saw them as an alternative to the atrophying universalism of functionalist theories (fig. 25). Fortunately, the Casablanca of the 1930s had anticipated on this concern for authenticity, and constitutes nowadays a vast corpus of innovative and spectacular urban buildings (fig. 26).

1. "Nouveaux immeubles à Casablanca," *Chantiers Nord Africains*, March 1932, pp. 231-235.

2. See the chapter on the decor in the author's book, *Architecture de la vie privée—La belle époque de l'habitation parisienne, 1880-1914*, Tome II (Brussels: Archives d'Architecture Moderne, 1993).

3. Léandre Vaillat, *Le visage français du Maroc*, op. cit. , 1931, p.12.

4. "Les innombrables visages de l'architecture casablancaine," *Chantiers Nord Africains,* December 1931, p.1208.

5. R. d'Arcos, "L'urbanisme au Maroc," *Chantiers Nord Africains*, October 1929, pp.583-4.

6. Jean Cottereau, "La maison mauresque," *Chantiers Nord Africains*, June 1930, p.538.

7. Henri Descamps, "L'architecture française au Maroc, introduction: la création marocaine," *Chantiers Nord Africains*, October 1930, p.911-2.

8. Jean Gallotti, "Une nouvelle rue à Paris (la rue Mallet-Stevens)," *L'Art Vivant*, n°64 (August 1927).

9. The *zelliges* are enameled terra-cotta tiles, cut by hand according to the required pattern.

10. Marius Boyer, "La construction moderne," unpublished lecture, 23 February 1929, pp.18-19.

11. Edmond Pauty, loc. cit., p.142.

12. "28 garçonnières dans un immeuble," *Chantiers Nord Africains*, February 1932, pp.151-152.

13. *Réalisations*, April 1936, p.153.

14. *Chantiers Nord Africains*, December 1931, pp.1213-1221.

15. *Réalisations*, June 1936, p.162.

16. Michel Ecochard, "Habitat musulman au Maroc," *L'Architecture d'aujourd'hui*, n° 60, June 1955, pp.36-40.

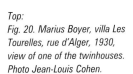

Top:
Fig. 20. Marius Boyer, villa Les Tourelles, rue d'Alger, 1930, view of one of the twinhouses. Photo Jean-Louis Cohen.

Bottom:
Fig. 21. Marius Boyer, villa Benazéraf, rue d'Alger, 1930, view of the entrance. Photo Jean-Louis Cohen.

Top:
Fig. 22. Edmond Brion, workers'
quarter of the Compagnie
Sucrière Marocaine, 1937, general plan.

Center:
Fig. 23. Edmond Brion, workers'
quarter of the Compagnie
Sucrière Marocaine, 1937,
view of an interior street. Photo
Jean-Louis Cohen.

Bottom:
Fig. 24. Edmond Brion, workers'
quarter of the Compagnie
Sucrière Marocaine, 1937,
view of the square. Photo
Jean-Louis Cohen.

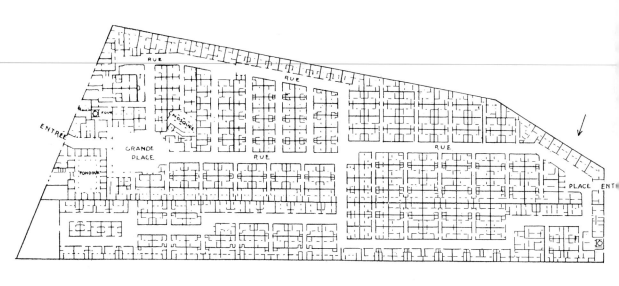

Top left:
Fig. 25. ATBAT-Afrique (George Candilis, Shadrach Woods, architects; Vladimir Bodiansky, Henri Piot, engineers), patio house "nid d'abeilles" (bee-house), district of Carrières Centrales, 1953, detail. Photo Jean-Louis Cohen.

Right:
Fig. 26. Léonard Morandi, Liberté building, 1951, general view. Photo Jean-Louis Cohen.

HENRI PROST & CASABLANCA

THE ART OF MAKING SUCCESSFUL CITIES

Jean-Louis Cohen

The universal aura of Casablanca is rooted in the homonymous movie, whose fiftieth anniversary was celebrated in 1992 and in which the economic capital of Morocco does not appear, whether physically or visually. Its success was such that the Warner Bros almost succeeded in keeping the exclusivity of the city name when they tried to prevent the release of the Marx Brothers' own *One Night in Casablanca* (1946). The unexpected cinematographic resonance of Casablanca doubled the echo already created by numerous and edifying sagas, whose inspiration laid in the French realizations in Morroco as early as 1912. "Fraught with all what the modern industry can provide," Casablanca represented, in the definition of Pierre Mac Orlan, "the spontaneous phenomenon of the 'French energy.'"[1] The city begot rife literary critics while the concrete transformations transformed it into one of the most mythical crucibles of architecture and, above all, of the urbanism of the twentieth century.

The rapid and surprising emergence of Casablanca as the most important North African city of the first decades of the twentieth century could not but marvel observers and artisans alike of France imperial expansion; indeed, the imbalances and the conflicts linked to its growth remained extant in the representations, be they naive or cynical, of that developers' Eldorado. Whereas its historical core, originally called Anfa, had been standing for centuries with its Jewish (*mullah*), Muslim, and European sections, Casablanca belongs, to the major urban creations of our century.[2] With the extensions that the core underwent after 1912, it is actually the main genuine urban area built in the French controlled territories, including the Metropolis, until the advent of the *Villes Nouvelles* of the 1960s.

In reply to numerous commissions of Moroccan and French clients committed to the innovation and the modernization of the city and the country, exceptional teams of technicians and professionals contributed to the blossoming and the development of the economic capital of Morocco. By doing so, they turned the city into a regulatory, technological, and cultural laboratory. When in 1929 Léandre Vaillat noticed not without a hint of frustration that "what is forbidden to the size and the

soil of Paris is allowed with the gigantic and the rocky Casablanca," he acknowledged the ambition of a city to propound a new form of metropolis that could teach a lesson to the Capital of the Empire.[3]

Far from being a mere overseas French city, inscribed in the exclusive relationship of "metropolis-periphery," Casablanca was at once, because of the political specificity of the Protectorate and the profile of the immigrant population, an international as well as a Moroccan city. It was a motley where multifarious prodigies, whether national or local, coalesced. Parallel to an efficient policy of segregation that quickly showed its double visage—the refined one of the new *medina* and the cruel one of the dire and precocious slums—a certain blend of social, national, and cultural elements occurred. In the early years of the Protectorate, Casablanca was the juncture of many Mediterranean cultures and it alloyed the immigrants from Tunisia, Algeria, Italy, and elsewhere. Soon a new phenomenon appeared, i.e., the rampant Americanization, later reinforced by the allied landing in November 1942.

Discovered by French urban planners in the early twenties, the urban policy implemented by the administration of General Lyautey (1854-1934) seemed at first to tackle on the objectives of the Protectorate (instituted in 1912), i.e., to "regenerate" a France which was then on the brink of collapse. It was with lucid determination that Lyautey relied on the nascent urbanism, in an attempt to restore to a humdrum France, its fleeced and wasted "energy." As early as 1924, engineer Edmond Joyant cited as an example in his *Traité d'urbanisme*, the mechanisms that had permitted the transformation of Casablanca "from a sleepy Moorish town into a large, modern mercantile city."[4] The rigorous zoning and land distribution control made it a genuine model, applicable to the metropolis and of which it is essential to understand the basic principles.

Before the Protectorate, the city of Casablanca had a relatively compact initial core, but already from 1907, the establishment of many commercial activities outside of the walls had generated a strong process of expansion. The administration of Lyautey, who was named Resident General on April 26, 1912,

Top left:
Marius Boyer, boulevard de la
Gare, Glaoui building and pas-
sage. Photo Jean-Louis Cohen.

Bottom:
Jean-Claude Nicolas Forestier,
project of a garden for the
Sultan of Morocco,
Casablanca, 1916. Institut
Français d'Architecture.

inherited an urban agglomeration whose development was well under way: thus the planning work in Casablanca did not involve the creation of a new city, but rather the management of its growth. To the east the station of a first railway line toward Rabat began to polarize activities of trade and storage, while discontinuous subdivisions took shape around the old city. The French military had reserved two large enclaves around the camps which were built for the campaign of 1907-1908. In the immediate vicinity of the walls, the construction of the department store France-Maroc, designed by Auguste Perret, and of the Excelsior Hotel soon marked an initial change of scale in the urban fabric.

At first the process of land occupation took place without any form of control on the part of the French administration, whether the settlements were industrial installations scattered near the port, new railroad lines, subdivisions platted by newly arrived French developers, or any other private initiatives. A first plan of land division and street opening was prepared in 1912 by engineer-surveyor Tardif. It called for the construction of a wide circular boulevard, considered very important by the army as it was to connect most of the camps, and passed about a third of a mile beyond the existing urban expansion to the south and the southeast. Yet the larger landowners soon urged Lyautey to prepare a long-term plan. The question was debated by the *Section d'Hygiène Urbaine et Rurale du Musée Social* in Paris, and

Donat-Alfred Agache was entrusted by private developers with the drafting of an initial document.[5]

In 1913 the *Conservateur des Promenades de Paris*, Jean Claude Nicolas Forestier (1861-1930), was invited to Morocco to study the issue of open spaces. In his work, Forestier focused primarily on existing cities such as Fez, Marrakech and Rabat, for which he designed new roads and gardens. His suggestions for the new districts and, in particular, for the design in section of the new streets and arteries, influenced the work of the administration of the Protectorate in the later years.[6] Back from Morocco, Forestier communicated his reflections to the *Section d'Hygiène*. It is at this time, on Forestier's suggestion, that Lyautey nominated Henri Prost (1874-1959) as director of the *Service Spécial d'Architecture et des Plans des Villes* (Department of Architecture and City Plans), with the assignment to work on the entire country.

Upon his arrival in Morroco, Henri Prost was bequeathed a judicial apparatus elaborated by Paul Tirard and Guillaume de Tarde, and which aimed at controlling the urban development in all its aspects.[7] Having moved to Rabat in 1914, Prost found himself faced, in Casablanca, with a situation quite different than in other cities like Fez, Marrakech, Rabat, or Meknès, where he could easily apply the "Lyautey Doctrine" of separate communities. In Casablanca he encountered a city which had been "already substantially built and subdivided without any overall plan." Hence his task aimed, as he later confessed, at "containing damages."[8]

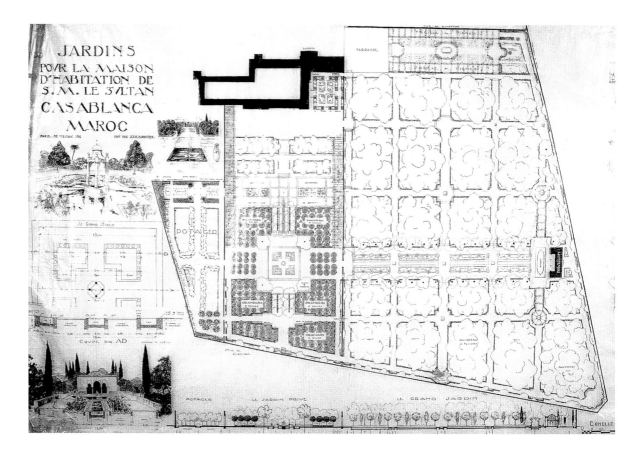

CASABLANCA
EN 1912

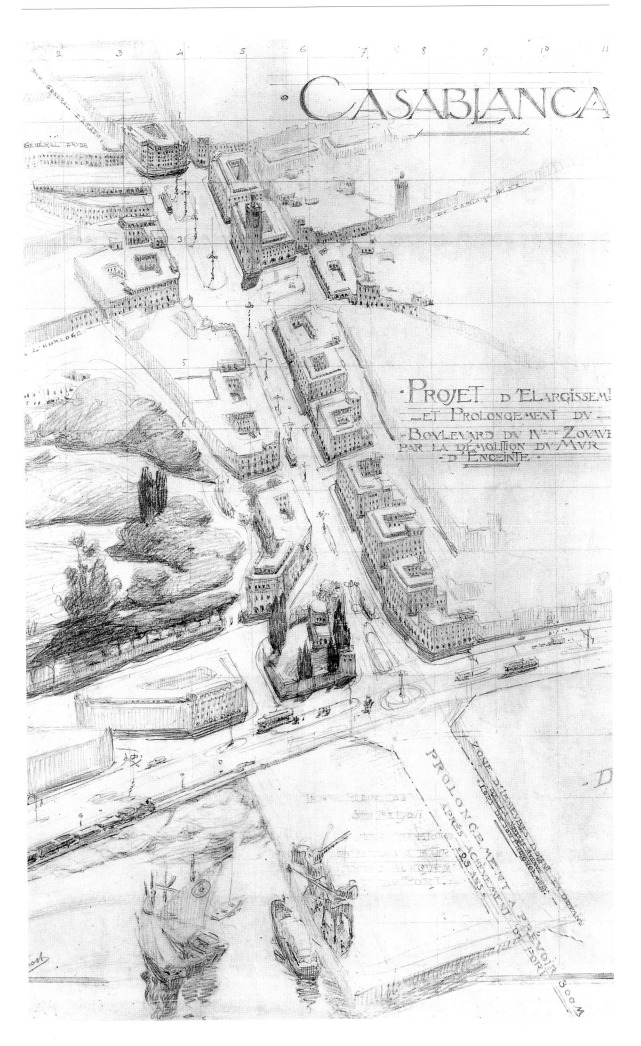

Top left:
Casablanca, plan of the city in 1912. Note the military camps to the south and, to the east, the first railroad station.

Center left:
Donat-Alfred Agache, "Survey of Casablanca by the Syndicat Français des Intérêts de Casablanca," 1914. Note the permanence of the camps and the expansion of the city toward the east.

Right:
Henri Prost, the "Canebière de Casablanca" (future avenue du IV-Zouaves and place de France), October 1914. Fonds Henri Prost, Académie d'Architecture. Note to the right the Medina and in the background the department store France-Maroc.

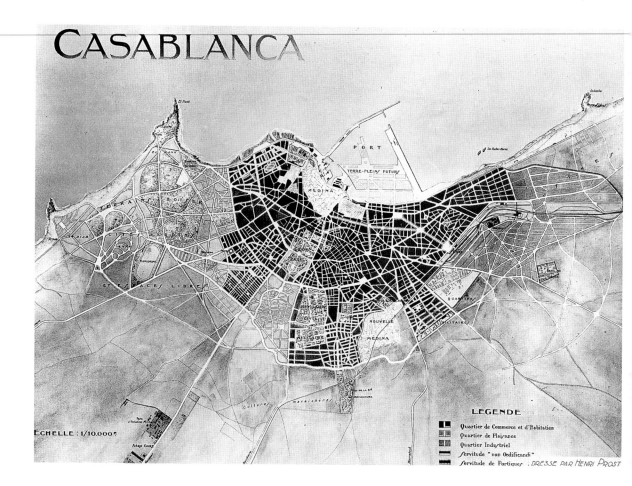

CASABLANCA

Top:
Henri Prost, "Plan d'aménagement et d'extension de Casablanca, 1915, zoning. Fonds Henri Prost, Académie d'Architecture.

Bottom:
Henri Prost, "Plan d'aménagement et d'extension de Casablanca," 1915, aerial perspective. Fonds Henri Prost, Académie d'Architecture.

CASABLANCA

*Aerial view of the city center
toward the north, 1928. Photo
Flandrin.*

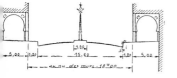

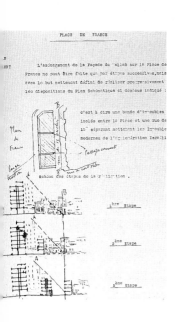

The methodological purview of Prost's work can be seen in the research conducted concomitantly with the development of the plan for Casablanca, in order to create a manual of urban design for all Moroccan Cities. Prost relied on a wide range of foreign experiences, particularly those in Germany, to critically assess the "French Tradition." The formulation of a methodological definition of "what is a city" occupied much of his research work; it was for him a necessary condition to define the urban regulations:

The study of the street network does not constitute per se the city plan. Of equal if not of greater importance is the delimitation of the form of the blocks placed between the public arteries (...).

It is on these blocks that the various buildings, factories, stores, houses, etc.—all the elements that constitute the city—will be erected. The best utilization of the land and the salubriousness of the buildings are contingent on the proportions of the blocks, their dimensions, and the conditions of adjacency of lots and party walls (...).

The problem of creating a new city does not consist only in the layout of the streets and the spatial distribution of the districts, the determination of the parks and public gardens, the positioning of administrative buildings, schools, post offices, hospitals, etc., of the protection of historical monuments and sites; but also of the rational study of the blocks best befitting their function (...).[9]

It is around the very definition of these "buildable blocks"—inspired by the plan of Lausanne and its regulations that Prost had studied thoroughly—that most of his book project was structured. As a follow-up Prost suggested a wide range of models of urban blocks, classified by their density and their volumetric limitations on the streetfronts and interior courtyards; all aimed at achieving a certain degree of morphological homogeneity.

To strengthen the multipolar structure of the city, Prost's plan proposed a unifying system that would "vertebrate" its growth: it was based upon two radial axes tangential to the Medina, respectively from north to south (boulevard du IVème Zouaves, avenue d'Amade) and from west to east (boulevard de la Gare), and a double ring of boulevards.[10] Undoubtedly, the street plan of Casablanca was one of the first to integrally take into account, not only its infrastructure and industrial problems, but also the needs of the rapid motorization of Morocco. Carved for the automobile, the large thoroughfares permitted to connect the center with its commercial density, the remote residential neighborhoods, and the industrial plants; as a consequence, the parking garages acquired an important place amidst the first "monuments" of the city.

The street network originated simultaneously at the port, then in full expansion, and at the main railroad station which, at that time, lied outside of the city. It was between the business district, close to the Medina,

Top left:
*Auguste Perret, Wallut ware-
house, boulevard de Ceinture
and route de Bouskara, 1917-
19, view of the storage area.*

Center and bottom left:
*Land assembling around the
boulevard de la Gare. From:
Edmond Joyant,* Traité d'urbanisme *(Paris, 1924). Plan before
and after the operation.*

Top right:
*Henri Prost, "Plan d'aménage-
ment et d'extension de
Casablanca, 1915, published in*
France-Maroc *in 1917.*

Bottom right:
*The boulevard de Marseilles,
1928. Photo Flandrin.*

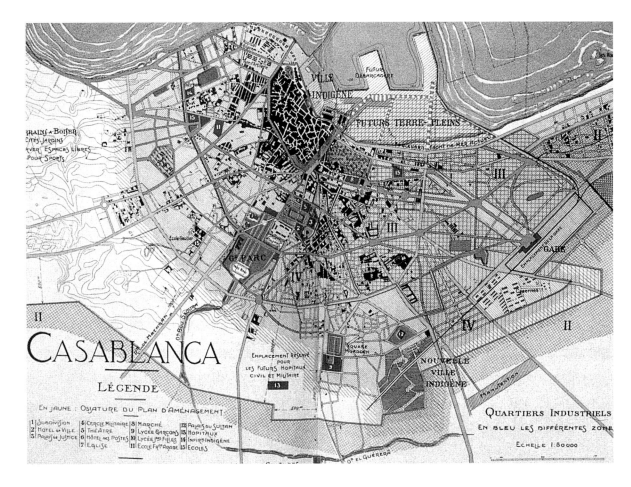

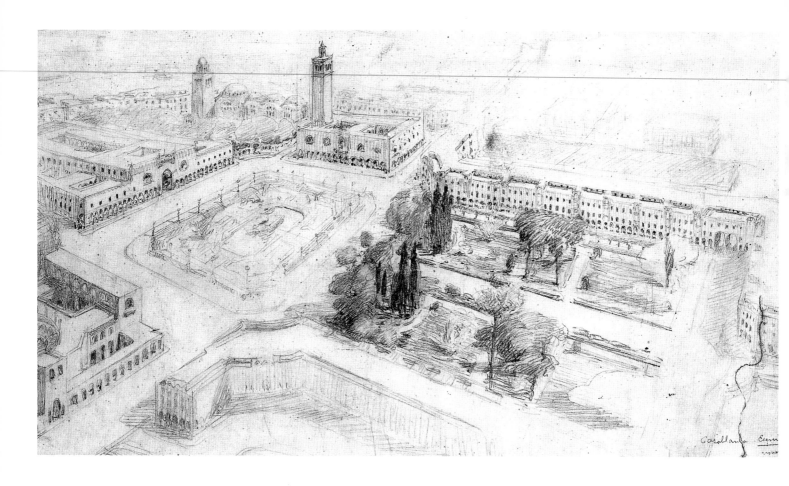

and that new peripheral center that the two and a half kilometers of the boulevard de la Gare were to unfold. From the place de France to the station, it followed a well-defined architectural program, based on the use of arcades, and gathered several of the main public buildings of the new city, including the central market. The very methodology of construction of the boulevard was conceived as a testing ground for the new policies of land consolidation for which Casablanca was to be a laboratory, uniting around common goals, the developers, city officials, urbanists, and architects.[11] The street section of its central segment was eventually handed over as a model to French urbanists during the interwar years.[12]

The plan also established a coherent structure of squares and other open spaces, primarily anchored on two urban poles, the commercial square and the administrative one. The place of France—that Prost had envisioned as early as October 1914, thus prior to his work on the masterplan, as a kind of Canebière of Casablanca (in reference to the renown street in Marseilles)—was articulated with the boulevard of the IVème Zouaves which linked the city to the port while passing along a front of large urban blocks that veiled the Medina. The administrative square was the setting for, among others, the central post office by Adrien Laforgue (1921), the courthouse by Joseph Marrast (1923), and the city hall by Marius Boyer (1937). A porticoed street, the avenue of General Amade, connected the place de France with the administrative square; it was part of the extended network of streets built according to a strict urban code mandating an uni-

tarian architectural composition for the ground floor and the facades. In accordance with the Dahir of April 1, 1924, about twenty squares and major streets were placed under the control of the Service des Beaux Arts between May 1924 and 1930. Layout plans and volumetric profiles were specified for each street, accompanied in some cases by sketches for "prototypical facades."[13]

The Prost plan was implemented through twenty-three "sub-plans," completed by neighborhood codes. These were subjected to public hearing before being enacted in specific Dahirs.[14] Not only did these codes permit to control the street frontage by defining the building section, but they also applied to the depth of the block itself, thus materializing Prost's discourse about the "buildable block."[15] Yet the most innovative element introduced by Prost was the definition of a series of functional zones, thus echoing a practice already initiated in Germany, common in America, and discussed at length within the *Section d'Hygiène Urbaine et Rurale du Musée Social* in Paris.[16]

In practice, two types of zones were established. On the one hand, and to address the "constraints to be imposed on property owners for the benefit of hygiene, circulation, and aesthetics," the European city was divided into three zones, "central," "industrial," and "residential," the latter dedicated to the construction of villas and private houses. On the other hand, to respond to the issue of insalubrity and nuisances, six other zones were defined. Prost's aim was quite clear: in the end, with the disappearance of the "indigenous city" which he believed to be of "no artistic interest, inadequate

for the needs of European commerce," the new city "would expand in direct contact with the port across its entire length." In order that this city be simultaneously "practical and healthy," two types of new quarters were defined, on the basis of criteria derived from the study of European and American cities. Clearly differentiated by the zoning, the main components of the city would be the business district, a notion which was still relatively rare in France, and the residential quarters with single-family houses, the only typology which "permits the population to live in good hygienic conditions."[17]

Looking back upon the development of Casablanca, in the destiny of which he remained involved after his departure in 1923 until the beginning of the 1930s, Henri Prost deplored the narrowness of the new streets and the limits of the land assembling process: "the application of this principle encounters insurmountable difficulties when the land needed for the large arteries absorbs almost all of the private land, without many possibilities of compensation."[18] Actually, it seems that these operations ceased after Prost's departure.[19] Yet it is obvious that the implementation of the architectural ordinances and regulations and the relatively high quality of the buildings created a truly exceptional urban continuity: particularly memorable were the public spaces of the city center, further ramified into arcades and passages, and the characterization of the streets with public buildings. When Prost left Casablanca, most of the street system had been put into place, and very specific urban sections or districts were identifiable: the residential neighborhood of Anfa and its first villas built from the top of the hill down; the business districts, the city center included; and those conceded to the Muslim population, like the new Medina of the Habous district.

Made rapidly obsolete by the constant influx of the Moroccan population, housed from the beginning of the colonization in the infamous *derbs*, the housing policy for the "natives" shifted to the construction of a new Medina, placed under the architectural sponsorship of the Sultan's Palace. The realization was entrusted to Albert Laprade, whose design, attentive to the integration of local Arab-Andalusian themes, was completed by Auguste Cadet and Edmond Brion. "A savorous meditation on the theme of Oriental life pursued by European artists," in the words of Léandre Vaillat, this new Arab city also aimed at "containing vice."[20] Soon the new Medina proved insufficient as well in the face of spontaneous settlements of constructions in the form of aggregates of gas cans, which received the nickname of *bidonvilles*.[21]

Contrary to the general preconception, the three decades that followed Prost's departure were not a mere and peaceful process of implementation of his plan. The city was essentially built during this period, in a rather controlled manner, and with a varied architecture, both in building types and forms. For the most part, the architecture remained within the defined guidelines, a fact which validated a posteriori the value and adequacy of the initial decisions. Begun by Prost at the beginning of the first world war, the work on the plan of Casablanca galvanized, after 1918, the interest of the pioneers of urbanism. When Edmond Joyant proposed, in his *Traité d'urbanisme*, the notion of "differentiated regulations" for neighborhoods—a concept comparable to zoning—he made use of two concrete examples: Casablanca and Metz. His "scheme of a city and its various zones" raised to the level of a generalized model the typological structure of the new city of the Protectorate.[22]

While the fame of Casablanca continued to expand, the new district projected between the place de France and the sea developed at the end of the 1920s as a business center; the goal was to give to the city in full portuary expansion a visage more in line with its avowed ambitions.[23] Prost himself had remarked that "the skyline of Casablanca, when one arrives from the sea, is quite discouraging. It is a mere horizontal line without any visual impact. But, if five or six large vertical "stripes" were to occupy the landscape, one could hope that the general impression made by Casablanca would be much more satisfactory than the current one."[24] In the search for a new image for the city, New York

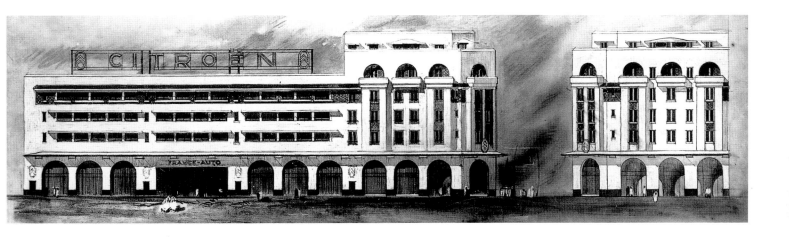

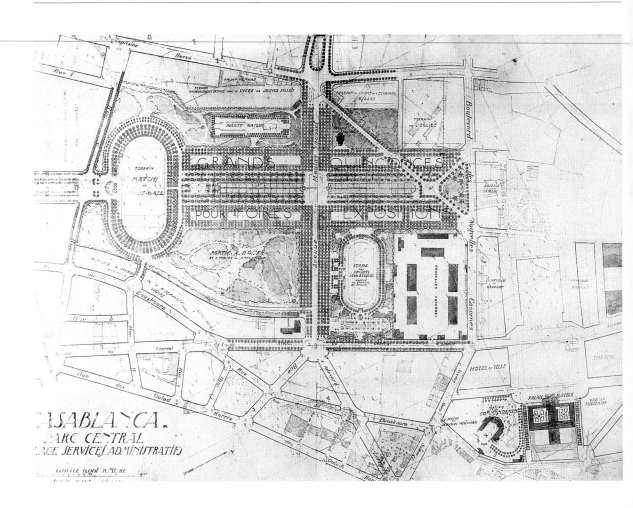

CASABLANCA.
PARC CENTRAL
PLACE SERVICES ADMINISTRATIFS

Translated from the French by
Jean-François Lejeune and
Roselyne Pirson.

became the obliged point of reference. Already in 1914, many saw in the impetuous development of Casablanca, signs of an "American city,"[25] while Walter Berry, president of the American Chamber of Commerce of Paris, breathed the air of a "Yankee atmosphere."[26] In the words of General d'Amade, the comparison reached the status of a cliché: "before the end of the century, the North African France will be the United States, and Casablanca 'New York.'"[27] As for Léandre Vaillat, he expected "to see rising, at the heart of this city of conquerors, with its violent soul, a group of skyscrapers."[28]

The theme acquired another dimension when the decision to build a denser center, and thus to relax the height regulations around the place de France, was taken at the end of the 1920s. While Prost continued to send precise directives from Paris, architects such as Antoine Marchisio, Edmond Brion, and Marius Boyer designed unabatedly North American proposals for the new center.[29] Yet the discussed hypotheses referred more clearly to the model of operation epitomized by Donat-Alfred Agaches's plan for Rio de Janeiro, in which he combined the third dimension and the Beaux-Arts methods of composition in the creation of the administrative center linked to the harbor.[30] In 1929, the Service des Beaux-Arts redefined the ordonnance of the Place de France: it introduced "buildings with multiple setbacks, without interior courtyard, allowing a larger development of usable area," and prescribed for the port district "a grandiose ordonnance" to be designed by Marchisio with "fifteen-story buildings linked by porticoes and bridges."[31] One year later, a new and more ambitious scheme was presented to the municipal commission, a city district whose "high constructions" would fill "the dispersed and surprising skyline, the lack of ordonnance, and the apparent disproportions, producing in contrast a powerful stage set, expressive of the character and decidedness of the city, as an affirmation of power and will."[32] Pierre Jabin's Moretti building was the first operation to respond to the new volumetric regulations *(see fig. 11, p. 100).*

During the second world war and until the allied landing of 1942, Casablanca was more than ever the *plaque tournante* of French and North African mutual relationship, a privileged position that would ensure its prosperity up to the time of Independence. The 1945-1955 urban transformations followed two distinct processes: on the one hand, the urbanists of the Protectorate, whose leader from 1945 to 1952 was Michel Ecochard, proposed a new, functionalist approach of the urban structure;[33] on the other hand, a group of young architects from diverse origins—among whom the ATBAT-Afrique was the most cohesive team—radically transformed the approach to the question of housing, schools, medical, cultural or industrial infrastructure, while remaining within the general urban framework defined by Prost forty years earlier.

Opposite page:

Top:
Albert Laprade, project for the Lyautey Park, 1919. Fonds Albert
Laprade, Archives Nationales. The administrative square is the lower
right corner.

Bottom:
Albert Laprade, central alley of Lyautey Park, 1919. Fonds Albert
Laprade, Archives Nationales. At the end of the alley is the
commandant's headquarters.

This page:
The boulevard Moulay-Youssef. Photo Jean-Louis Cohen.

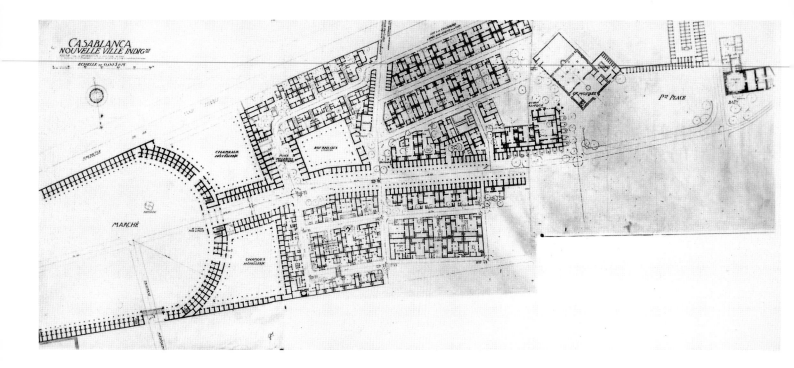

CASABLANCA
NOUVELLE VILLE INDIGNE
ECHELLE de 0.005 P.M.

MARCHÉ

Top:
Albert Laprade, project for a
new indigenous city,
Casablanca, 1917, general
plan. Fonds Albert Laprade,
Archives Nationales.

Bottom:
New indigenous city, view of a
commercial street, circa 1925.
Fonds Albert Laprade, Archives
Nationales.

1. Pierre Mac Orlan, "Bouzbir," *Rues secrètes*, Paris: Arléa, 1989, p. 46.

2. On the history of the city before the Protectorate, see: André Adam, *Histoire de Casablanca (des origines à 1914)* (Aix-en-Provence: Ophrys, 1968); *Annales de la Faculté des Lettres d'Aix-en-Provence*, nouvelle série, n° 66; Jean-Louis Miège, "Les origines du développement de Casablanca au XIXème siècle," *Hespéris*, n° XL, 1953, pp.199-255.

3. Léandre Vaillat, *Le visage français du Maroc* (Paris: Horizons de France, 1931), p. 6.

4. Edmond Joyant, "Casablanca," *Traité d'urbanisme* (Paris: Eyrolles, 1924; 1928, 2nd. edition), vol. 2, p. 95.

5. The Agache plan is reproduced in: Michel Ecochard et al., *Rapport préliminaire sur l'aménagement et l'extension de Casablanca*, Rabat: Direction de l'Intérieur, Service de l'Urbanisme, 1951, p. 10.

6. Jean Claude Nicolas Forestier, *Des réserves à constituer au dedans et aux abords des villes capitales du Maroc*, Paris, December 1913 (typewritten).

7. First among the legislative measures was a law (Dahir of August 12, 1913) that regulated the land division market while condoning egregious despoilment, and which was accompanied by the creation of an extremely precise cadastre controlled by a special department; second was the Dahir of April 16, 1914, which addressed the issues of "alignments, regulating plans and plans of expansion, urban regulations, and and taxes." In addition was the Dahir of August 31 which allowed mass expropriation and recovery of speculative gains, thereby granting municipalities extra profits. Finally, the Dahir of November 13, 1917 regarding the union of landowners, authorized land assembling operations which were impossible at the time in France.

8. Henri Prost, *L'urbanisme au Maroc* (project of publication), undated, circa 1920, Fonds Henri Prost, Académie d'Architecture, E6 15.

9. Ibidem, E6 36-37.

10. On the state of the city in 1914, see *L'essor industriel de Casablanca, enquête sur les entreprises industrielles de Casablanca* (Casablanca: Editions de La Vigie marocain, 1914).

11. On the boulevard de la Gare, see Amne Alaoui Fdili, *Casablanca 1913-*

1940, un plan, une percée (Paris: Ecole d'Architecture Paris-Villemin, 1986).

12. See the two versions of these drawing in: Jean Raymond, *L'urbanisme à la portée de tous* (Paris: Dunod, 1925), p. 66; id., *Précis d'urbanisme moderne* (Paris, Dunod, 1934), p. 147.

13. See the list of some twenty arteries controlled by specific regulations in: "Service des Beaux-Arts et des Monuments Historiques," *Historique (1912-1930)* (Rabat: Direction Générale de l'Instruction Publique, des Beaux-Arts et des Antiquités Historiques, 1931), p. 287.

14. Edmond Joyant, "Le plan d'aménagement de Casablanca," loc. cit., p. 166.

15 Examples of urban regulations can be found in: Edmond Joyant, *Traité d'urbanisme*, op. cit., vol. 2, p. 105.

16. Upon the elaboration of the zoning process in Germany, see Franco Macuso, *Le vicende dello zoning* (Milan: Il Saggiatore, 1978).

17. Henri Prost, "Le Plan de Casablanca," France-Maroc: 15 August 1917, p. 11.

18. Henri Prost, "L'urbanisme au Maroc," *Chantiers Nord Africains*, February 1932, p. 119.

19. *Rapport préliminaire sur l'aménagement et l'extension de Casablanca*, op. cit., p. 6.

20. Léandre Vaillat, *Le visage français du Maroc* (Paris: Horizons de France, 1931), pp. 12 & 16.

21. Pierre Mac Orlan, "Bouzbir," op. cit., p. 47.

22. Edmond Joyant, *Traité d'urbanisme*, op. cit., vol. 1, plate 253.

23. Jean Eyquem, *Les ports de la zone française du Maroc, leur rôle économique* (Alger: Ancienne Imprimerie V. Heintz, 1933), pp. 33-145.

24. Henri Prost, "L'urbanisme au Maroc," loc. cit., p. 119.

25. *L'essor industriel de Casablanca*, op. cit., p. 35.

Top:
Albert Laprade, project for a new indigenous city, Casablanca, 1917, study sketch for the streets. Fonds Albert Laprade, Archives Nationales.

Center:
"Bidonvilles" in the periphery of Casablanca. Postcard. Courtesy Jean-Louis Cohen.

Bottom:
Albert Laprade, project for a new indigenous city, Casablanca, 1917, study sketch for the blocks. Fonds Albert Laprade, Archives Nationales.

26. Alfred de Tarde, "Le Maroc école d'énergie," op. cit., p. 60.

27. Général d'Amade, letter prefaced to J. Goulven, in *Casablanca de 1889 à nos jours* (Casablanca: Flandrin, 1928; reprint Casablanca: Serar, 1988).

28. Léandre Vaillat, *Le visage français du Maroc*, op. cit., p. 5.

29. *La construction moderne*, 14 December 1930, p. 170.

30. See Donat-Alfred Agache, *Cidade do Rio de Janeiro, extensaõ, remodelacaõ, embellezamento. Organisacaõ projectadas pela administracaõ, Antonio Prado Junior* (Paris: Foyer Brésilien, 1930).

31. "Service des Beaux-Arts et des Monuments Historiques," op. cit., pp. 287-288.

32. "Procès-verbal de la réunion officieuse de la Commission Municipale pour échanges de vues sur le projet d'aménagement des quartiers voisins du port," *Bulletin Municipal Officiel de la Ville de Casablanca*, February-March 1930.

33. Michel Ecochard, *Casablanca le roman d'une ville* (Paris: Editions de Paris, 1955).

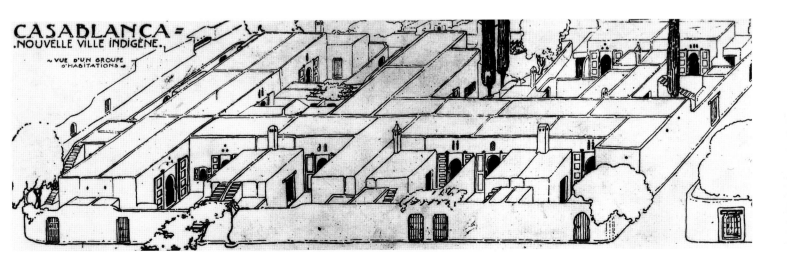

Top:
The main avenue of the
European section of the city of
Fez. Masterplan by Henri Prost.
From L'oeuvre de Henri Prost,
op. cit.

Henri Prost was born in Paris on February 24, 1874. He studied at the Ecole Spéciale d'Architecture, and later at the Ecole des Beaux-Arts. In 1902, he won the Grand Prix de Rome with a project for a National Printing Office. Along with his contemporaries Tony Garnier and Léon Jaussely, he became interested in urbanism, a nascent discipline in France. During his residence in Rome, he traveled to Istanbul, where he made extraordinary survey drawings of Haghia Sophia. In 1910, he won First Prize in the international competition for the expansion of the city of Antwerp in Belgium, while participating with Eugène Hénard and the *Musée Social* to the study of the first expansion plan of Paris.

Lyautey called him to Morocco in 1913, where he directed during ten years the Department of City Planning. Free from the bureaucratic weight of the metropolis, he worked on new city plans for Fès, Marrakech, Meknès, Rabat, and Casablanca. His plans took in consideration, in a well differentiated manner, the landscape and history of each city, and proposed to regulate their growth through a rigorous set of urban regulations. In Casablanca, his efforts concentrated on the creation of large public spaces and on the development, in collaboration with major landowners and developers, of a street system to prepare future growth.

Bottom:
View of Rabat with the 300-ft
wide access avenue through
the European town from
Casablanca. The masterplan
was done by Henri Prost; the
experimental gardens were
designed by J. C. N. Forestier.
In the background the medina
and the walls of the Arab city.
From L'oeuvre de Henri Prost,
op. cit.

Back in France, he developed the regional plan of the Coast of Var in the South of France (1923-26), with a particular attention to the layout of roads and the protection of the landscape. In 1928, he was commissioned to draw the first general plan of the Paris Region, in collaboration with French engineer Raoul Dautry. Completed in 1934, the plan proposed not only the introduction of zoning at the regional scale, but also the development of an ambitious freeway and parkway system.

In the 1930s, Prost made new plans for Algiers and Metz. In addition to his teaching career, he spent much of his time working in Istanbul, whose development he supervised until 1951. He was director of the Ecole Spéciale d'Architecture from 1929 until his death in Paris in 1959.

J.-L. C.

Opposite page:

Top left:
Henri Prost. Extension plan of the city of Fez.
From L'oeuvre de Henri Prost, *op. cit.*

Top right:
Henri Prost. Extension plan of the city of Casablanca.
From L'oeuvre de Henri Prost, *op. cit.*

Bottom left:
Henri Prost. Extension plan of the city of Rabat.
From L'oeuvre de Henri Prost, *op. cit.*

Bottom right:
Henri Prost. Extension plan of the city of Marrakech.
From L'oeuvre de Henri Prost, *op. cit.*

Red: housing and commercial district (mixed-use).
Green: residential district.
Light brown: industrial district.
White: indigenous Arab city.

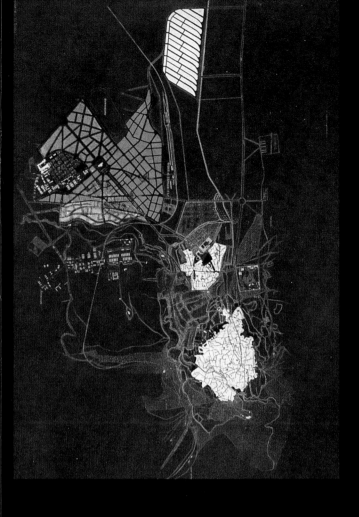

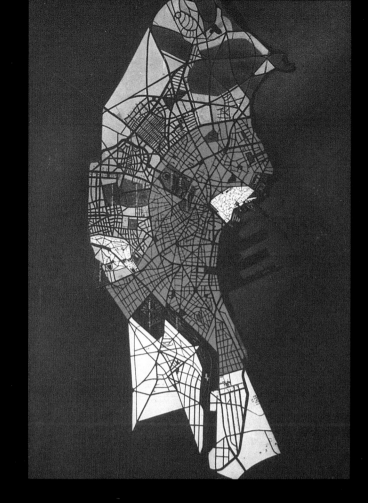

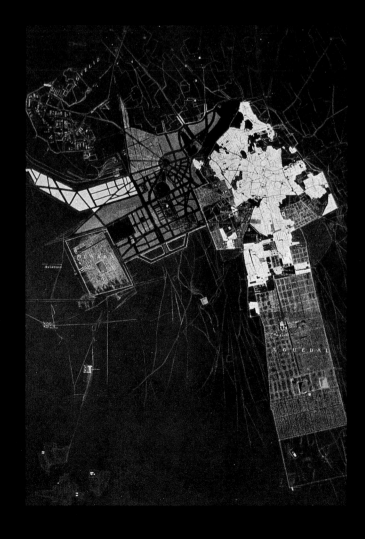

What is God? It is length, width, height, and depth, all at once. These four divine attributes are the objects of as many contemplations.
Bernard de Clairvaux, quoted by Fernand Pouillon in Les Pierres Sauvages (Paris: Le Seuil, 1964).

This page:

Bernard Bellotto de Canaletto. Die Altstadt von Dresden vom Neustädter Brückenkopf (The Old Town of Dresden seen from the bridge on the New Town side), *1765. Oil on canvas, 99.5 x 134 cm. © Staatliche Kunsthalle Karlsruhe, Inv.-Nr. 2518.*

Opposite page:

Bernard Bellotto de Canaletto. Der Neumarkt in Dresden von der Jüdenhofe aus (The new market in Dresden seen from the Jüdenhofe), *1749. Detail. Oil on canvas, 136 x 237 cm. © Staatliche Kunstsammlungen Dresden, Gemäldegalerie Alte Meister, Nr. 613.*

Right:
Hans Kollhoff & Helga
Timmerman (Jasper Jochimsen,
project director). Daimler Benz
Project Potsdamer Platz,
Building A1. CADD perspective
by Dieter Gretscher with Bojan
Blecic.

Center:
Eduard Gärtner. The
Bauakademie, Berlin (Karl-
Friedrich Schinkel, 1832-35).
Oil on canvas, 1868.
© Nationalgalerie Berlin.

FIN-DE-SIECLE

Editorial
Jean-François Lejeune

I

The third volume of THE NEW CITY series was first discussed four years ago in the atrium of the Archives d'Architecture Moderne in Brussels. One interlocutor was the author, a resident of Miami Beach, the other was Philippe Lefebvre, now Brandeis, who a couple of years earlier left Brussels and its "luttes urbaines" to reclaim his Mediterranean roots in Israel. Exchanging impressions and "scientific" descriptions, we came to the conclusion that Miami Beach and Tel Aviv were quite similar cities, genuinely urban yet marked by a "horizontal" architecture that had as much to do with the International Style than with the rules of "traditional" architecture. Hence the idea was born to investigate further how traditional urbanism and modern architecture adapted to each other, lot by lot, but as detached structures. This convergence was academically recognized when the City of Tel Aviv decided to organize the 1994 International Style Architecture Conference (May 22-28) and made the City of Miami Beach a co-sponsor of the meeting.

The conference developed a broad and "revisionist" agenda, that contrasted strongly with previous events such as Terence Riley's a-critical reconstruction of the International Style Exhibition in 1992. First, it acknowledged the contribution of the anonymous or forgotten "masters" who built our cities and neighborhoods of the 20th century, often in the modern style and for the middle-class. It is in "everyday architecture" that these architects invented the "vernacular modern"—a mix of classicism and modernism—that the International Style architects refused to recognize. Secondly, it stressed the urgency to pursue an aggressive agenda of preservation of this fabric—a task that associations such as DOCOMOMO or the MIAMI BEACH PRESERVATION LEAGUE have successfully embarked upon. Lastly, it denounced the anti-democratic equation made in the 1920-30s—and even more so after the war by the orthodox voices of history—between the socio-architectural goals of modernism and the destructive, libertarian agenda of the "open city" and the "end of the street." Thus it made clear that the idea of universality implicit in the modern project was not incompatible with an architecture established in its context, and that the "traditional" city of streets, squares, and blocks was and remained the truest and richest receptacle of modern architecture.

Miami Beach, Tel Aviv, Casablanca, and the German garden cities of Schmitthenner, Taut, Schumacher, etc.—analyzed in this book—were not unique and isolated cases. In districts and cities such as Copacabana, Messina, Guidonia, Sabaudia, Cairo, the Bronx's Grand Concourse—to name a few—traditional urban culture and realities of real estate prevailed and enticed the modern-oriented architects to mediate between the urban scale and the individual expression. As early as 1970 historian David Gebhard argued that neither the International Style nor any other European-based transplant was widely built in the US, whereas a broader "Moderne" was, that absorbed International Style elements such as horizontality and white-stuccoed facades.[1] A similar conclusion could easily be reached for many countries, including the cradle of modernism, Germany. Recent books such as John Zukowsky's The Many Faces of Modern Architecture Building in Germany between the World Wars (Munchen-New York, 1994) and Vittorio Magnago

Lampugnani's exhibition and catalog Moderne Architektur in Deutschland: 1900–1950—Reform und Tradition (Frankfurt, 1992) clearly demonstrated that the Bauhaus was but one small stream of German modernity. The "discovery" of the reconstructed Bauhaus-Dessau at the heart of a genuine garden city district and the very existence of the modernist fabric of Tel Aviv have closed the circle; the last myth of "Giedonesque" reading of history has been dismantled.

II

Between Jerusalem and Berlin looms the huge figure of Eric Mendelsohn. It is a pity that his works in Israel have been unjustly overlooked, for they embody the genuine encounter of the spirit of European modernism with the Mediterranean roots and soil. The debate between North and South, led in words and projects by Hugo Häring, Alberto Sartoris, Gruppo 7, and others is a fascinating topic of history-theory that deserves further examination. In Israel their encounter led to true synthesis, to architectural syncretism. Mendelsohn did not abandon any of the modern principles that he had put into use in Germany; he fused them in the language of stone—its use was imposed by the British Mandate in the 1940s and is still in force today—thus reinventing modernity. In a similar way but on a grander scale, Fernand Pouillon metamorphosed the housing bars and the open space of modern planning through the use of stone. But one should not err: drawn in their context, his districts are thoroughly and unabatedly modern. Here stone and other traditional materials salvaged, transcended, elevated his housing districts to the pinnacle of "new urban foundations."

III

At the end of a century which saw architecture and city destroyed by ideology and greed more than by military acts and natural disasters, how can one resist quoting Alan Balfour's assessment of the Berlin of the Future published in World Cities–Berlin, a jewel of "perverse" criticism: "A city formed from simple, unambiguous orders of streets and squares, formed also from what might be described as post-industrial consciousness—egalitarian, pedestrian, organized for social stability, asserting civil order over corporate speculation, opposed to change, opposed to speed, opposed to the city as machine, as social experiment."[2] This book is not the only one about present Germany to be saturated by the discourse of the current avant-garde—mostly the American propaganda machine of Daniel Liebeskind, Peter Eisenman, and allies such as Philip Johnson. Liebeskind's jeremiad against the "staggering degree of regimentation and control" in Berlin edges on the ridiculous: "in certain circles in Berlin, and elsewhere, there is an ugly atmosphere which resembles the pathology of the time in which the notion of 'degenerate art' was born."[3] Balfour raves against codes, limited building heights, respect of block structure, all principles that are the lot of civilized societies and cities such as Paris, Barcelona, or Washington DC. Furthermore he goes as far as to mourn and 'rehabilitate' the spaceless, prefabricated suburbs where East German planners encased the workers to "free" them from "the oppressive conventions of nineteenth century urbanism."[4] Instead of such outdated ideological reading, one should rather question why, under similar regulations, the buildings of the 1990s cannot match the

1 David Gebhard quoted by Terry Smith, Making the Modern: industry, art, and design in America (Chicago & London: The University of Chicago Press, 1993): 395-6 and note 35.

2 Alan Balfour, World Cities–Berlin (London: Academy Editions, 1995): 309.

3 Daniel Liebeskind, in World Cities–Berlin, op. cit.: 36.

4 Alan Balfour, op. cit.: p. 308.

5 Claus Käpplinger, "Mélange berlinois," L'architecture d'aujourd'hui 297 (Feb. 1995): 89.

6 Fritz Neumeyer, "Head first through the wall: an approach to the non-word 'facade,'" Hans Kollhoff (Berlin: Ernst & Sohn, 1995): 87.

7 Bullett paragraphs reproduced from Hans Stimmann, "Urban Design and Architecture after the Wall," World Cities 3–Berlin, op. cit.: 48-53.

8 The reconstruction of the church and its financing are coordinated by the Gesellschaft zur Förderung des Wiederaufbaus der Frauenkirche Dresden, e.V., Dresden.

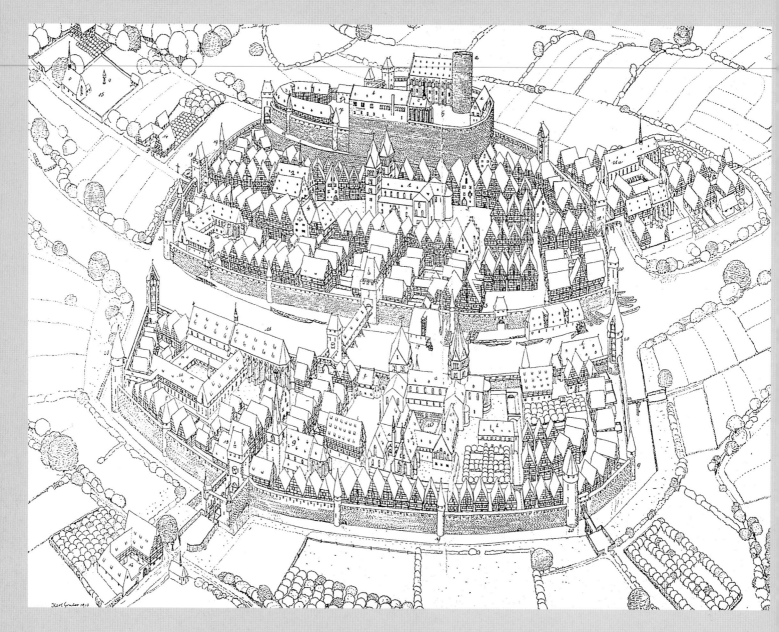

These four drawings belong to Karl Gruber's thesis *Eine deutsche Stadt–Bilder sur Entwicklungsgeschichte der Stadtbaukunst published in Munchen in 1914. They were republished in 1952 in Die Gestalt der deutschen Stadt (see next page). They narrate the evolution of a generic city of Germany, located for instance on the Neckar or the Main river.*

The four "moments" can be considered as the most characteristic of its history: the city after its foundation around 1250, at the apex of the medieval bourgeoisie in the middle of the fourteenth century, at the advent of princely power in the sixteenth century, and finally during the Absolutist period around 1750.

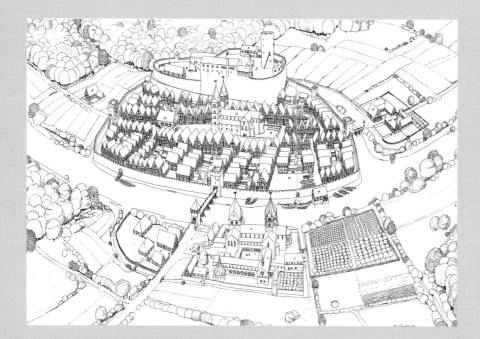

Left:
Karl Gruber, 1913. German city around 1250.
1. Parish church; 2. Town hall; 3. Castle (a: dungeon; b: central building; c: kitchen; e,f: rooms); 4. Advanced fortress; 5. Town gates; 6. Warehouse; 7. Mill; 8. Cemetery; 9. Inns; 10. Hospital and chapel; 11. Benedictine convent (a: church; b: atrium; c: cloister; d. dormitory; e: refectory; f: kitchen; g: hospital; h: abbey-house; i: hostelry; k: gate; l: lay chapel; m: toilets; n: domestic courtyard.)

Top:
Karl Gruber, 1913. German city around 1350.
1. Parish church; 2. Town hall; 3. Wheat market; 4. Wedding hall; 5. Stone house; 6. Castle (a: dungeon; b: former central building; c: chapel; d: new central building; e: housing wing); 7. Advanced fortress; 8. Town hall of town extension (vorort=suburb); 9. Parish church of town extension; 10. Benedictine convent (a: church; b: cloister; c: dormitory; d. refectory; e: kitchen; f: lay monks house, to become the abbey house; g: hostel; h: hospital; i: wheat warehouse; k: mill); 11. Dominican convent (l: stone dormitory; m: half-timbered temporary building; n: toilets); 11a. Franciscan convent; 12. Nuns convent; 13. Hospital with church; 14. Inns; 15. Cemetery (p: chapel; q: lantern of the dead; r: ossuary); 16. Leperhouse; 17. Mills; 18. Gates (s: barbican); 19. Flanking towers; 20. High towers.

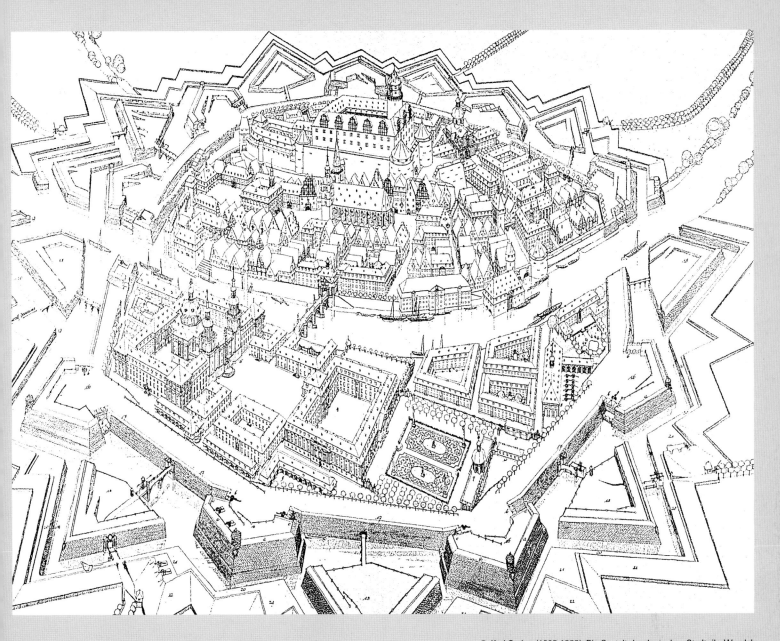

© *Karl Gruber (1885-1966),* Die Gestalt der deutschen Stadt: ihr Wandel aus der geistigen Ordnung der Zeiten *(Munchen: Callwey, 1952).*

Top drawings photographed from original prints. Bottom drawings photographed from French edition under the title Forme et caractère de la ville allemande *(Bruxelles: Archives d'Architecture Moderne, 1985). Courtesy AAM, Maurice Culot.*

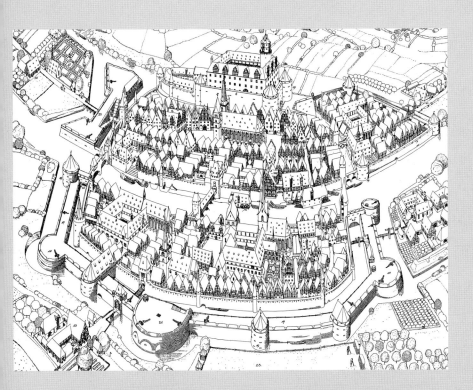

Left:
Karl Gruber, 1913. German city around 1550.
1. Parish church; 2. New town hall; 3. Wheat market; 4. New warehouse; 5. Nuns convent; 6. Castle; 7.Benedictine convent (a:new choir; b:chapter house and library; c: new abbey-house); 8. Dominican convent; 9. Franciscan convent; 10. Parish church of town extension; 11. Parish hospital of town extension; 12. Mills; 13. Inns; 14. Infirmary; 15. Cemetery; 16. Capuchin convent; 17. Walls; 18. "Rondell" or round bastion; 19. Battery towers; 20. Moats; 21. Big bastion; 22. "Horn" bastions; 23. Fire range.

Top:
Karl Gruber, 1913. German city around 1750 after the Wars of Religion.
1. Parish church; 2. Town hall; 3. Old castle (Alte Schloss); 4. New castle (Neue Schloss); 5. Jesuit college; 6. Jesuit church; 7. Orangery; 8. Arsenal; 9. Stables; 10. Guard house; 11. Hospital with church; 12. Convent of minor friars; 13. New town gate; 14. New parish church; 15. Nuns convent; 16. Bastions (a: face; b: flanks; c: ears); 17. Curtain; 18. Raveling; 19. Counterscarp; 20. Protected walk; 21. Place d'armes; 22. Glacis.

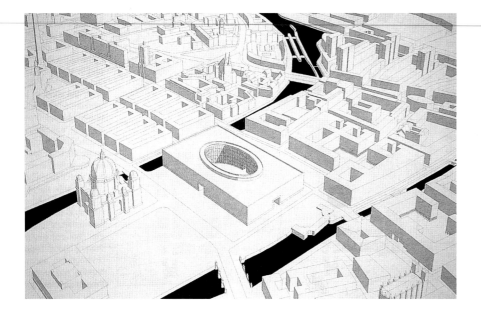

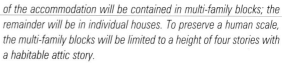

masterpieces of Mendelsohn, Poelzig, and others of the pre-war era; why in spite of the return to commonsense urbanistical rules of "critical reconstruction," the syndrome of "experimentation" continues to dominate the architectural practice and to ostracize even the slightest return to classicism.

The position of Hans Kollhoff—who cannot be accused of being a classicist—is the right one, i.e, the re-definition of the "Berliner vernacular." He echoes historian Fritz Neumeyer's who, from 1991 onward, urged to adopt rules "to counterbalance the international architectural pluralism" with a specific Berliner architecture, inscribed in the classico-rationalist tradition of Schinkel, Messel, Behrens, and Mies. At the same time he pleaded for the construction, next to Friedrichstrasse Bahnhof of Mies' skyscraper of 1921, arguing that contemporary architecture had nothing better to offer.[5]

About Kollhoff's & Timmerman's portfolio of "houses of stone" Neumeyer wrote: "Now that a decision has been taken in favor of the block and the historical ground plan, the wall as element of the cubically ordered space of the streets and squares, has again become something that design must address. A task for which we are very badly prepared. We will have to learn to understand the wall on the "row site" again, after being broken of the habit by the architectural ideal of the free-standing and -floating buildings of Modernism and the abstract seriality of linear buildings."[6]

IV

As defined by Hans Stimmann, the rules of the Senate of Berlin for city growth in the periphery—directly applied at Berlin-Oberhavel, indirectly at Kirchsteigfeld and Falkenhöh—share a striking resemblance with the Charter of the New Urbanism adopted in Charleston in 1996. Hence the recognition of this convergence should be a prime objective of their respective sponsors. The rules are as follow:

• The model for mass housing is no longer the high-rise development, but the suburb of around 5,000 apartments and houses. Each new suburb will become a new part of the existing structure of Greater Berlin. Set next to the sixties' high-rise developments, the old village centers and the 'garden city' schemes, the new suburbs will express the discontinuity of the cityscape and raise it to an aesthetic principle.

• The developments differ in their social and functional composition. In each case, an average of twenty per cent of the overall floor area will be designated work space. Of the residential accommodation, one third will be public housing, one third will be subsidized at market rates, and one third will be privately financed and/or owned. For economic reasons, a minimum of eighty per cent

of the accommodation will be contained in multi-family blocks; the remainder will be in individual houses. To preserve a human scale, the multi-family blocks will be limited to a height of four stories with a habitable attic story.

• The new suburbs will have their own district identity in keeping with the historical fabric and use of the sites. The quality of the land and the traces of historic building lines will influence the urban design.

• The suburbs will follow a rather traditional urban planning model. The basic framework is formed by streets and squares which serve as points of orientation. The streets follow a conventional pattern, being divided into driveway, curb, pavement, tree/hedge/front, garden, house.

• It is the responsibility of the public authorities to build schools and nurseries. There will be located at prominent sites, wherever possible in squares. The architecture of the buildings will reflect their public nature.

• The fabric of the new suburbs will be reinforced by landscaped spaces: parks, playgrounds and sport fields.

• The parking spaces required by regulations will not be placed inside the block, but on the street. However planners must avoid putting parking on both sides of the road perpendicular to the driveway, as this makes the street look like a car park.

• While a large number of the projects are being undertaken by private developers, the public authorities are retaining overall responsibility for their management.[7]

V

Nowhere has the concept of the Radiant City been implemented with more inflexibility than in the late 1960s reconstruction of Dresden. In spite of this planned devastation, the partial reconstruction of the monumental city center by the former GDR created a fascinating "city of monuments," that gives a surprising resonance to Rossi's theory of the city. With less media attention and ideological noise than in Berlin, the reconstruction of the city has accelerated since 1989, filling building gaps in the fabric and producing masterplans for major sections of the center. Many of these successfully propose to narrow streets, reconstitute squares, and return to the original urban structure wherever possible. Most impressive is the "identical" reconstruction of the castle (as a museum) and of the Frauenkirche (as a church and concert hall).[8] Built in 1726-43 by the architect George Bähr on a centralized plan, the latter was the most important Baroque church of German Protestantism before its destruction on February 13, 1945. On the basis of the drawings produced during the restoration of 1938-43, the Frauenkirche is being rebuilt using historic building techniques coupled to advanced computer-based stereotomy. When it is completed in 2006, along with the castle for the 800th anniversary of the city, the church will once again dominate the skyline from the Neustadt or the Brühl terrace. But will the desolated landscape that disfigures the church on the city side remain? Will Bellotto Canaletto's "vedute" continue to haunt the collective memory? I hope, suggest, dare believe that, sixty years after, the inhabitants of Dresden will finally follow the example of Warsaw: In 1945, its citizens wisely decided to reconstruct their historic center "as it was," using the views that the same Canaletto painted in the Polish capital.

VI

The Frauenkirche, the New Williamsburg, Helge Syperecht's "Rotunda," Rob Krier's "Rondell," the "new" Rue de Laeken in Brussels, the hypostyle halls under Highway 836 and the "M" of Miami, the reconstructed theater of Sagunto, all partake equally of "the modern city." With their contemporary programs, without guilt or prejudiced rejection of style, in a revitalized understanding of Regionalism, in the respect of the necessary urban rules, they show the way to genuine freedom in the twenty-first century.

Opposite page:

Right:
Bernd Niebuhr, with K. Teutsch, G. Hinrichsen, M. Waltero, H. Helmer, U. Mangold and G. Möckel. Spreeinsel, Berlin, 1994 competition. Winning entry. Like many others, this project included the reconstruction of the former Bauakademie.

Below:
Views from Schinkel's Altes Museum. The demolition of former GDR's Ministry of Foreign Affairs has now liberated the site once occupied by Schinkel's Bauakademie. Photographs Jean-François Lejeune: top (May 1995); bottom (November 1995).

Bottom:
Karl Gruber. Panorama of a German City around 1350. © Karl Gruber, Forme et caractère de la ville allemande (Bruxelles: Archives d'Architecture Moderne, 1985). Courtesy AAM, Maurice Culot.

On Gruber as architect, teacher, and artist, see Andreas Romero, Baugeschichte als Auftrag : Karl Gruber, Architekt, Lehrer, Zeichner: eine Biographie (Braunschweig: Vieweg, 1990).

Coming from many countries of Europe, America, and Asia, the participants to the International Conference "The City of the New Renaissance," held in Bologna (Italy) on March 28-29-30, 1996, at the initiative of A Vision of Europe and with the collaboration of:

- The Prince of Wales' School of Architecture, London
- The *Archives d'Architecture Moderne*, Brussels
- The *Escuela Técnica Superior de Arquitectura*, San Sebastián
- The *Fondation pour l'architecture*, Brussels
- The Institute for the Study of Classical Architecture at New York Academy of Art, New York
- The University of Miami School of Architecture, Coral Gables
- The University of Notre-Dame School of Architecture, South Bend
- The Journal *ARCHI & COLONNE INTERNATIONAL*, Bologna

have adopted the following resolution:

The participants express their appreciation of the critical works that have been developed in the last years through writings, projects, built works, and didactic initiatives at universities and educational institutions, by courageous colleagues in every part of the world, in favor of the recognition, preservation, and continuous use of the authentic values which, for more than two millennia, have characterized, at all the scales, the primary forms of residence and organized community. Consequently, they want to emphasize that:

1. The present-day chaotic and uniform appearance of our urban and suburban environment is not the consequence of uncontrolled processes, but clearly the result of the ideologies that have promoted the pursuit of a "mass society," now obsolete.

2. The recent activity of many architects around the world has established a new architectonic and urbanistic culture, which rejects the anonymous peripheries and the 'melancholic' suburbs of the last fifty years. In contrast, it privileges, firstly, the creation of villages, neighborhoods, cities and even metropolises, marked by new structural and formal qualities that will make them comparable to their historic counterparts; secondly, it advocates a process of 'urbanization' of the suburbs, which aims, among others, at redimensioning streets, arteries, and squares according to traditional measurements and characteristics, while enriching them with new functions and with the structures that they are generally lacking.

3. The emerging element of this new urban renaissance is the reorganization of the urban conurbations into mixed-use neighborhoods and districts to be constituted of buildings that have no more than four floors above the street ground level.

4. Through the process of land subdivision into parcels of a great diversity of dimensions and functions, both at the level of the district and the block, it will be possible to develop an urban economy which shall no longer be based exclusively on industrial activities, but shall equally rely on a network of productive and merchant activities at all scales of entrepreneurship, thus including the small and medium-sized enterprises;

5. As a result, the new urban and rural architecture will no longer be defined by self-referential 'innovative design,' but by the imitation of the constructive, organizational, and esthetic archetypes that are deeply rooted in every local culture.

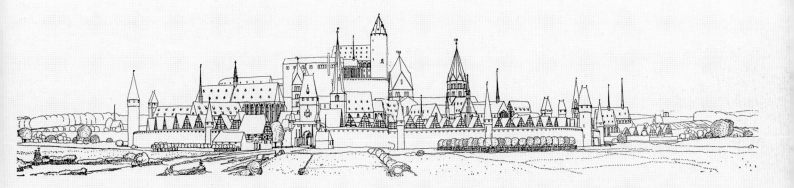

THE REGION: METROPOLIS, CITY, AND TOWN

THE CONGRESS FOR THE NEW URBANISM views disinvestment in central cities, the spread of placeless sprawl, increasing separation by race and income, environmental deterioration, loss of agricultural lands and wilderness, and the erosion of society's built heritage as one interrelated community-building challenge.

WE STAND for the restoration of existing urban centers and towns within coherent metropolitan regions, the reconfiguration of sprawling suburbs into communities of real neighborhoods and diverse districts, the conservation of natural environments, and the preservation of our built legacy.

WE RECOGNIZE that physical solutions by themselves will not solve social and economic problems, but neither can economic vitality, community stability, and environmental health be sustained without a coherent and supportive physical framework.

WE ADVOCATE the restructuring of public policy and development practices to support the following principles: neighborhoods should be diverse in use and population; communities should be designed for the pedestrian and transit as well as the car; cities and towns should be shaped by physically defined and universally accessible public spaces and community institutions; urban places should be framed by architecture and landscape design that celebrate local history, climate, ecology, and building practice.

WE REPRESENT a broad-based citizenry, composed of public and private sector leaders, community activists, and multidisciplinary professionals. We are committed to reestablishing the relationship between the art of building and the making of community, through citizen-based participatory planning and design.

WE DEDICATE ourselves to reclaiming our homes, blocks, streets, parks, neighborhoods, districts, towns, cities, regions, and environment.

WE ASSERT the following principles to guide public policy, development practice, urban planning, and design:

The Charter was adopted by the assembly of participants (architects, urbanists, planners, city administrators, etc.) at the Fourth Congress for the New Urbanism held in Charleston South Carolina, May 3-5, 1996.

The First Congress took place in Alexandria (November 8-11, 1993), the Second Congress in Los Angeles (May 20-23, 1994), and the Third Congress in Francisco (February 17-20, 1995).

1

Metropolitan regions are finite places with geographic boundaries derived from topography, watersheds, coastlines, farmlands, regional parks, and river basins. The metropolis is made of multiple centers that are cities, towns, and villages, each with its own identifiable center and edges.

2

The metropolitan region is a fundamental economic unit of the contemporary world. Governmental cooperation, public policy, physical planning, and economic strategies must reflect this new reality.

3

The metropolis has a necessary and fragile relationship to its agrarian hinterland and natural landscape. The relationship is environmental, economic, and cultural. Farmland and nature are as important to the metropolis as the garden is to the house.

4

Development patterns should not blur or eradicate the edges of the metropolis. Infill development within existing urban areas conserves environmental resources, economic investment, and social fabric, while reclaiming marginal and abandoned areas. Metropolitan regions should develop strategies to encourage such infill development over peripheral expansion.

5

Where appropriate, new development contiguous to urban boundaries should be organized as neighborhoods and districts, and be integrated within the existing urban pattern. Noncontiguous development should be organized as towns and villages with their own urban edges, and planned for a jobs/housing balance, not as bedroom suburbs.

6

The development and redevelopment of towns and cities should respect historical patterns, precedents, and boundaries.

7

Cities and towns should bring into proximity a broad spectrum of public and private uses to support a regional economy that benefits people of all incomes. Affordable housing should be distributed throughout the region to match job opportunities and to avoid concentrations of poverty.

8

The physical organization of the region should be supported by a framework of transportation alternatives. Transit, pedestrian, and bicycle systems should maximize access and mobility throughout the region while reducing dependence upon the automobile.

9

Revenues and resources can be shared more cooperatively among the municipalities and centers within regions to avoid destructive competition for tax base and to promote rational coordination of transportation, recreation, public services, housing, and community institutions.

THE NEIGHBORHOOD, THE DISTRICT, AND THE CORRIDOR

1

The neighborhood, the district, and the corridor are the essential elements of development and redevelopment in the metropolis. They form identifiable areas that encourage citizens to take responsibility for their maintenance and evolution.

2

Neighborhoods should be compact, pedestrian-friendly, and mixed-use. Districts generally emphasize a special single use, and should follow the principles of neighborhood design when possible. Corridors are regional connectors of neighborhoods and districts; they range from boulevards and rail lines to rivers and parkways.

3

Many activities of daily living should occur within walking distance, allowing independence to those who do not drive, especially the elderly and the young. Interconnected networks of streets should be designed to encourage walking, reduce the number and length of automobile trips, and conserve energy.

4

Within neighborhoods, a broad range of housing types and price levels can bring people of diverse ages, races, and incomes into daily interaction, strengthening the personal and civic bonds essential to an authentic community.

5

Transit corridors, when properly planned and coordinated, can help organize metropolitan structure and revitalize urban centers. In contrast, highway corridors should not displace investment from existing centers.

6

Appropriate building densities and land uses should be within walking distance of transit stops, permitting public transit to become a viable alternative to the automobile.

7

Concentrations of civic, institutional, and commercial activity should be embedded in neighborhoods and districts, not isolated in remote, single-use complexes. Schools should be sized and located to enable children to walk or bicycle to them.

8

The economic health and harmonious evolution of neighborhoods, districts, and corridors can be improved through graphic urban design codes that serve as predictable guides for change.

9

A range of parks, from tot-lots and village greens to ballfields and community gardens, should be distributed within neighborhoods. Conservation areas and open lands should be used to define and connect different neighborhoods and districts.

THE BLOCK, THE STREET, AND THE BUILDING

1

A primarily task of all urban architecture and landscape design is the physical definition of streets and public spaces as places of shared use.

2

Individual architectural projects should be seamlessly linked to their surroundings. This issue transcends style.

3

The revitalization of urban places depends on safety and security. The design of streets and buildings should reinforce safe environments, but not at the expense of accessibility and openness.

4

In the contemporary metropolis, development must adequately accommodate automobiles. It should do so in ways that respect the pedestrian and the form of public space.

5

Streets and squares should be safe, comfortable, and interesting to the pedestrian. Properly configured, they encourage walking and enable neighbors to know each other and protect their communities.

6

Architecture and landscape design should grow from local climate, topography, history, and building practice.

7

Civic buildings and public gathering places require important sites to reinforce community identity and the culture of democracy. They deserve distinctive form, because their role is different from that of other buildings and places that constitute the fabric of the city.

8

All buildings should provide their inhabitants with a clear sense of location, weather and time. Natural methods of heating and cooling can be more resource-efficient than mechanical systems.

9

Preservation and renewal of historic buildings, districts, and landscapes affirm the continuity and evolution of urban society.

HOUSES OF STONE

*Hans Kollhoff &
Helga Timmerman,
architects*

Architects married to an ethos of individualistic design without limits, when saw themselves called upon to deposit abstract white volumes on cleared green fields and, particularly, to create "exciting relationships," are now obliged—in city centers—to have their buildings join the ranks of fellow-sufferers, fit in with the old building line and rub shoulders with their neighbors.

Has everything which young architects were taught, which was philosophically underpinned and sanctioned by the great examples, suddenly become obsolete? How can I manage to attract attention in the glossy journals which demand new images? And, above all, will all those people, whose faith in the fact that they understand something about architecture must not be shattered, still understand me? A corkscrew as a building is at best good for causing a media sensation.

The fact that we think we can do anything today using concrete, polystyrene and plastic, with the result that architecture is slowly disappearing into nothing more than packaging, has led me to believe that architecture has an inherent tectonic principle and that the architecture of the city center needs to look solid. That is why I talk of "stone architecture," knowing very well that I am really talking of layers added to a wall and in absolute knowledge of the fact that a great deal of nonsense can also be instigated with stone. This urban need is more important to respect than the modern dictate of "honesty."

The major European cities, and also the early American ones, evolved on the basis of a precise typology in urban design and architecture and within a more or less explicitly agreed canon of rules. And who would claim that these limitations hindered great architecture! Who believes that architects in Paris, Milan, and New York should have been given a freer rein? Maybe it is precisely these very subtle nuances that characterize metropolitan architecture. In reference to the conventions of urbanity and with the desire for simple architecture, I turn my attention to those buildings and spaces which function quietly without fuss: we do not need an architectural wonder on every corner. I see the city once more as a community of buildings which know that they are not alone in the world.

I would recommend anyone who still believes that modernism took place on the green fields with a lot of glass and white paint, to read Werner Hegemann's book *Reihenhaus-Fassaden, Geschäfts-und-Wohnhäuser aus alter und neuer Zeit* (Facades of terraced houses, commercial and residential buildings of today and yesterday), published in Berlin in 1929. This book contains a collection of architects—from Höger to Ochs, Taut, Kaufmann, Behrens, Strumer, Hans and Osker Gerson, Schumacher, Mendelsohn, Messel, Mebes and Emmerich, Kohtz, Salvisberg, Muthesius, Bernoulli, Sehring, Mies van der Rohe, Ludwig Hoffmann and Poelzig—all architects who stand for nothing less than German metropolitan architecture. If we make this great tradition of modern architecture into a taboo we cannot complain about the disastrous developments in the architecture of our city centers, apart from those which were rebuilt after wartime bombing.

There is probably nowhere in the world where the members of the international architectural elite have been able to realize their ideas so extensively and with such variety as in Berlin from the time of International Building Exhibition (IBA) of 1987 to the present day. It was here that some of these avant-garde architects were given their first chance to build something. We should remember this before leaping into the fray with accusations of self-opinionated dogmatism.

Now that we are building a new capital city, there is a desire to learn from a post-war architectural history which is anything but satisfactory. In the process, people have come to realize that not everything is possible everywhere. What may be absolutely convincing at the Schöneberger Kreuz may be completely out of place on Unter den Linden and there are schemes which might be better built in Tokyo or Los Angeles than in Berlin. Yet, what we have absolutely no need to fear is the spectre of monotony. The extent of the Senatsbaudirektor's ambitions, Hans Stimman, in this respect and his scope for intervention can easily be deduced from the contractors' boards at building sites at Checkpoint Charlie and the Friedrichstadt-Passagen. Even the IBA would never

*Opposite page:
Hans Kollhoff and Helga
Timmerman, architects.
Competition Daimler Benz
AG/Potsdamer Platz (1992).
Perspective from terrace of the
new blocks.*

Top left:
Model of the Potsdamer Platz
project now in construction.
Master plan by Renzo Piano,
architect. Hans Kollhoff's sky-
scraper is visible as a dark vol-
ume to the right.

Bottom left:
Aerial view of Potsdamer Platz
now in construction. Master
plan by Renzo Piano, architect.

Right:
Hans Kollhoff and Helga
Timmerman, architects.
Competition Daimler Benz
AG/Potsdamer Platz (1992).
Street level perspective of the
new blocks.

Editor's note:
Hans Kollhoff's text was
originally published in
Domus nº770 (April 1995,
pp. 106-7) under the title
"Against the taboos of an
urban architecture." It has
been reedited for this publi-
cation.

have produced such a potpourri. Our eyes will smart at these places but it will not be due to monotony.

In Berlin the dilemma of modern architecture in the urban context can be seen like nowhere else in the world. Here questions are being asked about the nature of the center of an European metropolis, whereas in other places it is simply a matter of filling in gaps or developing the periphery. I imagine that we will not be able to tackle this task successfully without picking up the thread of the early modernist tradition of urban architecture, in other words all those attempts which did not turn their backs on the city in the hope for salvation in the open. The emphasis is on picking up, but not wholesale adoption, since it cannot be our aim to churn out replicas of historical architecture, even if it will be difficult to immediately find convincing solutions in this process which is as difficult as passing through the eye of needle.

Competition Daimler Benz AG/Potsdamer Platz
Berlin, 1992
Collaborators Tobias Nöfer, Götz Kern

There may be no doubt that a house is different from a car: houses are static and permanent, owe more to conventions than to creativity and are more like a household object than a machine. So houses have to be built solidly, their cost-effectiveness has to be calculated on a long-term basis and not in short, depreciation terms. So a house cannot be a fashion object. A house offers security, safety, and is representative of its residents and users. A large house is also a collective phenomenon, at variance with individualist behavior. A number of such houses put together can form a town. Our project for the new city area at the Potsdamer Platz is made up of small blocks and large houses. So measurements are postulated which, in line with the requirements of the current programs, are larger than those of the traditional houses on the plot, but smaller than those of a traditional housing block because these programs cannot be fragmented into anonymous units.

So we start with a square housing element with a maximum of four entrances. Each of the sides forms a separate whole. The squares are stretched into rectangles and there appear a front, a side, and a back. Finally, the street plan forces the rectangles into an irregular form. This means that the street has priority over private interests. In order to emphasize this, the housing units show a great regularity despite their irregular ground plan. The other basic problem that must be solved is to bring a rectangular structure of individual buildings into harmony with a radial block pattern. The irregular structure of the individual buildings seems ideal for this purpose too: it absorbs the structure of the separate blocks in the east with playful ease and in the same way connects with the large individual buildings to the west. In addition the ground plan of Mies Van der Rohe's National Gallery conforms to the ideal original type, while the twisted rectangle reproduces the block type of the fan-shaped Friedrichstrasse.

If this zone is to develop into a genuine link between the older parts of the city and not just into a gigantic 'shopping center,' traditional town-planning norms have to be taken into account. An European city is not a city for pedestrians only. That is why we propose a completely normal street pattern, even though the traffic here may be limited to delivery and pick up. We are consciously abandoning the 'housing design' of the streets and are opting for a cultivated big-city space that is clearly distinct from the domestic living room. We reject a neighborhood square in the inner area of a street block because that makes it too confined, and we are also abandoning town-planning accents, since, with the given height limitations, they would appear unnatural and forced.

The gutter height of 35 meters is made tolerable in all buildings by means of the deep extension of the terrace at the ninth floor level. Above that there are two recessed floors, forming a delightful terrace-shaped roof landscape. We assume that the terraces will be intensively planted and give the impression of the hanging gardens of the Potsdamer Platz. Although our work has a highly uniform expression of buildings and urban spaces in mind, we are nevertheless thinking about very individual, varied forms of architecture. The necessary condition is that these respond to the rules and regulations whose purpose is to pick up again the thread of the traditional forms of building and city design.

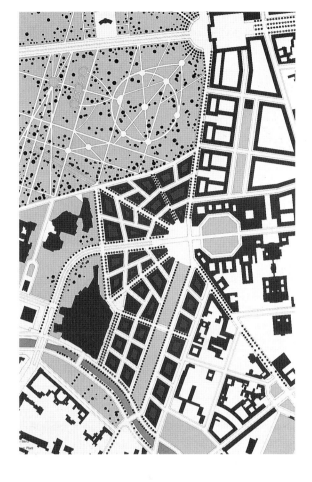

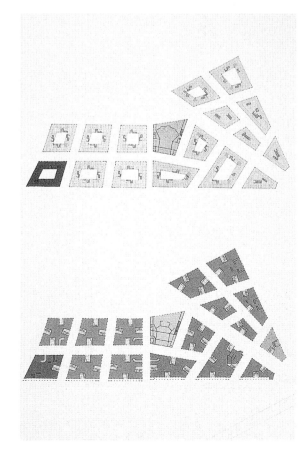

High-rise office building on Potsdamer Platz

Berlin, 1993
Collaborator Jasper Jochimsen

At the north end of the Daimler Benz terrain there is the representative office and flat building A1, right next to the Potsdamer Platz. Together with the Sony tower to be built at the opposite side, this building forms the entrance to the new Potsdamer Strasse. In the building's immediate surroundings there are the entrances to the underground railway, to the regional train system, and also to the streetcar and bus stops.

The mass of the building drops away step by step down the twenty-two floors tower and links up on the west side to the highest points of the adjacent buildings. Towards the rear, between the wings of the building, there is a five-floor atrium.

Office space is provided on all upper floors of the building, except on the ground floor which will be occupied by retail businesses. The reconstructed cafe Josty opens immediately on the Potsdamer Platz. One enters the two-floor-high entrance hall from the old and new Potsdamer Strasse. From there one can reach the atrium by means of escalators. The atrium is destined to house busy public facilities or a booking hall. The office floors are accessible from a centrally placed upper foyer and can be subdivided into various independent rented offices.

The material for the front facade is brick and for the base gray-green granite. Walkways are provided with marble paneling and granite floors. The doors and windows on the first two floors are in steel with applied bronze extrusion; on the office floors they are made of bronze-colored anodized aluminum with countersunk wooden covering. The apex of the tower narrows like a crown. At night the building will be spectacularly illuminated.

Top right:
Skyscraper at the Potsdamer
Platz. View of model from
Potsdamer Platz. Photo
Uwe Rau.

Center left:
Plans (from bottom to top:
ground floor, 7th-8th floor, 13th
floor, 20th-21st floor).

Bottom left:
Skyscraper at the Potsdamer
Platz. View of model from the
new Potsdamer Strasse.
Photo Uwe Rau.

Commercial and Residential Building Project
Berlin, 1993
Collaborators Norbert Hemprich, Jean Lamborelle, Bärbel Müller

The new city square is proposed between the Wieland and Leibnitzstrasse: it is 100 feet in width and 330 feet in length. With the buildings on its periphery which match the traditional Berlin roof line, the square forms a type of big city space that is frequent in other European metropolises.

This urban space is kept free of traffic. Restaurants and cafes look out on the square. In the summer the square can be used for public events. A fountain closes off the space from the Leipziger Strasse and the sound of its water covers the traffic noise. Double-height galleries make the square broader, offer protection in bad weather, and form an elegant border between the shopping area and the green public area.

The buildings around the square, which are, by code, seven floors high, contain dwellings and offices, as well as shops on the ground floor. The roof surfaces are arranged as green roof gardens. On the sixth floor of the southern wing there is a day-care center with its own entrance hall and elevator.

The Leibnitzstrasse is given an extra accent by two ten-floor buildings, used as an office block and a hotel. The galleries that run around the corner provide spacious entrances. The buildings are executed in brick, with load-bearing outer walls and ceilings with structural supports in reinforced concrete. The facade facing the square is clad with sheets of natural stone and connected by narrow mortar joints. The dwellings look out over the square, with double glass doors in natural wood. The facades on the inner yard are covered with mineral lime plaster in a bright color. The inner yards without underground levels are planted with large trees and so have the same character as the adjacent inner yards.

The square is paved with large granite slabs (Charlottenburger pavement tiles). Underneath, there is a two-floor parking garage with four hundred and eighty spaces. The entrances and exits are on the side of the busier Leibnizstrasse.

Top:
Commercial & residential building at Wielandstraße and Leibnitzstraße. Street perspective.

Center:
Section through project and new street with underground parking.

Bottom left:
Aerial view of model. Photo Uwe Rau.

Bottom right:
Street perspective of model. Photo Uwe Rau.

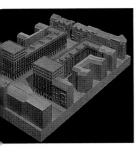

Office and Shop Building on Friedrichstrasse
Berlin-Mitte 1994
Collaborator Michael Vöchting

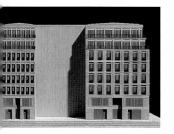

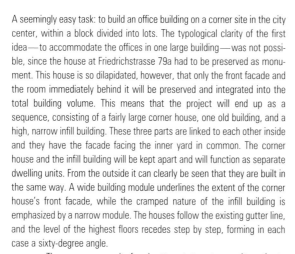

A seemingly easy task: to build an office building on a corner site in the city center, within a block divided into lots. The typological clarity of the first idea—to accommodate the offices in one large building—was not possible, since the house at Friedrichstrasse 79a had to be preserved as monument. This house is so dilapidated, however, that only the front facade and the room immediately behind it will be preserved and integrated into the total building volume. This means that the project will end up as a sequence, consisting of a fairly large corner house, one old building, and a high, narrow infill building. These three parts are linked to each other inside and they have the facade facing the inner yard in common. The corner house and the infill building will be kept apart and will function as separate dwelling units. From the outside it can clearly be seen that they are built in the same way. A wide building module underlines the extent of the corner house's front facade, while the cramped nature of the infill building is emphasized by a narrow module. The houses follow the existing gutter line, and the level of the highest floors recedes step by step, forming in each case a sixty-degree angle.

The gray-green granite facade attempts to act as an alternative to the usual indented, "tiled facade" type, and to continue the tradition of the pre-war office and shop buildings in Berlin. The front facade is conspicuous for its tectonic sections with low-relief work. The stone slabs covering the facade do not meet flush. To avoid open grid joints whose width is determined by the required tolerance, they overlap each other without conspicuous expansion joints, which gives the whole a solid appearance. The ground floor and the first floor are closed, monolithically conceived, and act as a base upon which the wall panels, pilasters and cornices of the other floors are built. The vertical, double oak windows with mounted bronze facing give the houses a certain aloofness. Inside, the functionality of the standardized office spaces contrasts with the liberal use of marble in the ground floor lobbies. The intention is to create a conventional building in a positive sense: i.e., to form, together with the other buildings, a street of the city. Passers-bys will only notice them at a second glance.

Top:
Office and residential building at Michaelkirchstraße. Perspective along canal (computer: Dieter Gretscher with Bojan Blecic).

Bottom from left to right: Office and residential building at Michaelkirchstraße. Two views of model. Photos Uwe Rau.

Atrium am Spreeufer, Michaelkirchstraße 22 & 23
Berlin-Mitte 1995

For years, important efforts have been undertaken to bring the city of Berlin back to the river that gave it once its name of "Athens-on-the-Spree." Where the industrialization has left behind huge port installations, silos, scrap yards, and other production facilities, new and attractive urban districts are ready to rise from the new government district in the Spreebogen, to the Wasserstadt Spandau. Along the Spree the city will in the future show its most relaxing and serene side.

Our project—"Atrium on the Banks of the Spree"—stands near the Michaelkirche Bridge, which connects the district Berlin Mitte to the Kreuzberg quarters, with a splendid view on the Spree, the old and the new city, in walking distance to the Jannowitz Bridge, Alexanderplatz, and Unter den Linden. Coming from the center and crossing the renovated Michaelkirche Bridge, one reaches the new promenade of the Holzufer which gives its address to the complex. Both buildings, one of which displays a conspicuous corner with a tower, face the water and are organized in the traditional manner of Berlin, around quiet and planted inner courts. Shops are planned on the ground floor, with a restaurant at the corner of Michaelkirchstraße. Offices floors will take place directly above the large, representative entrance hall while the upper floors, completely independent from the office circulation, will be reserved for apartments.

To lend a noble discretion to the buildings the facades will be covered in gray sandstone. Ground floor windows and doors will have bronze frames, whereas aluminum will be used in the upper floors. Special care will be given to the workmanship of the selected materials. The solidity of appearance and the precise tectonics of the facades construction clearly range these two buildings within the pre-war tradition of office and commercial buildings in Berlin.

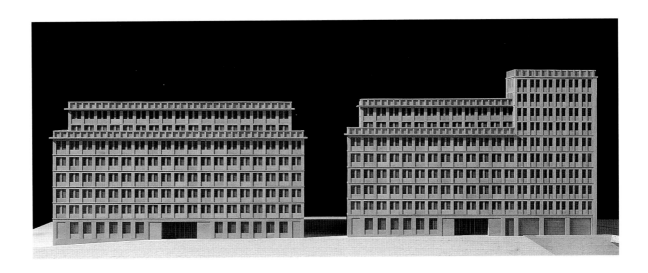

Between a housing estate and a loosely-knit single-family area, this housing project consists of sixteen identical buildings organized around two interior courtyards. The approximately square site, located in former East Berlin and measuring about 125,000 sq. ft., is subdivided by residential streets, in fact private roads and passageways with public access. The two blocks were raised five feet above ground level, with brick retainer walls along the sidewalks: this solution improves the living conditions at the ground floor level and creates a more private situation with a common garden all around the buildings. A three-foot high privet hedge provides additional visual protection. The garden has a natural and discreet presence: a grass lawn and leafy trees with bright autumn colors. Parking is located along the residential streets.

In keeping with the area's typology—mainly single family houses—each block is composed of eight compact buildings with four stories and eight apartments each floor. The buildings' organization is conventional: each house is divided in the middle; the layout is symmetrical in order to obtain a reflected image changing with the orientation; hence, the verandas oriented towards the south, southeast or southwest, respectively. The entrance halls were designed with a special attention to comfort and image. The width of the stairwells, the wood paneling in the entrance areas, the choice of a quality stone paving, the natural wood of the handrails and the doors, and the overall attention to detail, all combine to create an atmosphere of simplicity and solidity. The exterior is characterized by traditional, solid brickwork marked by horizontal prefabricated concrete strips. The window frames are made of wood with a natural finish. All the materials are durable, keeping maintenance costs low. The flat roofing made of sheet zinc has a marked overhang that contributes to create an overall impression of secluded protection in a "hard" neighborhood.

Top:
Malchower Straße housing blocks. Location plan.

Bottom:
View of several edifices along a side street. Photo Ulrich Schwartz, Berlin.

Top:
View of the interior street. Photo Ulrich Schwartz, Berlin.

Bottom:
Typical top floor plan; typical floor plan; typical ground floor plan.

Das Schloß? Project for the site of the former castle
Berlin, 1993
Collaborator Carsten Vogel

Top:
Berlin Schloß and Schloßbrücke (Berlin castle and bridge). Postcard. Collection Jean-François Lejeune.

Bottom left:
Aerial view of the Museuminsel around 1920 with the Berlin Schloß and the Schlossplatz (right and extreme right), the Dom and the Altes Museum (center), Unter den Linden (bottom right edge). Alexanderplatz is out of the picture near the top center. © Staatliche Museen Berlin.

Bottom right:
Diagram of typological transformation illustrating Kollhoff's & Timmerman's project.

As can be seen on the aerial photograph here below, the Berlin Schloß occupied an urban position of fundamental importance at the historic heart of the city. Built in many successive phases—from 1443 to its reconstruction by Andreas Schlüter (1704-07) and the final extensions of the mid-1800s—this huge "container" or "urban artifact" was the main articulation between the medieval city (partially reconstructed in the 20th century), the 18th century rational grids of the Friedrichstadt and Dorotheestadt, the works of Schinkel and Lenné on Unter den Linden and at the Lustgarten, and the Museuminsel built by August Stüler, Alfred Messel, and Ludwig Hoffmann. Built around two courtyards the Schloß was about 650 feet long and 380 feet wide; the 19th century cupola was 200 feet high. Severely bombed in 1945, the Baroque structure was partially renovated in the immediate post-war years; its ideologically motivated demolition in 1950 by the authorities of East Berlin was carried out despite major opposition by renown architects and citizens alike. The so-called Palast der Republik which was built on its site was not only a classic example of 1960s architectural banality—what Klaus Herdeg described perfectly in the term *dekoriertes Diagramm*—but it also destroyed the subtle and fragile urban equilibrium established by Schlüter, Schinkel, and Lenné.

If the Palast der Republik is, as most Berliners hope, to be demolished soon, there are, in principle, three possibilities for the reconstruction of the site. The first is to accept a sort of inversion of figure and background, and allow for a "creative" solution to replace the former castle. This means that the city is no longer characterized by the delicate relationship between anonymous, compact structure as a background and the individual public buildings and spaces that set themselves off against it, but that they can now only be seen as chance collections of individual buildings cast adrift, all desiring or actually having, the same importance. As a consequence the inter-related structures would no more merge into the homogeneous urban whole, once defined by the subtle spatial relation established by Schinkel.

The second possibility—favored by many in Berlin as demonstrated by the success of the *trompe l'oeil* reconstruction initiative during the summer of 1994—is to rebuild the castle as it existed and so demonstrate that the city's old street plan continues to exercise a determining influence on the image that the city has of itself, despite the wartime destruction and the post-war architecture which was inimical to the very notion of the city. The "identical" reconstruction would be a testimony to our readiness to revive the very heart of the city, to give it a life that corresponds to its historical and urban importance. It would be the serene and accepted acknowledgment that our decision-making processes, the clients and the architects are no longer capable of producing a work of architecture that comes anywhere near restoring the obvious presence, meaning the uniformity and the harmony, of the old castle.

The third alternative, presented here, is to take a chance on a new building, and see this act as a challenge, as a return to a comprehensible architecture that is capable of being an authentic, collective expression. Such a requirement implies that the architecture reflects on the means that are mostly its own, and draws a precise dividing line between art and "media spectacular." What would it be like if, on this historic site, the cradle of the new architecture should arise, of an architecture able to blend art and convention and remind us of the existence of the architectonic, to which Berlin owes its most prominent buildings, from Schlüter through Schinkel to Mies.

Thus, if it should be decided not to reconstruct the former castle after all, then we should be able to agree on the construction of a new building whose volume is in tune with the original site. Yet, the open space to be created within this large mass of building shall not necessarily become a private courtyard as in a city block—on the model of the former castle. Other manners of organizing the building mass is possible as illustrated in our diagram *(bottom)*. For instance it seems sensible to accommodate large auditoria, reception rooms and congress halls in a spacious central building, while the numerous smaller rooms, regardless of their purpose, can be accommodated in the narrower sides of the building.

There are many arguments for not closing the building off on the east side, i.e., toward Alexanderplatz and the City Hall (the castle had always turned its back to the east). Such an opening in the form of a large open court would create an attractive link to the water, the park, and the eastern districts of the city. The opening of the second inner courtyard towards the western districts, Unter den Linden, and Schinkel's reconstructed Bauakademie will be a reminder of the historical situation, now rid of the pomp and circumstance of the monuments from the period of Wilhelm II. On the south side, facing what used to be and should be reconstructed as the Castle square or Schloß Platz, the central frontal extension shall emphasize the north-south orientation of the larger hall and the unity of the building. And who would object to the integration of Andreas Schlüter's portals, or what is left of them, into the eastern inner court? Finally, on the northern side facing Schinkel's Altes Museum, the neutrality of the long facade would be emphasized through the projection forward of both extremities.

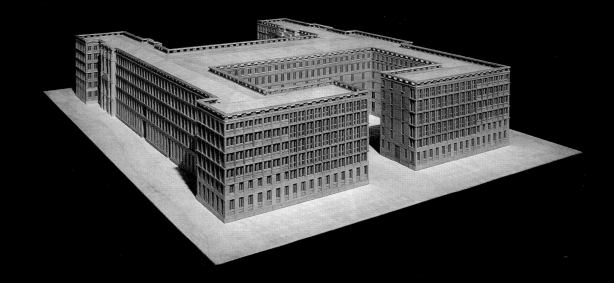

Top:
View of model from the east.
The courtyard opens toward
Alexanderplatz.
Photo Uwe Rau.

Center:
Facade model on reconstructed
Schlossplatz. Photo Uwe Rau.

Bottom:
View of model from Unter den
Linden. The left facade faces
the Altes Museum; the right
one faces the canal and the
Bauakademie. Photo Uwe Rau.

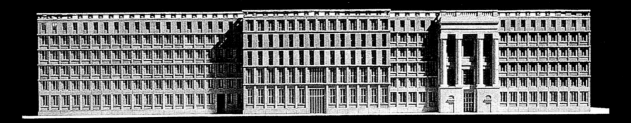

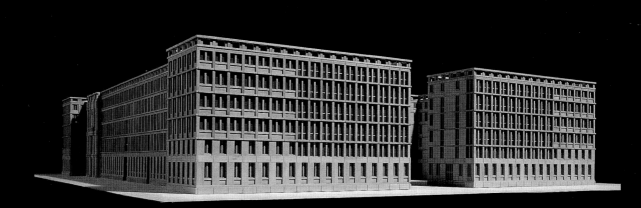

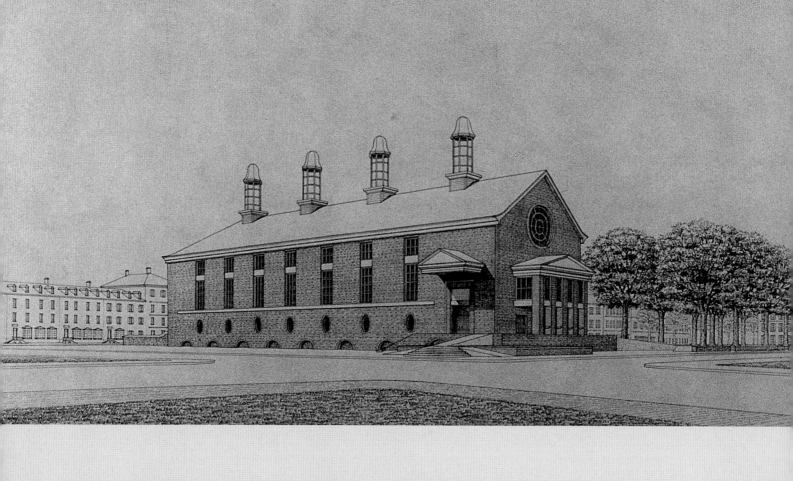

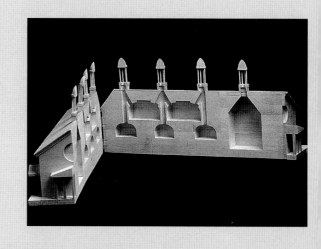

THE NEW WILLIAMSBURG, VIRGINIA

University of Miami School of Architecture faculty

This introductory text was adapted from the competition brief. The competition was organized by the Casey Company in coordination with James County, Virginia.

Opposite page:

New Courthouse for James County (Williamsburg expansion). Winning design, 1996. Architects: Jorge Hernandez & Francis Lyn. Collaborators: Mohamed R. Abd-Razak, Simone Chin, Adib Cure, Carie Penabad, Christopher Ritter.

Top:
Perspective of courthouse in new town context (project Barrett, Alvarez-Martinez-Caruncho, Duany & Plater-Zyberk: see pp. 148-9).

Bottom:
Courtroom chambers in section. Model Gregory Saldaña.

The competition challenge is to develop a Town Plan for the 600-acre parcel known as the Casey property, that must not only achieve design excellence, but also demonstrate economic effectiveness, environmental responsiveness, engineering practicality, and market flexibility. The site is located within a rapidly growing regional development pattern spurred on by tourism, the advent of retirement communities, and an appealing environment for new businesses. Tourism is associated not only with Colonial Williamsburg (just 2.5 miles away) but also with the Busch Gardens theme park, Jamestown, and a wide variety of other attractions in the region. New growth has brought a large amount of typical suburban development patterns, especially roadside strip malls and some major national chain stores. Much of this has occurred along Highway 60 as well as in other fringe areas around the City of Williamsburg. The local road system dates back two centuries and includes an elaborate network of smaller roads handling large volumes of traffic. Road improvements have not kept up with the new growth. This is part of the reason for the extension of Highway 199—the limited access highway that bisects the site and will have an interchange providing immediate and principal access to the site.

As new development evolves, the competition site may eventually be conceived of as a new downtown for the City of Williamsburg and James City County. It may also be perceived as part of a larger urbanized area which includes both the current downtown of the City of Williamsburg, the College of William and Mary, and other developments nearby. Indeed, the College of William and Mary has nationally recognized programs in computer science, applied science and physics, which provide the catalyst for related economic development activities on or near the competition site. The five goals and criteria for judging are:

1. *High quality model of Town Planning.* The Town Plan should become a landmark development and a national model of the highest quality of the visual, social, and economic aspects of town planning.

2. *Economic feasibility & development flexibility.* The Town Plan should accommodate a range of different market scenarios, options, and constraints for long term use of the site. Implementation of the plan should be economically feasible from a short term and long term perspective. The town plan should embody flexibility in the development sequence.

3. *Physical functionality and practicality.* The Town Plan should be practical, realistic, and achievable. It should effectively integrate the infrastructure of roads and utilities, the new courthouse and its associate civic space, other public spaces, and a wide range of land uses including diverse residential patterns, commercial, cultural, recreational, institutional, and possibly industrial uses. The infrastructure of roads and utilities should allow different densities of residential and commercial markets on the same parcels depending upon future market conditions. The same approach might apply to some open spaces, civic buildings, etc.

4. *Compatibility with local history, culture, and environment.* The Town Plan should be responsive to, and compatible with local traditions, history, culture, and neighboring land uses. Most residential and diverse commercial buildings will be low-rise. The unique role of Colonial Williamsburg should be preserved; new development should not replicate its buildings. New development should also be responsive, and compatible with the natural environmental features of the site and the region. The Town Plan should respond to the increasing concern for creating long-term sustainable development patterns by minimizing negative environmental impacts, and by emphasizing the conservation of energy and the use of renewable resources.

5. *Humanistic and urban approach.* The Town Plan should demonstrate a humanistic approach to the integration and mixture of land uses, social and economic activities, and environmental concerns. This should be evidenced in the scale and details of architecture, landscape, public spaces. The Plan shall encourage pedestrian and bike activity, realistic opportunities for mass transit, and, at the same time, respect the continued reliance on automobile usage as the primary mode of transportation. A "main street" could link the new courthouse and its civic space—to be built within the Town Plan—with other retail activities, cultural facilities, and perhaps, some residential uses.

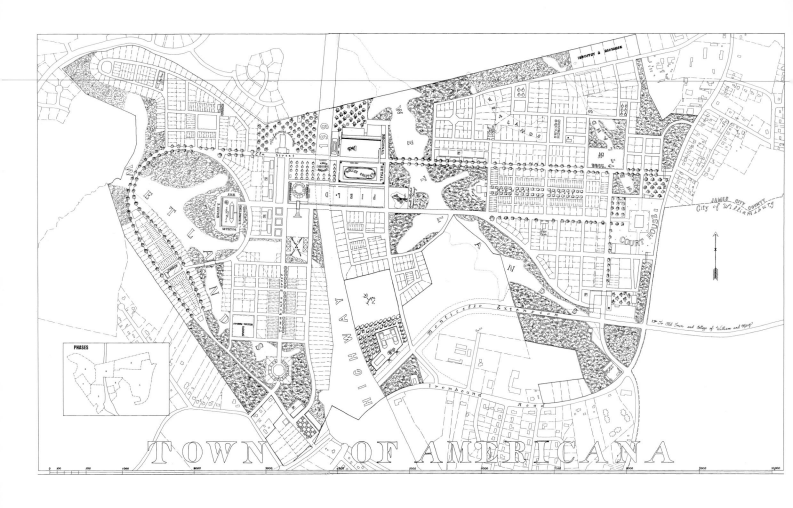

The Town of Americana

Architects: Roberto Behar, Jaime Correa.
Collaborators: Claudia Bancalari, Suzanne Perez, Kevin Storm.
Honorable Mention, Stage 1, Town Plan Design Competition.

The Town of Americana provides a unique American urban experience in the tradition of Williamsburg, the University of Virginia, and Mount Vernon. The town plan is composed of a collection of urban events based upon colonial American town planning principles and the permanent American desire for the new.

In this regard, common American spaces and monuments, ranging from Elm Street to the Ferris Wheel, are used in the construction of the image of the place. Like in pieces of American folk art, the Town of Americana merges a wide range of spatial experiences with complete independence of mind: as duck decoys, they are simultaneously contemporary crafts, colonial pieces, and native American inventions. Hence, the Town of Americana is a contemporary urban assemblage of shared memories and common desires. The drawings on the left illustrate two of these "moments:" the Meeting House planned at the end of an avenue of townhouses; the Roller Coaster and Ferris Wheel proposed on top and near a shopping mall.

The plan is organized in a number of independent, yet interrelated, neighborhoods. The architecture is based upon traditional Virginia building types. Public buildings and landmarks add elements of wonder at the termination of important vistas. The civic and the domestic realm are woven to produce a quilt of extraordinary and everyday life experiences.

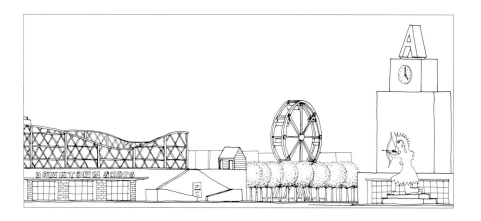

The architecture of the urban plan repeats, without reproducing it, the "grand miniature plan" effect of Colonial Williamsburg while reintroducing William Penn's original idea of a "greene country towne." The Town of Americana is a model for a new generation of American cities where freedom and imagination are discovered again as essential American values.

The Peaceable Kingdom

Architects: de la Guardia Victoria, Trelles Architects.
Principals: Jorge Trelles, Luis Trelles, Teófilo Victoria.
Collaborators: Adib Cure, Carie Penabad.
Assistants: Muayad Abbas, William Cate, Eric Osth, Shawn Seaman, Vincent Yueh.
Honorable Mention, Stage 1, Town Plan Competition.

THE PEACEABLE KINGDOM

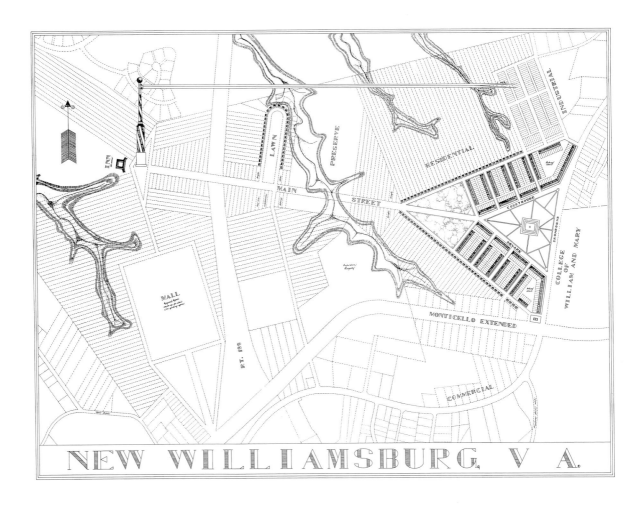

NEW WILLIAMSBURG, V A.

The Williamsburg Extension Plan & Neo-traditional Town Planning

Architects: Partnership of Charles Barrett, Architect; Juan Caruncho, Frank Martinez, Ana Alvarez, Architects; Andres Duany & Elizabeth Plater-Zyberk, Architects and Town Planners.
Competition team: Ana Alvarez, Charles Barrett, Juan Caruncho, Andres Duany, Frank Martinez, Iskandar Shafie, Galina Tahchieva.
Collaborators: Mario Abanto, Claudia Bancalari, Alisa Block, David Celis, Manolo Fernandez, Ludwig Fontalvo-Abello, Jorge Planas, Kevin Storm, Estela Valle, Adriana Veras.
Finalist, Stage 1, Town Plan Competition; 2nd Prize, Stage 2.

The Williamsburg Extension Plan embodies the most advanced principles and techniques of Neo-traditional Town Planning. The Plan is structured on four elements: Natural Preserves, Corridors, Neighborhoods, and Districts.

The Natural Preserves are areas designated to remain open and intact permanently. These areas are scientifically designated wetlands and endangered species habitats, as well as certain subjectively determined areas, such as steep slopes and hardwood uplands of aesthetic merit.

The Corridors are linear systems of two types: first, the Greenway Corridors which interconnect the Permanent Preserves and systematically incorporate miscellaneous open areas such as parks, playing fields and detention/retention ponds to form a comprehensive green space system; second, the Transportation Corridors which are right-of-way reservations for highways, rail lines and bicycle paths. The Transportation Corridors may coincide with Greenways to form Parkways and major bicycle trails. Monticello extended will be such a parkway.

The Neighborhoods are the primary, normative, urban structure. This plan incorporates five neighborhoods, one of which is dominant and shown as the "core plan." Neighborhoods are limited in size, ideally by a walking distance of five minutes to their center; they are multi-functional, including a full range of housing types, adequate to older and younger, as well as richer and poorer people; they have civic equipment, including a central open space and sites reserved for public buildings; they have edges, albeit coalescing with adjacent neighborhoods to form a town or city.

The Districts are areas which, by size or use, justified the a single use. They are an exception to the urban fabric. This plan has two such districts: one is a sector reserved for "big-box" commercial at the southwest quadrant of the intersection of Monticello and Ironbound Roads; the other is a sector at the northeast corner of the site, which is reserved for segregating industrial buildings, incompatible with the delicate fabric of the neighborhoods. The core section provides space for one new courthouse, three religious institutions, one meeting house, and one day-care center. It contains 439,000 sq. ft. of commercial and office space, and provides 425 housing units mostly in apartments.

The new town of Williamsburg

Architects: Maria de Leon-Fleites, Cesar Garcia-Pons.
Collaborators: Natasha Alfonso, Abdulla Al-Awadi, Oscar Mauricio Castro, James Dougherty, Diosdado Perera.
Honorable Mention, Stage 1, Town Plan Design Competition.

The specific goal of this proposal is to develop a community, or more exactly, a community of neighborhoods each with its individual identity, spiritual existence, and source of local pride. This is actualized by "urbanizing the suburbs." Each neighborhood was designed as a small all-class city with a different identity, convivial self-sufficiency, and aesthetic charm. This loosely federated community of communities has the potential to reduce its local residents' daily movements to a leisurely two or three miles by concentrating their socially necessary activities to their pedestrian-scaled neighborhood. People can again live close to where they work, or seek work close to where they live, while also enjoying all the other institutions they need for a full-fledged life—shops, schools, churches, recreation and sport facilities—in their immediate neighborhood.

We must remember that the amenities that draw people to a specific place are not only the environmental issues, the labor pool, the traffic facilities or superhighways, but also the narrow streets that slow down traffic and encourage pedestrian activity, the taverns which foster an environment of social interaction between people of all classes and ages, and the theaters which allow individuals to be entertained in the company of others—in short, the intensity and excitement of a town whose planners thought in terms of conviviality, religious belief, and politics.

Top left:
Partnership Barrett; Caruncho, Martinez, Alvarez; Duany & Plater-Zyberk. Masterplan of the area around the new Courthouse: see winning project Hernandez-Lyn p. 144). Second prize, stage 2.

Bottom right:
Ibidem. Detail of masterplan, western section. Second prize, stage 2.

Opposite page:
Top and center line:
Partnership Barrett; Caruncho, Martinez, Alvarez; Duany & Plater-Zyberk. Masterplan and three street perspectives. Winning entry, first phase.

Bottom:
Maria de Leon Fleites & Cesar Garcia-Pons, architects. Masterplan. Honorable mention, first phase competition.

Neo-traditionalism is a non-ideological, eclectic, pragmatic selection of whatever is best. It is distinct from the secondary, parallel trend of Traditionalism, which is ideological. The term Neo-traditionalism was coined by Stanford Research and Times-Yankelovich in 1985 to identify the state of mind of the Baby Boom Generation. Neo-traditionalism is manifested in housing by period exterior style combined with modern, airy, open-plan interiors; in construction, by vinyl clapboard; in planning, by the streetscape of the traditional small town combined with the convenient parking of suburbia; in social culture, by the corner cafe plugged into the Internet; in high culture, by the Louvre Museum on videodisk at home; in retail, by the centrally-managed Main Street.

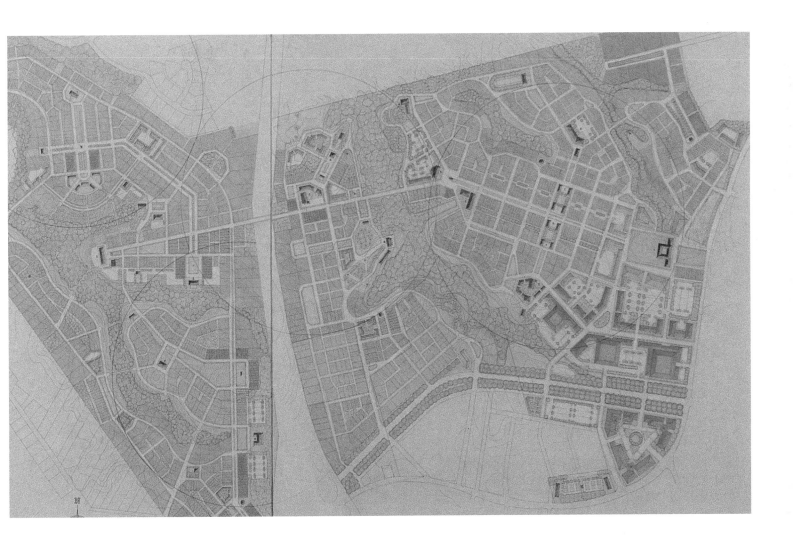

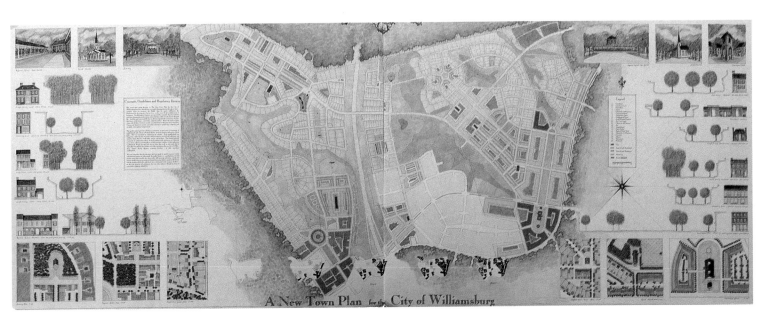

A New Town Plan for the City of Williamsburg

MANIFESTO FOR AN ORDINARY BLOCK

THE RECONSTRUCTION OF THE RUE DE LAEKEN IN BRUSSELS

Caroline Mierop

Ten new townhouses now line a section of the Rue de Laeken, one of the oldest streets in the historic city center of Brussels. Two of them are single-family houses, while the others contain thirty-nine apartments of varying size, from studios to a four-bedroom penthouse. They have shops on the ground floor as well as private gardens; some include small office areas; and they share a common underground parking garage. Thus it is a small-scale development, not in any way exceptional.

The project was conceived at the beginning of 1989, the result of a partnership between a major property owner and developer—the AG-1824 company—and a cultural association—the *Fondation pour l'Architecture*, located in Brussels and internationally known for its program of exhibitions and publications. The rare nature of this alliance is not in itself enough to explain the relatively long period of gestation—five years no less—before the project was finally brought to fruition. The reconstruction of the Rue de Laeken is indeed an experimental project: it involved the division of the buildable site into small lots, a competition process in two phases, a typological exploration around the concept of the "apartment house," and contemporary variations upon neo-classical language. The scheme assembled seven different European architects (or teams of architects), a restoration adviser, the developer-owner's consulting architect, and a tenth player, a Brussels-based architect responsible for the overall coordination. All the architects were under forty years of age and, in some cases, the Rue de Laeken was their very first construction site. But the most exceptional aspect of this reconstruction is that it involves the "renaissance" of a true urban block: a quite ordinary block indeed, typical of the Brussels morphology. This had not been seen since the immediate post-war era.

The block in discussion is an archetype of the historic urban fabric: a slightly elongated square (about 360 feet long), built and densified house by house along the centuries, lining up an old road linking Brussels to the suburban town of Laeken and further to the city of Antwerp. Originally traced *extramuros*, the street became part of the city of Brussels at the time that the

Opposite page:
The new houses of the Rue de Laeken by night. Photo Sylvie Desauw, 1995.

Top:
Atelier de Recherche et d'Action Urbaines (ARAU). Axonometric view of the center of Brussels (Pentagon, detail), 1987. To the right of the site (marked with a black dot) is the Beguinage Church with its square. On the right top corner is the Administrative Center of the City of Brussels (cross-shaped); on the bottom right is the neo-classical Hospital of Grand Hospice.

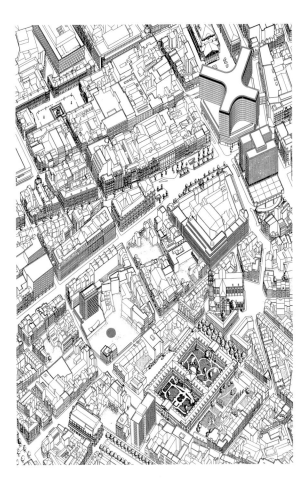

second and expanded ring of walls was built in the 14th century. Behind a row of houses, agricultural plots and small industrial buildings could be found. The opening of three new streets in the first decades of the 17th century established the definitive edges of the block and initiated the first phase of urbanization, marked by the characteristic gable houses (as late as 1960, a series of these still remained).

The golden age had yet to come. As a result of the large and ambitious campaign of public works led in the area at the end of the 18th century, the street was modernized. Houses were rebuilt or, in many cases, a new and "fashionable" facade was applied on the old structure: around 1840, the street had become one of the most elegant neo-classic streets of the city.

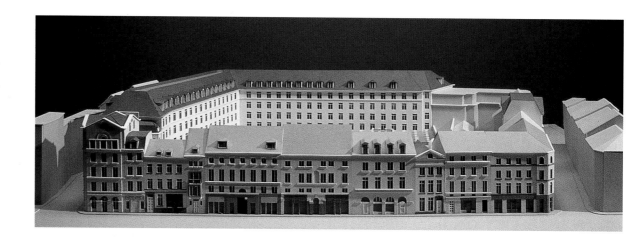

Technical datas:

Developer: AG 1824, Compagnie Belge d'Assurances Générales.
Consulting architect for the developer: Joanna Alimanestianu.

Consultant: Fondation pour l'architecture. Executive director
Caroline Mierop (with Diane Hennebert from 1992).
Coordination: Françoise Deville & Barbara Szternfeld.

Coordinating architects: Olivier De Mot &
Jean-François Lehembre (ATLANTE s.p.r.l.), Brussels.

Ground floor area of the operation: 27,000 sq.ft.
Total floor area of the operation: 120,000 sq.ft.
Housing area: 50,000 sq.ft. (usable).

Center:
General model of the block with the new houses in the foreground and
the office building in the background. Model by J.Ph. Caufriez, 1995.

Bottom right:
Facades onto the Rue du Laeken (Lot 6). On the left, the "identical"
reconstruction. Painting by J. Hart Dyke. Liam O'Connor, John Robins,
architects, London.

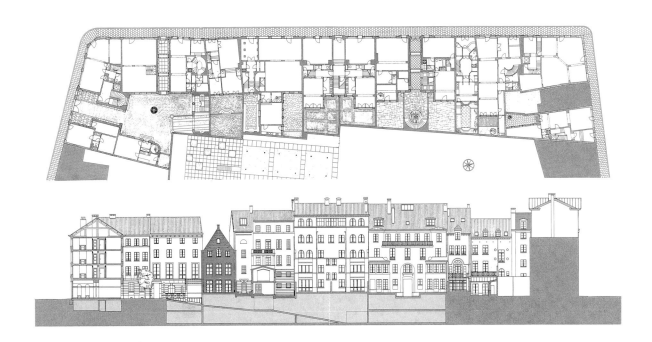

Top of spread:
General elevation of the houses on the Rue du Laeken, from the Rue Du Pont Neuf (on the left) to the Rue du Cirque (on the right). Drawing by Atlante (Y. Breithof, 1994).

Center top:
General ground-floor plan, indicating the public passageways, courtyards, and gardens. Drawing by Atlante (Y. Breithof, 1994).

Center bottom:
Cross section and general elevation of rear of the houses, from the Rue du Cirque (on the left) to the Rue du Pont Neuf (on the right). Drawing by Atlante (Y. Breithof, 1994).

Bottom right:
View of the new block interior. Photo Sylvie Desauw.

Today, behind the peeling facades of abandoned houses and despite the anarchic transformations that affected them after the war—here a large aluminum shopwindow, there the thin glazed brick veneer, etc.— it is still the neoclassic, "black and white," smooth and regular ordonnance of houses that dominates the Beguinage neighborhood.

A couple of blocks could not resist the repeated assaults of post-war urban renewal: among other casualties, an office tower surrounded by parking ramps, missing "teeth" at various street corners, and along the Rue de Laeken a large empty site, bordered by a couple of abandoned and decrepit buildings. Looming over the street in the background, askew on top of a parking plinth, was the modernist, twelve-story high, "Blue Tower," the 1960s "landmark" of the AG insurance company.

It is that ordinary Brussels block that was rebuilt from 1990 to 1994.

The block

The new block is densely built: a floor/area ratio of 3.2, superior to the one prevalent in the surrounding historic area (for instance, the adjacent Beguinage district has an average ratio of two.) Such a density does not exclude the presence, at the very heart of the block, of a new private garden, whose size is unique in this central section of the city. A wall, similar to those generally found at the back of Brussels houses, separates the garden from the inhabited parcels and is approximately one floor high. This system, invisible from the street, recalls the organization of the Beguinage of medieval Flanders: an analogy that is reinforced by the surprising tranquillity of the interior garden.

The reconstruction also reestablished the traditional mixed-use character of the block: along the Rue de Laeken, the ten houses with shops on the ground floor and some annexes at the back (a drugstore storage area, the concierge's apartment, the access pavilion to the underground parking garage, etc.); the L-shaped office building (approximately 140,000 square feet) with auditorium, galleries, and restaurant, that replaces the now destroyed "Blue Tower"; on the opposite side, the peaceful "red-lights" of the rue du Cirque which

also comprises old houses, bars, artisans workshops,…; in the center, a large underground parking for the office building, topped by the garden.

The advantages of mixed-use functions are well-known, particularly in terms of security and space management. This operation also demonstrated how important the mixed-use concept is nowadays for the financing of an urban project: in this case, the large office areas "payed" for the added housing, and the operation is expected to have a positive economic impact on the neighborhood as a whole.

The typology

Although it is owned by one single company, the block was redivided to conform as much as possible to its historic configuration. As a result, it is now made up of individual lots whose different sizes and shapes are linked to their mode of occupation and their epoch: first, the lots "en lanière", long and narrow, of the oldest houses (literally "in bands"; the two historic houses identically rebuilt belong to this category); secondly, the residential lots for houses "de rapport" (i.e., houses built to produce a revenue, generally by building additional housing units with the owner's one), obtained by absorption of two or three medieval parcels; thirdly, the corner lots, larger and generally more compact; and finally, the modern and administrative parcel, covering almost half of the block, and commanding the interior garden.

In relation to the new houses built along the Rue de Laeken, these typological variations have allowed to naturally prolong the irregular rhythm of the historic street: the division of the block in architecturally autonomous lots, and the insertion of two existing houses within the new complex, reproduce, to some extent given the shorter time frame, the traditional process of development of an European street.

The typological challenge did not stop there. Indeed, with the exception of two single-family houses, the new buildings invent a residential typology in the historic center: the "apartment house," organized around a staircase hallway and, necessity dictates, a small freight elevator. This residential scale allows to maximize the use of the vertical distribution stairwell

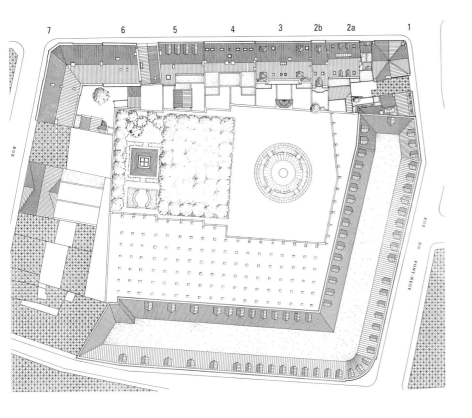

by avoiding corridors, elevators, and other public spaces, expensive to build and to maintain. Depending on the size of the reestablished parcels, four to twelve apartments are therefore distributed around a single staircase, with a single street entrance, thus creating a large and modern storefront space. This aspect is important to point out, as, too often, mixed-use configurations have been set up to the detriment of the residential organization: for instance, besides the complex issue of the entrance doors, the location of a store in the ground floor is usually incompatible with the presence of a back garden.

The reconstruction of the Rue de Laeken has attempted to resolve this quasi-historic contradiction. Three types of solutions were applied: first, the combination store/apartment, directly adjacent back to back; second, the housing unit conceived as an outbuilding, and opening on a private side courtyard; third, the small office space, placed at the back and opening on a public inner court—in this case, the paved courtyard that houses the access pavilion to the underground parking garage.

Top:
Site plan of the renovated block. On the top, the reconstructed houses on the Rue du Laeken (with lot numbers); on the bottom, the L-shaped office building of the AG 1824. Drawing by Atlante (Y. Breithof).

Bottom left:
Street view of the new AG 1824 office complex. Michel Polak, architect. Photo Sylvie Desauw.

Bottom right:
Street view of the new block with house 7 in the foreground. Photo Liam O' Connor.

Top:
The reconstructed houses (on the left) and the new office building (on the right), viewed from the central garden. Photo Sylvie Desauw.

Bottom left:
Access to the underground car park (lot 6), Liam O'Connor, architect. Photo Sylvie Desauw.

Bottom right:
Rear side view (lot 5). In the foreground, the rear house against the shop store room and first floor balcony. Photo Sylvie Desauw.

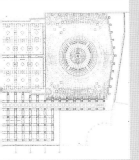

The Garden

Dan Kiley,
landscape architect

The walled gardens of the French middle ages may not seem to have much in common with the inner courtyard of the new AG Company Headquarters building at the Rue de Laeken, but it is from that tradition that the garden takes its inspiration. The courtyard is limited by the building on two sides, and by seven-foot high walls on the other two. Like its medieval counterpart, it is a place of peaceful containment, with opportunities for contemplation, relaxation and socializing.

To avoid a sense of confinement, and to give the space more variety and interest, the garden is divided into three distinct parts. The first is a large open courtyard space, paved with concentric circles of granite blocks. The courtyard is suitably sized for large receptions as well as for more informal gatherings of people. There is a center fountain, ringed with benches. The fountain, backed by low yew hedges, catches the light and provides liveliness and brilliance. Accents of color will come from the containers of seasonal flowers.

A symbolic canal, originally intended to be of water, demarcates the courtyard from the middle section of the garden, an "island" of honey locust trees. In marked contrast to the urban quality and paved surface of the main courtyard, the tightly planted grove of forty eight honey locusts is interspersed with benches to encourage one to linger in the dappled sunshine. The ground cover of vinca provides a dark green color and rich texture.

The third and smallest part of the garden is located over a further symbolic canal. This section features a pavilion with a smaller fountain at its center. There are small gardens flanking the pavilion. The garden to the east has a circular seat set amidst ferns and other ground covers; the one to the west has a simple crushed rock surface with four small flowering trees in loose array (*Amelechier canadensis*, the shadbush). Since it is seen through the trunks of the locusts, the view back down the length of the garden from the pavilion is not only interesting, but even a little mysterious.

A low-roofed portion of the building becomes part of the view when seen from above. Usually roofs are very barren and deadly looking; this one, however, is a vine garden trained to a low wire grid, a simple but visually engaging composition of voids and greenery.

The choice of plant materials is very much influenced by the garden's urban site. Honey locusts and ginkgo are among the very best city trees. This is due to their resistance both to disease and the effects of pollution. Their light, lacy, and delicate foliage and open branching structures make them also highly suitable for an urban environment. The ginkgo is the oldest tree known coming from the dim past of the Pre-Cambrian age.

The garden then, besides affording a variety of sensory and visual experiences, completes the shape of the building and is in a way almost an architectural extension of it.

*Work in progress for the recon-
struction of the Rue de Laeken.
Photo Liam O'Connor.*

*Opposite page:
Liam O'Connor & John Robins,
architects. Study of the cornice
(lot 6B), sketch, 1992.*

THE RECONSTRUCTED STREET OR THE EXACT NAME OF THINGS

Maurice Culot

Contemporary European architecture is the victim of metaphor. In other words things are no longer called by their right name and they gradually lose their own meaning and reality.

For many architects a street is no more a street but "a sequential dialog of autonomous facades" or "an aleatory escape toward the daily illusoriness"; a residential building is "a receptacle of life," "a sidereal cruise ship"; a neighborhood becomes "a fractal dynamic-chaotic fragment."

The metaphor, glory of the Roman speculative rhetoric, has been used to transfer the image of a given element to another, lightening the effect. Nowadays the metaphor has been reduced by architects, professors, and critics of architecture, to a "word game," a childish poetics, an amalgam of fragments, borrowed indiscriminately from philosophical, scientific, and economic discourse. Thus, against the epidemic of metaphors I see only one remedy: the recourse to styles.

Why? Every desire is made of a part of nostalgia and of a part of project, a part of projection in the past, and a part of projection in the future. Yet one can only desire a human being, an object, a sensation, a city, that one knows already, that one has seen before, or of whom one has heard evoke the quality or the beauty. Nobody desires an abstraction.

In a civilization where the arts and the craftsmanship constitute an important and recognized value, many men and women do appreciate beautiful monuments, urban perspectives, picturesque, classical and baroque squares, medieval and orthogonal city plans. And when I draw a project of architecture, or advise students and clients, I always start with this question: Will this project be appreciated by many people, will they adopt it, will they like it? Thus I request information about people's tastes in a particular neighborhood, city, region, or country, and I try to penetrate them. I also naturally believe that well formulated images—i.e., where the context is always taken into consideration—speak for themselves, for their implicit motivation, for the principles that guide them, for the social values that they imply. For the general public—in Europe one would say, for the bourgeoisie—architecture is first

and foremost a question of style and context. My first preoccupation, as architect, is thus style and context, understanding that the context usually determines the selection of style. In which style to complete this neighborhood, construct this street, build this public building,...? Which style is compatible with the existing environment, particularly when, as often, the latter is heterogeneous and results from successive additions.

I have of course my own taste and my own ability to work the styles. For instance, I avoid the utilization of the classical orders, pediments, colonnades, and other classical elements for which my architectural education and personal know-how were and are still insufficient. If I had to use them I would look for the help of a competent colleague.

Thus my favorite styles are the following, and in order of preference:

The Spanish-Mediterranean style. I appreciate it for its picturesque, its capacity to resolve complex programs such as a house, and also—I must confess it—because the mistakes in composition are less visible than in the classical style where they are usually unforgiving. The beauty of the style was revealed to me by Alfred Hitchcock's movie's *Vertigo*, by my mother's village of Higueras de la Sierra in Andalusia, and by Coral Gables in South Florida.

The Basque regionalist style. The style is characterized by large red-tiled and double-pitched roofs, thick white-painted walls mixed with wood panels, and red (originally beef's blood) or green louvers. In the 1920s architects gave it a modernized look, full of freshness and grandeur, under the guidance of Henri Godbarge on the French side and Leonardo Rucabado in Spain.

The Art-Deco Modern style. For its double character, cosmopolitan and aware of local traditions, and for its capacity to associate the Decorative Arts (stained-glass windows, wrought-iron works, wood works, etc.) it is the most optimistic of the styles. If, as one often says, the color of the curtain wall of the Seagram's building causes thirst, Art Deco invites to the cocktail hour.

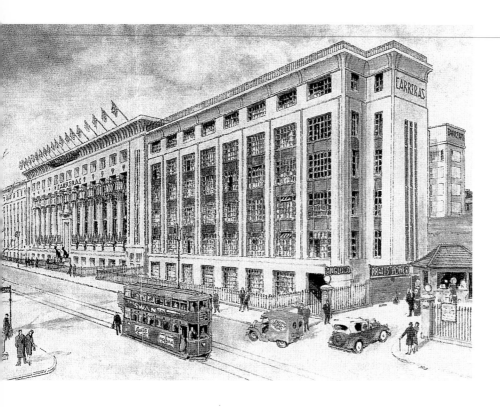

The Exotic Styles. Chinese, Turkish, Aztec, Mozarab, etc. They can only be used on rare occasions when one needs to bring an exotic accent in a characterless or very homogeneous neighborhood. As an example I will mention the Carreras building erected in Neo-Egyptian Art Deco in the early 1930s in the district of Camden Town, London. It was the production place of the renown cork tipped *Craven A* cigarettes, whose packet figured the image of a black cat. Two giant sculptures of black cats flanked the entrance of the building, built within a park ringed by a residential crescent. The style of the building rightly made up for this serious urbanistic mistake. Every morning the factory workers could rejoice at the view of this temple which invited to dream about Egypt. Unfortunately, in the 1980s, the Carreras factory closed its doors and the new owners hurried to eradicate all Deco-Neo-Egyptian motifs. In front of this massacre the cats also disappeared and the only thing left is a bad office building at the wrong place.

The discussion about styles—which will no doubt take a considerable importance in the years to come—reactualizes the historic creative concepts that are, the copy, the "identical reproduction," the pastiche, the mimetism, the imitation, etc. All these concepts have been irremediably banned from the European schools of architecture, where thinking has been sclerosed by the moralist heritage of the modernist ideology. This universe stands ready to be explored again, in the excitement of the discovery of past knowledge and of so many projects to realize. I think that is once again up to America, free from preconceived ideas and more open to research, to show the way.

The success of the reconstruction of a segment of the Rue de Laeken can be clearly attributed to the choice of style. It is an aesthetic success, plebiscited by the Brussels population, but also a commercial one, as the new apartments and their architecture, though located in a poor neighborhood, have immediately attracted a clientele. The neoclassical style was selected because it corresponded to the period of reconstruction of the neighborhood in the 1840s. Its use has clearly given a new homogeneity to a district whose streets had lost their character following on decades of transformations and substitutions.

This stylistic framework may appear rigid and constraining, but only to those who do not want to see. The interested eye notices immediately the particular accents that the young European architects have introduced. They have brought to the project exotic features and nuances, incorporated within a whole which is inherently "Bruxellois." Anyone who takes the time to look and listen to these houses can feel the unmistakable echoes of Bilbao, Bologna, London, or Toulouse.

The Basques have given the ground floor of their building a powerful arcaded base as found in the manor houses of their native regions. The English highlight the

The Vernacular styles. All the vernacular styles, particularly those of the 1920s. I include in this category the Pueblo style, the Art Deco Pueblo style, the Maya style, the Colonial American style, the Moroccan style, the Neo-Norman style, etc.

The Neoclassic style. This is the bourgeois variation of the grand style, simple and practical. Its power resides in its proportions. It is well adapted to the current period plagued by idle talk and gesticulation.

The Rationalist Style. The rationalism preached by Viollet-le-Duc in France, Andrade in Turin, Rubbiani in Bologna, Pompe in Brussels, Baude in Paris, Dom Bellot in Holland and in England, etc., shows many features of Protestant-ism: economy, structural evidence, simplicity of the plan, and absence of display. Ornament is often reduced to its most simple expression.

The International style of the 1920-30s. It procures deep emotions, similar to those of the period's painting. It requires an absolute precision and a lot of maintenance. It is better reserved for well-to-do persons and communities, preferably on the sea front where the whiteness of the facades against the blue of the sea warrants strong poetic effects.

The Beaux-Arts style. It does not seem to fit anymore in Europe, where the priority is more to reconstitute urban fabrics than to build public buildings. In contrast, the United States have the financial means and the talented architects to utilize it, as can be demonstrated by the new Chicago Public Library by Thomas Beeby.

details, much appreciated in these times when the—non-biodegradable alas—polyvinyl chloride finishings continue their seemingly unstoppable advance. France brings memories of the monumental proportions of the immense brick facades of Toulouse. Emilia-Romagna bestows a Baroque crown upon the street corner, beneath which lies an apartment which is as curious as it is unexpected. The Brussels teams have erected a tower house whose interior layout is reminiscent of the fluidity of interior spaces initiated a hundred years ago by Victor Horta, a successful contemporary homage to neoclassicism and to Art Nouveau on a lot measuring just four meters across.

Victim of metaphor, European architecture suffers equally from the loss of the client. In other words the client accepts everything and anything which is sold to him or her under the label of creativity or pure functionality. The three symptoms of this phenomenon are:

first, is the anonymous character of most contemporary clients (insurance companies, real estate speculators, multinational companies, etc.) for whom architecture is a merchandise like all others;

secondly, the idealization through the press, the exhibitions, and the educational system, of the image of the architect, whereas it is notorious that most of them are of limited talent;

thirdly, the absence of alternative to the fatality of "progress." Schools, architectural magazines, professional associations of architects, cultural institutions, are all, with rare exceptions, totally refractory to architecture and urbanism which affirm a link with tradition.

Thus the freedom that architects seem to have won from the disappearance of the client is of course illusory. Without a demanding and cultured client, architecture is completely under the law of maximum profit, and profit at all cost. And when the imagination of the architect is not controlled or structured by the enlightened debate with the client and with the civil society, it can only engender monsters, shapeless, ridiculous, and obscene creatures.

From the 1920s onwards, model streets and quarters began to be erected in Europe, a would-be testimony to the new world, to the new man, to the European man freed from nationalism, cleansed of all of the injustices of history, if not of history itself. The Weissenhof Siedlung built in 1927 in Stuttgart is without a doubt the most famous of these "housing exhibitions" (the irony of history: it is now a historical monument). Many leaders of the International Style were involved in this work: Le Corbusier, Oud, Mies van der Rohe, Mart Stam, Victor Bourgeois, etc.

Following Stuttgart, in 1930, the City of Liège projected to build a new housing development, but the depression limited access to the national architects. In 1932, it was the turn of the Austrian Werkbund to build an experimental new town in Vienna. The French architect, André Lurçat, made a notable impact here, before emigrating to the USSR, the presumed homeland of the new spirit of the age. In the 1950s West Berlin decided to build a model urban quarter and to teach a lesson in modernism to its Eastern neighbors. But the Hansaviertel is nothing more than an accumulation of constructions in green surroundings. Berlin made a further attempt in 1981-1987 with the IBA, although the result was scarcely more impressive, other than for the endless list of big names it succeeded in attracting. The Rue de Laeken development does not of course belong to this series of initiatives which were sometimes romantic, always dogmatic, and which endeavored—usually with the very opposite result—to convince a public which really needed no convincing at all.

Today, contemporary urban thinking is interested in the town rather than the housing project, in the neighborhood which lives and breathes rather than the zone, in urbanism rather than in ruralism. This is the thinking which lies behind the Rue de Laeken. There is no reason, however, not to trace a link back to the *Strada Nuova* in Genoa, and its palaces celebrated by the engravings of Peter Paul Rubens. This is not simply because it is very agreeable to have such an illustrious parentage, but also because the reconstruction of the Rue de Laeken exceeded the hopes of even its most optimistic promoters, as sometimes happens with works with no initial aspiration to posterity, but which are imbued with the lucidity of their age.

Bottom right:
View of the staircase in house of lot 5. Javier Cenicacelaya, Iñigo Saloña, Architects, Bilbao. Photo Sylvie Desauw.

Translated from the French by Jean-François Lejeune.

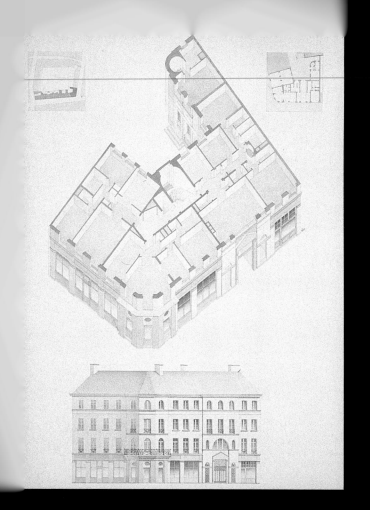

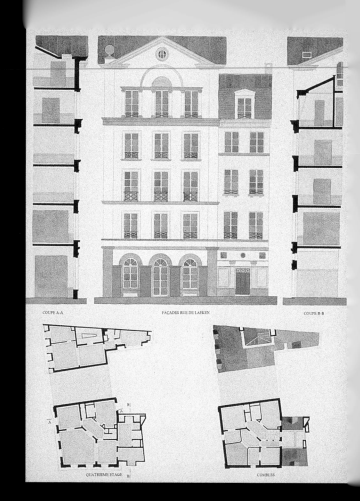

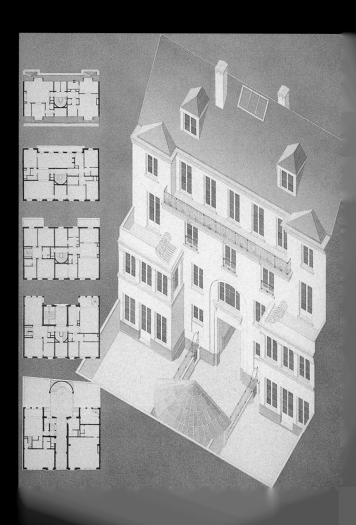

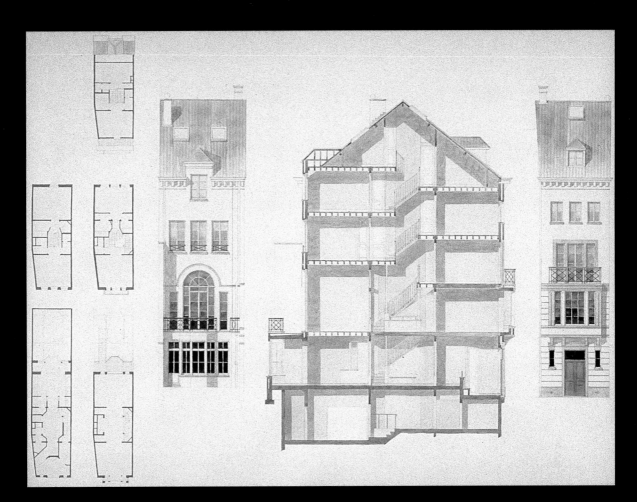

Top right:
The one-family house (lot 2B): facades, longitudinal section and plans. Atelier 55: Mark Heene, Michel Leloup, Brussels.

Top center:
Main facade, project of 1989 (lot 5). Javier Cenicacelaya, Iñigo Saloña, Bilbao.

Center left:
Facade onto the Rue de Laeken (Lot 4). Jean-Philippe Garric, Valérie Nègre, Paris.

Opposite page:

Top left:
Plans, ground- and first-floor, detail of the wall base (axonometric) and development plan of the street facades (Lot 7), Joseph Altuna, Marie-Laurie Petit, Tours.

Top right:
Facades onto the Rue de Laeken and sections through the tower house (lot 1B), fourth-floor and attic plans (lots 1A and 1B). Gabriele Tagliaventi & Associates, Bologna.

Bottom left:
Facade onto the Rue de Laeken. Section through the covered passageway and access to the underground car park (Lot 3). Sylvie Assassin, Barthélémy Dumons, Barcelona, & Philippe Gisclard, Nathalie Prat, Toulouse.

Bottom right:
Axonometric drawing of the garden facade with floor plans (lot 3). Sylvie Assassin, Barthélémy Dumons, Barcelona, & Philippe Gisclard, Nathalie Prat, Toulouse.

ARCHITECTURE ON THE STAGE

GIORGIO GRASSI
& THE RECONSTRUCTION OF SAGUNTO'S ROMAN THEATER

Alberto Ustarroz

*Giorgio Grassi
& Manuel Portaceli,
architects*

*Collaborators:
Jean-Luis Dujardin,
Lukas Meyer, Alfredo
Paredes, Rafael Duet.*

I want to emphasize, first of all, the principal quality of this project: a new, and certainly polemic, creative relationship between the architect and the ruins. Until Grassi and Portaceli's project for the reconstruction of the Sagunto's Roman Theater, the ruins seemed to increasingly belong to the ineffable and exclusive realm of the experts, historians, and archaeologists. During the twentieth century in particular, ruins have been perceived almost exclusively from the point of view of conservation or, at best, scientific detachment.

In fact, the history of architectural creativity within the ruins is long, at least as long as the history of western architecture during the last six hundred years, a topic I discussed in my doctoral dissertation, *Las Lecciones de las Ruinas*.[1] I must confess to be an "apprentice of the ruins." Nothing has helped me more in my development as an architect than the presence of the ruins and their study. I would add that so many architects have been apprentices of the ruins as to make up the list of the best of the discipline: from Brunelleschi to Palladio, from Raphael to Schinkel, from Soane and Le Corbusier to Louis Kahn, etc. Thus I want to address Giorgio Grassi and Manuel Portaceli's work in Sagunto within this context. As an insider, I will retain the personal tone of the text.[2]

Every historical period observes in the ruins whatever it wants to see in relation to its concrete architectural problems. It is also true that the ruins—understood as a theorem to be taken apart and comprehended—have been useful to formulate the everlasting questions of architecture: from the enigmatic beginning of the precise elements of composition, from the construction techniques to typology, from building character to the role of ornament.

As an initial warning, it is useful to remember that the architect's interest in the ruins is more varied than the historian's, archeologist's, painter's, or poet's. Instead of a vision bound to be objective, to immobilize, to classify, to describe or to be lyrical, the architect's view is based on a rediscovery of the rules of the Constructive Art, no matter how paradoxical this may seem. The ruins provide the most beautiful analogy to understand what is and how is architecture.

In the confronting of the ruins, I believe that architecture includes everything that the disciplines of archaeology and history would be unable to construct or explain. An architect who is an apprentice of the ruins is similar to a voracious reader who encounters and re-encounters a world full of creative analogies.

The ruins from the past are only bare bones which are no longer a reflection of their previous self, as their own world has vanished. The ruins' attractiveness, however, lies within their mere presence, as directional arrows that signal the point of departure of our thoughts and imagination. These fragments, like the talking stones of the Temple of Zeus at Dodona recorded by Plato, bring a message of prophecy, and imaginary maps open up to creation. When we look at them from the present, full of interest and questions, we become for a moment Greek or Roman: their creativity belongs to us and only us.

Every ruin, therefore, is, first of all, an invitation to the Art of Building. Often, when we look at the broken and disorganized architecture that has been reduced to simple marks on the ground—the footprint of a building and a few unconnected fragments—our imagination fills in the gaps and overwhelms the site, looking for formal and constructive order from the apparent chaos. An order that sometimes leads to a project of reconstruction—whether it is theoretical or will be built—and sometimes to a body of thought, drawings, and works that expand the practice and theory of the architectural discipline. At other times, construction will take place on or within the ruins, as in the case of Baldassare Peruzzi at the Theater of Marcellus or of Michelangelo with the Baths of Diocletian.

It is within such power—the capacity of action or the *virtù* of the ancients in the words of Palladio—that the architect finds the always fresh value of the ruins; they seem to have been made for the specific pleasure of the architects as the essence of the design process. On the other hand, the materiality of the ruin dominates in spite of its broken state. The unfinished ruin teaches things that we had forgotten: the synthesis of the most obvious elements of the Art of Building; the cross fertilization between the formal and material

*Opposite page:
View of access and rear facade
facing modern Sagunto.
© Photo Duccio Malagamba.*

Raphael, "Cavallo dell'Opus praxitelis di Montecavallo, profilo del pilastro di sostegeno sotto le figure." Sanguine drawing, pen & brown ink for measures. 218 x 272 mm. Chatsworth, Devonshire Collection. Inv. n. 657, U.K.

worlds shown from inside the ruins itself; a process, stopped at a magical moment, that teaches all that it exposes, as it provokes us to reconstruct.

One drawing by Raphael is an accurate illustration of this concept. It is a beautiful sanguine in the Chatsworth Collection of one of the horses of the Dioscuri, Castor and Pollux, in front of the Quirinale. It was a commission from Leo X, as a study for the restoration of the work, attributed to Phidias and Praxiteles, poorly preserved for hundreds of years and missing essential parts of the horses' bodies. This beautiful and precise drawing shows a new full horse. Its ancient components are drawn in sanguine red and Raphael's additions at the legs and the head in gray. Everything is carefully defined, as if it was a building. Raphael's operation attempts to reconstruct a perfect horse, molding all its parts whether new or old. Archaeological accuracy is not important: the horse lives and it is beautiful.

Raphael continues the horse where the fragment ends and suggests further paths for completion. This is co-authorship, an inspired creation which connects us with a past that becomes our present, our own work. It is not about arriving at unquestionable truths, which, fortunately, cannot come from the ruins, but about believable truths appropriate for action, for use in the building drama. In the words of Le Corbusier, "la pas-

sion fait de pierres inertes un drame."[3] I believe such is the tone of the Sagunto theater project.

However, when perceived from the point of view of romantic evocation or aloof historicism, the ruins are placed at a higher level, as if they had frozen on top of their native soil and become embalmed reproductions. The uselessness of their desolation appears to be good for nothing. Their life cycle, we are told, has ended definitively and from such insurmountable distance, the only appropriate thing to do is offer praise: "we have destroyed our idols to adore their remains" as Cioran would say.[4]

And now, the project by Grassi and Portaceli attempts to erase the distance right here, on top of the very remnants of Sagunto's Roman theater. From such novelty a scandal emerges. Should the thought of creating architecture from the ruins be for ever suspended in the realm of the idea for a project, or could it be realized in situ, as in this exceptional instance, to be something permanent and physical? This is the bold and rational wager of the project by Grassi and Portaceli. The result is the rebirth of the Sagunto's Roman theater, in the manner of Raphael's sketch.

Grassi's position should not be surprising because he has always searched in his work for the creative crisscrossing of the architecture of the present and the architecture of the past, ideally as fragments, as in the projects for the Abbiategrasso castle, Valmarina,

Teora's church, Berlin's Prinz Albrecht Palace, and even so for the new library of Groningen. In the Sagunto's theater, where both its interior and its exterior worlds were reestablished, the ruin is not consumed nor hidden, but its fragments, well fitted within the restored areas, shine again inside the completed work. Glimpses gain prominence and fragments remain as witnesses of an ancient order which captures us within its new orbit. Then, the ruin frees the poetry held within, in an architecture reduced to the bare essentials.

As the *cavea* has become anew a true *cavea*, the monumental *frons scaenae* is impressively reborn. The theatrical space is enclosed by the *post-scaenium* wall is capped again by the bright blue of the Mediterranean sky. The orchestra reoccupies the center of this reborn Vitruvian geometry and the sounding board perhaps echoes a joke from Aristophanes or some tragic verse by Seneca, as the gates await the actors whose voices will reverberate on the wood of the proscenium. Higher up, the mosaics, the altar stones, and the evocative inscriptions cover the backstage's wall, speaking Latin, *"the language of the builder-architects"* as Loos once said.[5] Two orders of the columnation of the *frons scaenae* have returned to their place, giving a sense of scale to the restoration. These column fragments, these full columns as they now appear, draw an unexpected articulation between the new and the old. Such articulation is seen within the geometry which overwhelms the complex: it is *"the appearance of the invisible,"* in the words of Anaxagoras.[6]

Here is the powerful demonstration that each fragment, randomly relocated by history, and the mutilations and forgeries that have affected the ruin, reveals a new sense of unity in the whole which is the Roman theater. It is simply architecture on top of architecture. Its bare purity, typical of Grassi as it is

well known, recalls all fragments, whether existing or no longer there, of a reborn monument. Unnecessary things do not distract. Purposely unfinished elements demand to be completed by the viewer. The rest of the ensemble shows no interest in *"the easy gesture,"* to use words of Valéry.[7]

Building here means emphasizing correctness and precision, which truly points out to the essential idea: the Roman theater as a building type. From the sunken ruin, Grassi has decided what should be salvaged, shown, hidden, or removed. This is a process of distillation, but similar to the process of architectural design. The result is the architecture of a Roman theater and its ruin, both present at once. As they are juxtaposed, they do not eliminate the ruin's evocative power; nor do they eliminate the emotion of the reconstruction, in the manner of Alberti in the Malatesta Temple of Rimini, where he builds roman arches which do not obscure the gothic windows, inaugurating the best tradition of architectural restoration.

The minimal presence of Grassi's architecture demonstrates eloquently the beauty of everything which is not there, a second secret life enjoyed endlessly by things from the past. Some are present, others are absent, all are creatively combined, without any limiting nostalgia. The void of the absent underlines the reasons for the manner and extent of the restitution.

The work is, in itself, a theater for the mind of the future spectator, a place for memories—connected to so many Roman and other western theaters which emerged from the modest means of reasonable construction—reminiscent of Loos' statement, *"I build as the Romans did."*[8] The theater repeats the act of Roman construction, i.e., concrete covered by brick. Everything else is left for the creative void of things absent. Such constructive statement dominates all the meetings of the old and the new, even when they are unpleasant, as in the *cavea*, without falling into the mannerism of fashionable design.

A tradition is thus extended: the Roman theater type, *"with the full sound of ancient bronze,"* as Le Corbusier once said.[9] Now, the ensemble becomes a Roman theater once again, a combination of things seen and things imagined, both here and in so many memorable places: Aspendos, Sabratha, Leptis Magna, Djemila, Mérida, etc. The discovery of the project's tone, over the white noise which is the ruin, is the most valuable characteristic of the work by Grassi and Portaceli: a respect and love for the past and the present of a place; a will to build on top of them that guarantees the depth and accuracy of the restoration, which is itself stylized, minimized, and almost open ended, and which creates a new architectural syntax that knots and supports the evocative images; a precise sense of responsibility, and a rigor of the mind which delivers an old-new Roman theater as a complete, clear and detailed analog. The mind can undo, with misleading

Bottom:
The Dioscuri Group (Castor & Pollux) of the Quirinale, Rome. Engraving by Antonio Lafreri. circa 1546. © Rome, Lanciani Collection.

OPVS FIDIAE   OPVS·PRAXITELIS

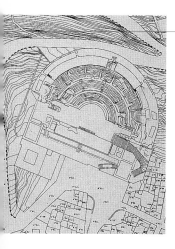

Top:
Site plan before construction.

Bottom:
Site plan of the project.

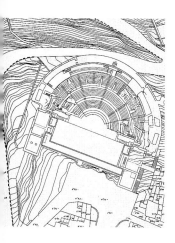

Previous spread:
The reconstructed Roman theater with modern Sagunto in the foreground and the Antique and medieval ruins in the background. © Photo Duccio Malagamba.

ease, such an obvious operation: building a shell for seating with stones that partially cover the old *cavea*, or separating the new stage. However, ruin and building appear to have emerged together, forever full of a superior oneness both as architecture and as theater. They are balanced, as far away from archaeological purism as from the arrogance of present day vandalism.

Everything is done with minimal tools, reduced to their essence: the stage, the shadow of the sounding board which frames the lyrical view of the sea of Sagunto through the *porta regia*. The sounding board unifies the elements that appear, on the surface, to be fragmented, through the elementary geometry of light and shadow. The scenic void thus created lights up on its own as a bright and poetic sphere fronting the neighboring Mediterranean sea. Light and shadow appear under the sounding board which mysteriously turns on and off, exposing in the air the invisible geometry of the curving *valvas*, the remains of ancient numbers subtly suggested by Grassi. Monumental light and shadow form the quality of the void of the scene, as they surround it with an aura. The sacred space retains the intangible mystery of an ancient play. The great shadow of the sounding board, the ghostly space of the scene, a persistent tradition which alters its appearance without locking itself in the past, open to the power of an analogy: *"where you see one I see one hundred"* to recall Paul Valéry.[10]

The scene is as surprising in its sense of scale as in its power of suggestion, something unexpected from Grassi's architecture. The Mediterranean light reveals this essential beauty based on the simplest constructive art: a powerful enclosing stone wall, large pillars, beams, and the wooden sounding board. Everything exists under the punishing sun and the mysterious shadows that come from it. Nothing is only itself: the slide of multiple images is appropriate to convey the purest scenographic effect of the theater and the ruin.

The most original feature of the project does not prevent evocative feelings, it does not fix the attention in a single image. The spectator is not constrained within a completed environment. Instead, he is an accomplice in the recollection of every non-existing element that is merely recalled. Reality and imagination add up, as do the unbroken building rigor and the poetical spirit, which crystallize on this project as on the edge of a blade. All that is unreachable in conventional restoration is substituted here by a project which retains all the possibilities of a dream within its essential bareness.

I think that every fragment cries for help. Here, Grassi's rescue does not eliminate the normal attractiveness of the fragment. Such characteristic emerges from the fragment's own incompleteness or from its partial promise of completion. Everything is found in a present which is acutely perceived as the temporal location of the rediscovery. Present things are not definitive because their essence is found in the moving images

that underscore the building. In Sagunto, the ruin perseveres, *"against time its strength is bold"* as in the powerful verse by Quevedo.[11] Ruin and fragment—memories during the age of oblivion—seems to be Grassi's statement. The project proposes a critical reading of history, where fragments are perceived as an architectural problem. The ruin, like all mythical structures, can expand our sensibilities, transport us instantly to the boundary of the present, can acknowledge our temporal prejudices and limitations, and can undoubtedly close the gap between the worlds of the past and of the present.

The road traveled by Grassi and Portaceli is challenging, as it is based on the assumption that architecture can still be built disregarding fashions or theories. The proposal comes from a mental dialog between memories and experiences, with the full realization that a few fragments, a ruin, and the project which encloses them, are unable to state all which must be said, as such pretense of comprehensiveness is now impossible. Unfinished architecture which awaits its missing parts, a fact typical of Grassi's, is in this case, more than ever in his work, necessary and illuminating. Asking questions of the past is about constantly looking back for the isolation of the present and finding common ground within the fragments, which are again humanized by daily use. It is not surprising that the restored theater presents a demanding challenge to a careful observer.

Everything is born out of the personal experience of the author confronting the ruin, which establishes the precise constraints for the elaboration of the message sent to the observer. This act is thus perceived silently, by itself, and full of questions. The silence results from the unique existence and presence of the fragments, which can only survive in the newly created organization. Fragments seem at once remembered and forgotten, as a prescription for remembering the whole because of the enlightenment of the observer. What was, what shall be, what has been in Sagunto? It is architecture on top of architecture which affirms itself by making apparent its missing parts. An architecture which firms up by presenting the problem of such missing elements, without eliminating the world of imagination which is found, fused with the shadows of the sounding board. An architecture of shelter, which is in itself a tribute to the space where western theater came to life. The presence of the additions—the mediators in this operation—is already a creative red flag, the means of demarcating absences as the reality of elementary construction is affirmed: a large portico supported solidly by two pillars. Something is brought to the present from a great distance, something which takes us closer to the original architectural myth, the theatrical myth, echoes of a relived experience. The chain of tradition, contains a first link where truth and certainty are kept. Building within tradition is Grassi's wager in Sagunto.

Some architectural critics are uncomfortable with the theater. It is indeed difficult to pigeonhole. Some repeat the well known *ritornello* about the impossibility of a dialog with the past, unless the past is denied or radically contrasted. The historical naiveté of the ruins is not accepted, which is more real and present than many controversial messages. Yet this has always been the role of the ruins in previous restorations: showing extremes, without regard to the art of construction or the architects' work. I acknowledge that no one is without prejudice when looking at the ruin and the lonesome observer is affected by his own impressions, desires, and memories, which constitute a practically unknown variable. Fortunately, the ruin allows no certainties, prejudices, or comforts. The added architecture not only established its language—here Grassi's—as it welcomes the ruin and its fragments as the foundation and decoration of its bare surfaces, but at the same time it creates another form of communication with the present. The project is searching for a specific type of existence: the one that results from the mind of the observer and is capable of building out thoughts and emotions. Creativity from within is what Grassi offers to the visitor in Sagunto's theater.

Imagining an intelligible form for the building type evoked by the project and building the architectural framework make the success of the project. Its architecture gives emphasis upon mediation and stimulates the recollection of the observer. Its Platonic interior populated by shadows is an echo of a theater born out of our experience as lived through it. The materials of the ruins speak to us, exist with us, and feed through us and through our memories. The intimate experience tied up to our perception is sustained by the radical solitude of the spectator on the *cavea* of Sagunto. The projects stimulates the memory of the ruin and it is also an immense receptacle that keeps it and protects it. The past is no more, memory does not exist out of the enlightenment of the present. Architecture is victorious over all kinds of anachronisms. It states without regard to time all the elements consumed by history.

I was particularly impressed, as I recently left Sagunto that I had visited for the first time in many years, by the memory of the theatrical scene and by the metaphysical wall which circumscribes it. The wall that guards the *antiquarium* presents to the outside world a genuine Levantine appearance. It is a belvedere wall which looks, in the way of its Roman predecessor, from its rhythmical voids and small overhanging balcony toward the eternal Mediterranean sea, which conveyed the myth and culture of the theater. A beautiful wall made of brick and stone—both ancient and new—similar to the castles and palaces of so many Spanish towns and cities. A visible wall, both on top of the rocks and of the past, and an important urban monument, which is a new symbol of Sagunto, crowned by the castle and the acropolis on top of the hill. A priceless image, full of all

the power and mystery of a memorable ancient site. It is a new space that may isolate "*one hundred people who are moved by a single act*," in the words of Musil.[12] A reconstruction from within which pulls on the observer, because it is, in itself, a theatrical object, and material for scenography. The project is full of meaning and the observer understands the message. Such meeting of the minds would not be possible without the observer's collaboration and understanding.

Memory, recollection, imagination. I would like to know why as Italo Calvino has said "*the perforated net of my mind catches some things as other go by.*"[13] Remembrance of tradition, an amphibious type of time which becomes in Sagunto a creative activity: a Roman theater where we are the Romans. All that is left from them, from the theater and the idea of the theater, is within us and only us, the spectators in Sagunto. Grassi provides the scene and he should be thanked. It is a project that follows his thoughts on architecture and acts as a tribute to what architecture could become. Grassi and Portaceli did what had to be done. The coherence and beauty of Sagunto's theater is everyone's reward.

Translated from the Spanish by Ramon Trías.

Bottom:
Site plan with roof plan of the project.

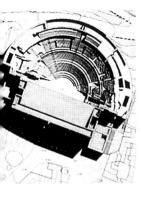

1. Alberto Ustarroz, "*La Leccion de las Ruinas,*" *(The Lesson of the Ruins)* Ph. D. Thesis, Universidad del País Vasco, Escuela de Arquitectura de San Sebastián, December 1989.

2. See also the beautiful text by Leon Krier, "L'amour des ruines ou les ruines de l'amour," *La Laurentine et l'invention de la Villa romaine* (Paris: Le Moniteur/IFA, 1982), pp. 149-163.

3. Le Corbusier, "Passion makes from inert stones a drama," *Vers une architecture* (Paris: Ed. Vincent et Freal, 1958), p. 121.

4. Emile Cioran, *Silogismos de la amargura* (Barcelona: Tusquets Ed., 1990), p. 96.

5. Adolf Loos, *Ornamento y Delito* (Barcelona, Ed. Gustavo Gili, 1970), p. 77.

6. Anaxagoras, *Fragmentos pre-socráticos* (Madrid: Jonathan Barnes, Ed. Catedra, 1992), p. 134.

7 Paul Valéry, *Cahiers* (Paris: Ed. Gallimard, 1973), Vol. 1. p. 34.

8. Adolf Loos, *Ornamento y Delito*, op. cit., p. 56.

9. Le Corbusier, *Vers une architecture*, op. cit., p. 121.

10. Paul Valéry, *Cahiers*, op. cit., p. 121.

11. Quevedo, *Obra Completa: Poesía* (Madrid: Ed. Aguilar, 1992), p. 92.

12. Robert Musil, *Ensayos y Conferencias* (Madrid: Ed. Visor, 1992), p. 90.

13. Italo Calvino, *Por que leér los clásicos* (Barcelona: Ed. Tusquets, 1992), p. 25.

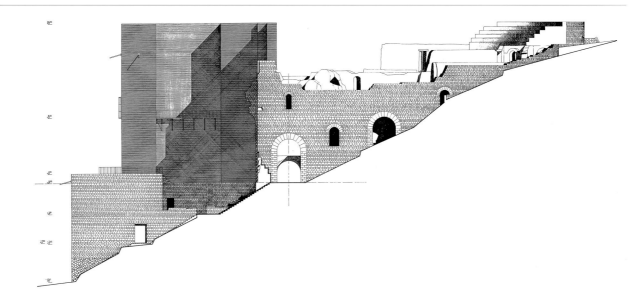

Top:
West and east facades.

Bottom left:
Plans of stage level and antiquarium level.

Bottom right:
Plans of second antiquarium
level and mezzanine level .

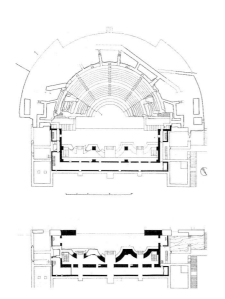

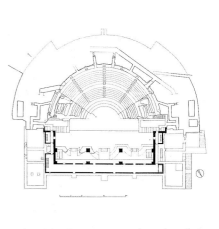

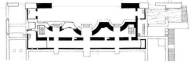

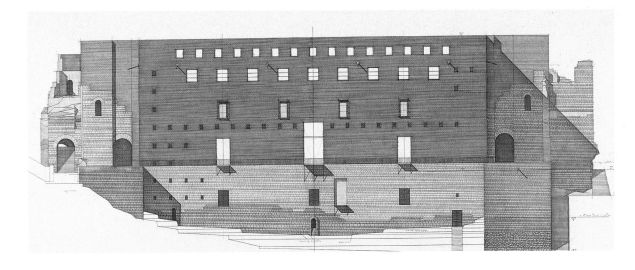

From top to bottom:

Cross section through the reconstructed stage building and cavea. © Giorgio Grassi Studio.

Rear facade facing modern Sagunto. © Giorgio Grassi Studio.

Stage front with Antiquarium on the second level. © Giorgio Grassi Studio.

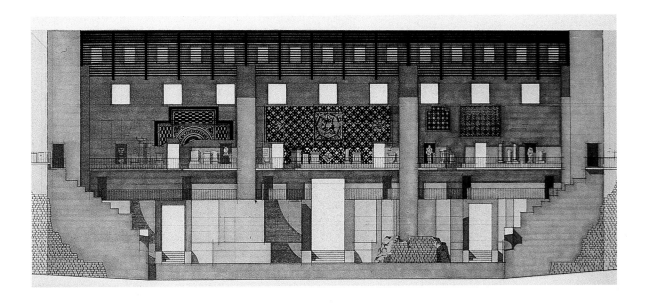

Miami magnetic melting man-kind meridional microcosm museum mambo maybe
melodrama mutual million muse mother monologue multiple materials moment
mutation magnanimous maze much more Minotaur movement myth Motezuma
montage mañana millenium monk mind **monument** mineral meticulous magnolia m
magnifico Marcello Mastroiani mixed message man mental magic mine manipula-
tion May metabolism megal Marciek matrix multiples mellow melody ma
mermaid manifesto matter market mamoth margin melange Mephistopheles
marvelous **meaning** marble magistral Mantegna model million mutation maritime
Morpheus must moon   mom meal mad muse   muse Mars mill
marionette member my   Madonna martyr   metaphore marriage
medieval melange mist   maharishi mimic   Merlin marihuana
meditation merengue might   maricchi manate   mercury Macbeth middle
migrant Mickey House   milestone m   monster mansion mescal
Matisse map **Metro**   modern meter   **Mover** method measure March morning m   metaphysic   main-shet meeting
milk melancholy m   Midas   medula mirage matchbox
maquette maraca mind   many   more Mardi-Gras melon
mana man-made me   mu   honchos muscular meta-
March mental mutable   mi   mild mural monastery
morphosis Medusa   movement mushroom
Malcolm X **magic**   meta mosaic music
mesmeric Mather m   moves magnanimos m
mountain mysterious   mood mythical me
metropolis millenary   mortality microscopic
Milky Way myried meti   meteors mobile mangoe
mice **mirrors** monumental   Michelangelo mythical
message merry minuters   Mayan magna machine
mathematics mirthful   maraca minimal mar
Minos medal manipulatio   medieval megalopolis
memorial Massaccis m   metaphysical melancholy
Mar del Plata monday   morning magistral mood
memorable metaphore   melodious manuscript
major meditative m   maxim Marco Polo
marathon methodic   motor medalion m
mania make main   maid mail maize
mind male mime   mate made marmalade
meteoric mouth mask   magnifier **multiple** mi
mirror marvelous m   metonymy metallic
marimba mature me   mentor magazine
M is miniature m   Mediterranean me
melange maraschino ma   mandolin mariposa
mestizo Malevich manifesto matriarchy minimal movable mimesis medium
maleable mask mundane magnitud multilateral monogram media mystery
milestone mission mitzvah modulation mortal meditation musical
meditation M C V Medusa momentum monastic mirror **memories** ....

THE BIGGEST M IN THE WORLD

*Roberto Behar &
Rosario Marquardt*

*Collaborators:
Claudia Bancalari,
José Jaén, Kevin Storm*

The aim of this project is to reconsider the notion of Art in Public Places from the point of view of Architecture as Public Art. The site is located in downtown Miami, at the foot of the Metromover Riverwalk Station, a newly inaugurated leg of the automatic train system, running 100 feet above ground. The site is a triangular traffic island of 1750 square feet., freely bound by the Metromover line, on the west; the skyline of downtown skyscrapers on the east; the Miami River on the south; and access and exit ramps for highway I-95 on the north. Thus, the site resides at the encounter of ships, elevated trains, highways, skyscrapers, and airplanes flying above; it participates of the wild, gray, unfinished beauty of ethnically diverse Downtown Miami.

To this atmosphere in motion, "the biggest M of the world" brings "e-motion." A pause for the eye where to fix a memory. An element of reference beyond doubt within the area, and a source of wonder in the ongoing collective invention of Miami. In the tradition of Diego Rivera, Andy Warhol, Haitian painting, and the best of modern times, the project expands upon the art of the streets of the Americas, and bridges across con-

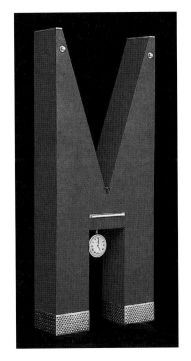

ventional denominations and expressions of culture. The "M" stands for Miami, Magic, Metro Mover, and so on; as a landmark in a land of immigrants, it may also celebrate Motherhood and Memory, and hence the birth of the first Pan-American city under construction. In this regard, the "M" is a Model of Multiple Meaning, the secret of which remains an open Mystery.

As a Monument, the "M" doubles as a toy, introducing human scale to the life of this part of the city, while simultaneously participating in the tradition of the "colossal" in America. Thus, the project gives identity to the area and mediates between the scale of the context and the huge size of the Metromover station. Like Alice in Wonderland, who changes scales to transform through dreams her perception of reality, the "M" of Miami provides physical evidence of the fantastic as part of everyday life.

The "M" is built in reinforced concrete blocks with red stucco finish. Color and texture bring warmth to the area, calling attention upon it as a future place of encounter. From the station open terrace, the concrete floor in ochre and black reveals the outline of an alligator and the trace of the natural archeology of the site.

*All drawings on this spread:
Roberto Behar & Rosario Marquardt. "M" for Miami.
Color pencil and pastel on paper.
Courtesy Art in Public Places of Dade County.*

*Top:
Roberto Behar & Rosario Marquardt. "M" for Miami. Model.*

THE 'ROAD 836' OVERPASS IN MIAMI

Monica Ponce de Léon
& Nader Tehrani

Collaborators:
Victor Sant'anna,
Colin Smith

The presence of massive infrastructure elements, such as highways, metrorail systems, or commuter stations, is a reality of the contemporary city. Contrary to the infrastructure of the 19th and early 20th century—the Berlin Stadtbahn, Otto Wagner's Stadtbahn and locks in Vienna, the 1930s works of Robert Moses in New York City, etc.—one finds few examples in recent history (the case of Barcelona is quite exceptional) where their colossal presence has been addressed in urbanistic or architectural terms. After the second world war, the realm of infrastructure has all too often been relegated to the domain of the civil and traffic engineer, whose disciplines do not have the means to fully address the complexities—architectural, urbanistic, social—involved in planning the large city.

As a result, while cities' infrastructures have developed a great deal in the past three decades, they have often done so to the detriment of the urbanistic and public aspects of the city. For instance, even though many highways have successfully connected the city's districts at a regional level, they have failed to account for the relationship between neighboring communities through (and over) which they have intervened. Furthermore, since they have been designed for the automobile (inevitably resulting in colossal dimensions), they have rarely been scaled to accommodate other forms of transportation, such as the pedestrian. This has resulted in the vast expanse of wasted space under, around, and between most major infrastructure interventions in the city.

In this context, our modern proposal—developed between 1991 and 1993—for the Road 836 overpass near Downtown Miami is the opportunity to explore some of the programmatic, urbanistic, and architectural potentials of public infrastructure. The proposal also operates at a general planning level, and aims at reorienting the development and the life of the city towards one of its main natural resources, the Miami River. The 836 overpass constitutes a unique moment on one of Miami's most traveled freeways. As it crosses the Miami River, the highway dramatically rises to great heights to allow for the mast of sailboats to pass below it. The space created underneath it is of monumental dimensions and bears an uncanny resemblance to what could be called a "hypostyle hall." The crossing of the highway also maintains an important adjacency between two significant public institutions on both sides of the river: the Orange Bowl Stadium and the Dade County Courthouse.

The proposal for the overpass uses the existing highway infrastructure as a means of connecting both these public buildings to the river. On the north bank, the unusual height of the highway becomes an opportunity for the creation of a public hall. This screened space which holds activities associated with the water, such as a public market and boat storage, serves to define a public plaza facing the existing courthouse. Similarly, on the south bank of the river, the underbelly of the highway is programmed with a parking garage and recreational facilities. These new programs open into a sport complex of playing fields and athletics buildings, working in conjunction with the existing stadium.

The iconographic specificity of this proposal was seen as rhetorically crucial to create a link with Miami's history, but also to give an air of reality and a sense of cultural immediacy to schemes that may otherwise remain utopian.

Opposite page:
Road 836 overpass. Model.

Top:
The 836 overpass in Miami
Photo Monica Ponce de Léon.

Top:
Road 836 overpass. Montage
of proposed intervention on
aerial view.

Center:
Road 836 overpass. Plan of
proposed interventions.

Bottom:
Road 836 overpass. Site section (north-south) with connection of parking facilities to the
Orange Bowl.

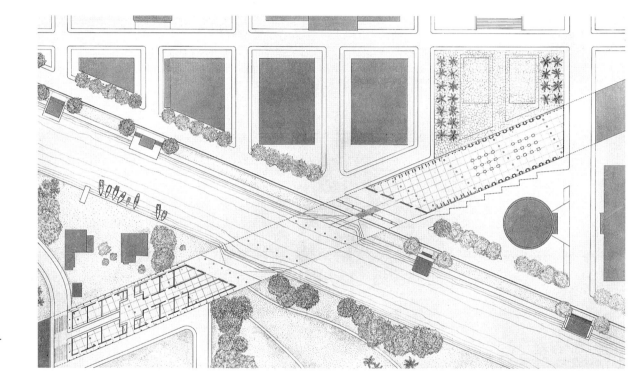

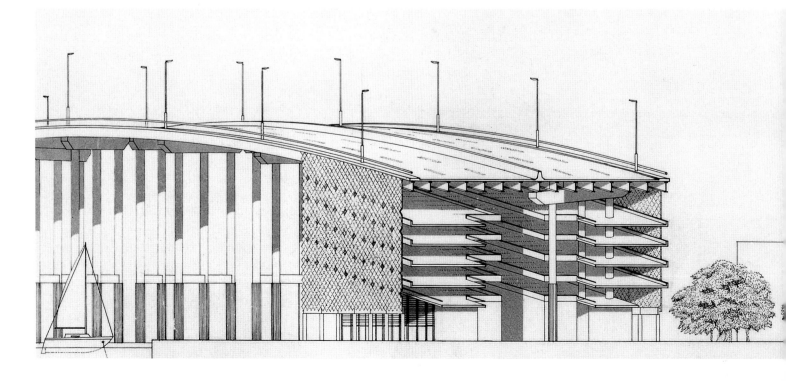

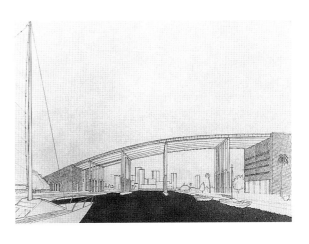

Top left:
View of 836 overpass.
Photo Monica Ponce de Léon.

Top right:
View of 836 overpass after
reconstruction.

Center left:
View of boat storage loading
dock under the overpass.

Center right:
View of public market hall
under the overpass.

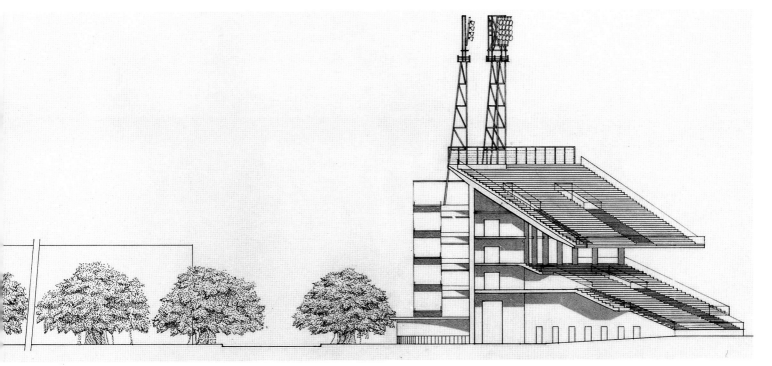

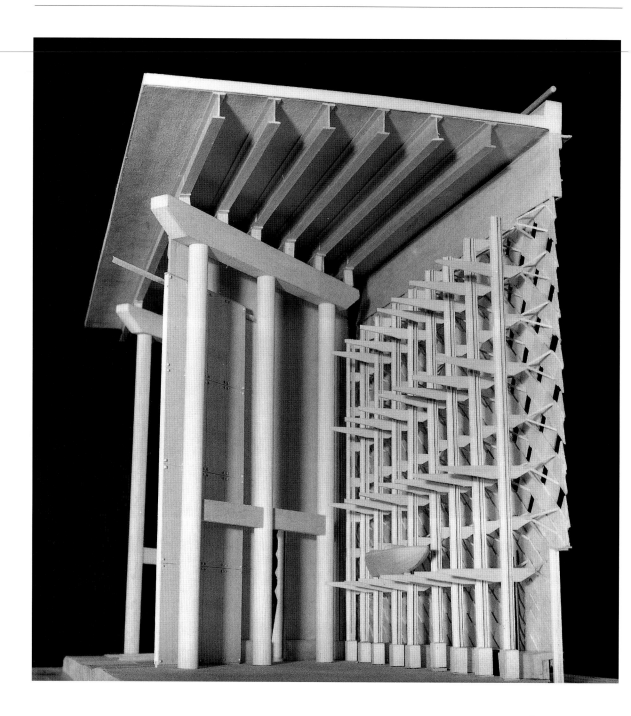

Top:
Road 836 overpass. Model of boathouse.

Bottom:
Road 836 overpass. Site section (east-west). Connection of Miami River to public boat storage and market hall.

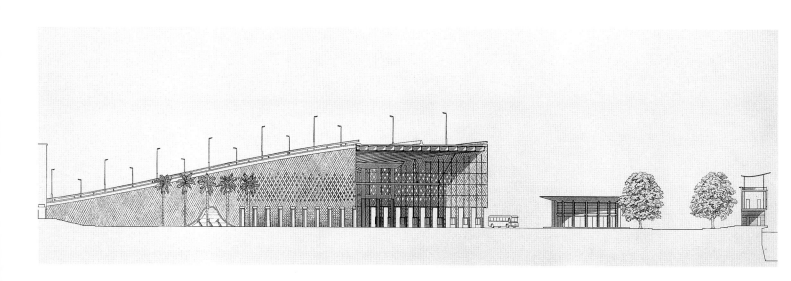

Top:
Route 836 Overpass. Model.

Bottom:
Road 836 overpass. Site section (north-south). Connection of courthouse to the Miami River.

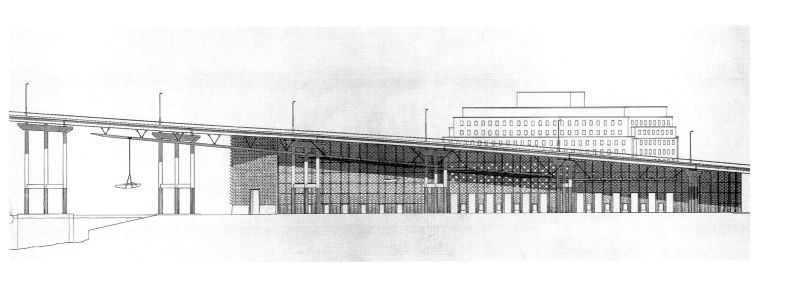

THE NEW TOWN OF KIRCHSTEIGFELD IN POTSDAM

Rob Krier &
Christopher Kohl

A century of urbanistic experiments is coming to a close, which by their sheer dimensions and their astonishing level of abstraction are unprecedented in history.

The inventors of these cities and districts—and many other supporting intellectuals—have spent their well protected life cocooned in the cozy quarters of our old cities, whereas they have relinquished the anonymous modern quarters to those who are not economically free to make choices. The latter and their children are the sacrificial victims of the far-reaching planning mistakes that we have committed not to repeat, here at the Kirchsteigfeld of Drewitz.

French municipalities are forced to squander every year more money for the renovation and the "therapeutic" costs necessitated by the quick obsolescence of the "villes nouvelles," than the French government spends for national defense. I don't know the numbers for Germany but I would not venture to say that they are better.

The risk implied by any new urban foundation is like a sword of Damocles swaying over our heads. What then gives us the force and what sustains our intellectual arrogance, that we hereby dare claim that we will do better and that we will never become addicted to the fashionable mistakes of the Zeitgeist?

I have dedicated my entire professional career to such a struggle. The criteria that I and my associates apply to urban design derive from the experience of life that the most beautiful European cities offer to our attention. We have not learnt the art of building cities from books and treatises, but directly through the patient study of the built reality of human cohabitation in the form of the most complex "total works of art," that our cultural history has produced.

In this new town—as we like to think of it—the foundation stone is once again the house, each one different from the other, created by many architects and coordinated, in size and in composition, harmoniously

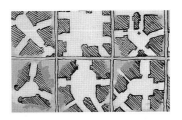

and to the best of our ability. Every resident will unmistakenly recognize his or her own front door; and even if we have to build apartments, mothers and fathers will call their children to dinner from their third or fourth floor, a simple family habit that can't be done from the eighth or tenth story.

In our new town the block is the basic unit of the urban structure. It defines the streets and the squares. Along the edges of the block the houses rise, here in close ranks, there in a more open order. The house is our yardstick, that one extrudes in length and height "as you like it." The public life in the alley as on the square can be enjoyed from countless windows, and it is herewith protected. This is the fundamental rule that one can observe in all "traditional" cities around the world. We have applied it here near Potsdam. It is the breeding ground for communal life in the urban neighborhood.

I must also mention that, through the network of streets, we have connected this new town to old Drewitz and that we have oriented it in the direction of the adjacent housing estate. Eventually we hope that all these parts will be united into a whole. We have located the so-called white-collar enterprises along the highway as a noise screen. In time there will be a job position in Kirchsteigfeld for every resident.

Kirchsteigfeld is neither a Siedlung, nor a dormitory or housing district, but a true town, where the residents and the following generations will share again the "there is a home here."

These dreams are not hanging in the clouds. We have captured them on paper; the owner-developer has tested the feasibility and assembled the financial means; the builders have set up a rapid program of construction. But it will be hard work and we all have many things to learn, for no participant can pretend to have ever been involved in such a true piece of city.

Inaugural speech, Rob Krier, December 2, 1993.

Opposite page:
Street intersection on
Hufeisenplatz (Horseshoe
square). Photo Waltraud
Krause.

Center:
Rob Krier. Charrette study of
the squares (December 1991).

Urbanism, urban form and character

The new town extends from the highway (an area built to the east in the form of a strict grid) toward the west, where the rigid structure breaks gradually and reorients itself along two other directions, towards the adjacent slab-housing district "Stern" and the old street-village of Drewitz. In addition to the linear business section to be built along the highway, the city is divided into two distinct neighborhoods, each with its characteristic interior streets and squares.

The most important "moments" of the townplan are the "gate" at the entrance of the town, the three open streets or "virtual axes" that will later connect to the adjacent housing district, the "tower building" at the intersection with the highway, and the "clothespin" that leads to the old village of Drewitz. From that important urban connection, the dividing line between the two neighborhoods follows the Hintergraben stream. A sequence of "natural rooms" establishes the urban character of this east-west axis, which consists of a central park and, to the south, of a boulevard parallel to the water.

Urban blocks make up the differentiated structure of the central area. The latter allows the creation of a varied network of streets and squares, that give to the different places their individual character and offer to the residents the familiar environment of a traditional town. As long as the streets and squares can be read clearly, street edges and corners can be left unbuilt at times in order to open up to the generous open spaces inside the blocks.

To the north of the town, the three open streets or "virtual axes" create varied opportunities of extension and connection to the existing housing district. Large houses, loosely sited and free-standing along the edge, guarantee the "transparency" of the town to the natural area called Priesterweg. Along the road on the eastern edge, small office towers accentuate and advertise the business section of the town. On the western side large free-standing multifamily houses present an open face to the old village. A large park defined by buildings will assure the genuine urban articulation with Drewitz. The private gardens of the houses along the western and southern boundaries protect the town from any infringement, and the linear business area will serve a sound barrier against the freeway traffic. The natural backbone of the project is the 2200-foot long drainage stream and canal whose presence will be urbanistically emphasized through several means: the tight edges of the business district to the east, followed by a section faced by open blocks, the central square near the civic center, and finally a reservoir pool near Drewitz.

The building density increases from the Drewitz edge to the center and the business section. Inside the neighborhoods building heights remain constant. Important locations can be visually marked by small angle towers or other architectural features. A total of 2500 apartments and houses—approximately three million square feet— will be accommodated in a regular four-floor configuration (R+3). Similar type of blocks permit a smooth transition between functions at the junction of the southern residential neighborhood and the business area.

The six required day-care centers are evenly distributed within the neighborhoods. A primary school and a comprehensive high school are located on the northeastern edge of town, in close proximity to the sport fields. The second primary school will be built to the south of the stream and will be combined with another civic building which should incorporate a multipurpose room, several public facilities, and eventually the main city hall. All the other cooperative commercial and communication spaces are situated within a block of the center. Directly to the south of this service center a site has been reserved for future cultural functions. Other public sites (church, etc.) are reserved throughout the town.

The large median-divided boulevard that parallels the "business belt" will distribute most of the traffic inside the town. The main interior circulation axis develops north-south along the streetcar line and services exclusive limited-traffic residential streets. Four secondary streets connect to the village of Drewitz, while the spacing of the detached multifamily houses on the southwestern edge permits the future opening of additional streets and pedestrian paths if necessary.

The streetcar coming from the adjacent housing district (Plattensiedlung) crosses the town from north to south. The main stop will be at the double turn in front of the civic center. The southern terminus loop wraps around a triangular square where one of the day-care centers will be built.

All streets and boulevards are lined with parallel or perpendicular parking spaces. Most of the residential parking takes place in half-sunken garages inside the blocks. They occupy seventeen feet of the ground floors at the back of the buildings and take up a 37-foot wide perimeter of the interior court. The garage is covered with terraces and private gardens accessible to the residents of the second and third floors. Openings between buildings are treated as raised gardens. A similar but more intensive system—occupying more of the larger ground floor surfaces—is scheduled for the business blocks. Additional parking faces the highway.

Top:
View from stream banks. Photo Waltraud Krause.

Bottom:
Krier & Kohl. Photomontage of the model on aerial view of the site (1993).

Translated and edited from planning report by Jean-François Lejeune.

Data sheet:

Housing units: approximately 2800; 800 of which will be individually owned.
Total housing area: 245000 sq metre or 2624000 sq. feet.
Service area: 100000 sq metre or 1070000 sq. feet.

Planning charrette (1991); Masterplan (1992); beginning of construction (September 1993); completion first phase (May 1995); completion second and third phase (May 1996).

Urban design & artistic coordination: Rob Krier, Christoph Kohl (Berlin).
Landscape design: Müller, Knippschild, Wehberg (Berlin).

*Top: Interior of block #6.
Photo Waltraud Krause.*

*Right:
Krier & Kohl. Kirchsteigfeld
Masterplan (1993). Landscape
plan by Müller, Knippschild,
Wehberg.*

*Bottom:
Krier & Kohl. Typical plan of a
"Stadtvilla" closing a large
block in the northeastern section.*

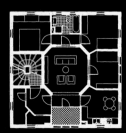

GRÜNORDNUNGSPLAN
zum Bebauungsplan Nr. 5803-001
Wohngebiet Kirchsteigfeld

Auftraggeber
Stadt Potsdam

Freie Planungsgruppe Berlin
Kurfürstendamm 62 W-1000 Berlin 15
mit
Garten- und Landschaftsarchitekten
C. Müller/E. Knippschild/J. Wehberg
mit U. Bresch, C.v. Haebler, A. Kauls, K. Meinale, T. Micke,
R.v. Geisten, P. Wollny
Derfflingerstraße 6 W-1000 Berlin 30

Städtebauliches Konzept
R. Krier / Ch. Kohl, Wien mit Moore, Ruble, Yudell, Santa Monica, Cal.

Datum
09. 11. 1992   Blatt 2 von 5

GESTALTKONZEPT   M. 1 : 5000

Top right:
"Rondell" Platz. Houses by Krüger, Schuberth, Vandreike (left) and Moore Ruble Yudell (right). Photo Waltraud Krause.

Center right:
Hufeisenplatz (Horsehoe Square), with houses by Moore Ruble Yudell (center end). Photo Waltraud Krause.

Bottom:
Aerial view of the town in construction (1995). © Luftbild & Pressefoto/Grahn.

Bottom left:
Krier & Kohl. Plan of the "Rondell" Platz (circle square).

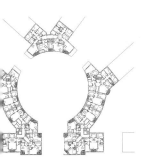

Top:
View of the bridge with mixed-use waterfront buildings in the background.

Bottom right:
Masterplan TET Wasserstadt Berlin-Oberhavel, October 1995. Notice the old fortress of Spandau in the lower left corner.

Center:
Joseph Paul Kleihues, architect. Perspective of a district (corresponds to the tip of land visible on the masterplan immediately north of the small island).

Bottom left:
Reichen and Roberts, architects. Proposal for the rehabilitation of an old brewery (at the bottom of the masterplan to the left of the island).

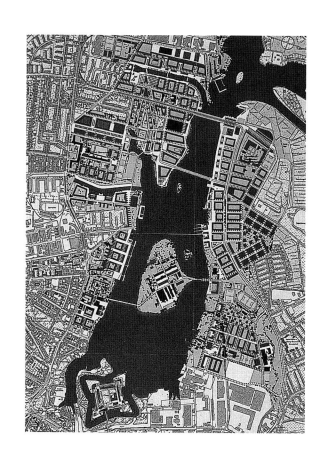

WASSERSTADT BERLIN-OBERHAVEL

*Jürgen Nottmeyer;
Hans Kollhoff &
Helga Timmerman,
Christoph Langhoff,
Klaus Zillich, Heike
Langenbach*

Above:
Model of masterplan (1992).
Since 1989 the project has survived all the ups and downs of
coordination with the different
authorities of the Senate of
Berlin and of the borough of
Spandau. It was formally designated in July 1992 as an urban
development area, and a
development agency (TET
Wasserstadt Berlin-Oberhavel
GmbH) was established. More
than 2500 housing units will be
ready by 1997.

Text and captions adapted from
project briefs.

The discussion related to the necessity to build new dwellings in large quantity after the reunification of Germany began in Berlin in the middle of 1989. At that time, a group of architects (Hans Kollhoff & Helga Timmerman, Christoph Langhoff, Jürgen Nottmeyer, Klaus Zillich) presented, in cooperation with the Senate of the Building Administration, a scheme for a suburb of unusual size and design. The project Wasserstadt Spandau—an industrial wasteland on both sides of the Havel river to the north of the Spandau citadel—broke several taboos, especially as regards the urban design concept, the process of design, and the way the scheme was to be realized. The architects requested a renewed consideration of the pre-modernist urban design concepts accompanied by a transformation and moderniza-tion of contents, methods, and architectural form.

The main aim was to create an urban atmosphere in a compact, pedestrian friendly urban structure. To achieve this aim the group chose to adopt high density, a mixture of different types of dwellings, services and commercial uses, and to include the topography and history of the site. The old design process was turned upside down: the architects did not start with laying down land uses and a road plan, but embarked on cre-ating a strong image of the future suburb encompassing urban spaces, squares, access, bridges, parks, and the

configuration of buildings, for a total of 13,000 dwellings and 22,000 jobs.

The water and landscape of the Oberhavel is defined as the characteristic element of the new town and determines the structure of urban spaces and build-ings; both are oriented towards the waterside. The prox-imity of the water should be felt even inland from the river. The most important arguments for traditional den-sity concern the quality of public space and, closely connected with it, a traffic concept aiming at avoiding traffic. The accessibility of all riverside areas, prome-nades, squares and streets for the inhabitants is the most decisive element of this quality. Most of the park-ing will be placed underground; individual vehicular traffic will be kept at a low level by installing a circular streetcar line giving access to all quarters and with stops within walking distance. The streetcar will be linked to the underground railway, thus ensuring access to the city center of Berlin, and to the train station in Spandau for long-distance travel. Traffic will also be reduced by the urban density, especially by the mixture of living, working, and leisure activities in all parts of the new town. As much as possible, the historic indus-trial fabric will be maintained and reused: the first pro-ject of this sort will include the rehabilitation of an old brewery and its insertion into a new mixed-use district.

GARTENSTADT FALKENHÖH

Helge Sypereck

The 100-acre site lies directly west of the municipal borders of Berlin and the city district of Spandau. It is surrounded to the east and the west by heterogeneous areas of single-family houses in a half-rural environment. The attraction of the formerly agricultural site resides on the one hand, in the protected natural areas that border it to the north and that are part of an extended green belt made up of lakes, wetlands, and forests; on the other hand, in its good connections to Berlin by road and by metro with the S-Bahn station of Albrechtshof, a quarter of a mile to the south.

The project was the result of a competition held in 1991. The geographic location between city and surrounding countryside suggested the concept and form of the garden city of the beginning of the 20th century: more specifically, Paul Schmitthenner's Gartenstadt Staaken (1913-1917)—less than a half mile away on the other side of the S-Bahn line—and Bruno Taut's Hufeisensiedlung and Wald Siedlung Zehlendorf (1926-1932) became the models of reference for a project that attempts to be at once site-specific and generic. The focal point of the plan—the four-story high "rotunda" in the manner of Taut's horseshoe at Britz—is located at the intersection of the east-west road that marks the southern limit of the site, and of the north-south axis that connects to the S-Bahn station.

The horseshoe houses about one hundred and fifty residential units, all with terraces; most ground floor apartments have small private gardens facing the inner park. In proximity to the gate connecting with the access road, the first floor is occupied by small shops including a cafe. The north side of the circle opens on two long, four-story high apartment bars that embrace the natural greenbelt that penetrates to the heart of the garden city. Gatehouses permit pedestrian passage to the greenbelt.

In the middle of the circle, two gates, marked with circular columns, connect to the preexisting axis of the Berlinerstrasse, now lined by multi-family residential villas, and redesigned as an avenue with a central tree-planted promenade. The main entrance to the garden city is from the Spandauerstrasse that runs on its southern side. There the mixed-use built front (two floors of shops and offices; two floors of apartments) is set back 100 feet to allow on-street parking and a planted screen of tall trees that maintain the semi-rural character of the road and protect the residents from the traffic noise. Some rental gardens are available in the middle of the blocks facing the villas. The alignment is interrupted at the central entrance of the district where two large-surface retail blocks with underground parking for 200 cars shield the circle and create a pedestrian link from the street to the shops and the inner garden.

Two residential neighborhoods expand on both sides of the horseshoe axis. The northwest section is organized as a grid of streets lined with single-family rowhouses (on lots 17, 20 or 33 feet wide). At the center is a four-sided square surrounded by apartments. The fan-shaped northeastern section consists of curved rows of individual houses of similar dimensions. Their asymmetrical street section recalls the "modernist" Siedlungen of the 1920s, with houses and back gardens facing each other in a rural pattern. A site for a day-care center has been reserved at the intersection of the fan with the street around the circle. In addition, some single-family detached houses can be found alongside the greenbelt to the north. A system of pedestrian walks meanders throughout the blocks and allows to interact with garden life. Despite its idiosyncratic shape, the new neighborhood can be accessed from all sides. Its street system establishes connections with the amorphous surrounding subdivisions. Most of the parking for the villas and apartments takes place along the planted streets; some rowhouses have individual garages on the property.

The varied housing conditions are intended to support the diversity of the social structure. Approximately 1500 apartments and houses are planned for a population of about 5000 residents. The private development will be partially rented and partially sold to individual property owners. It includes publicly funded social housing, and market-rate housing—some of which will be publicly assisted.

Opposite page:

Helge Sypereck, architect. View of the horsehoe or rotunda.

Above:
First, second, and third floor plans of rotunda (detail).

Translated and adapted from the planning report by Jean-François Lejeune.

Top:
Müller & Rhode, architects. The four-story mixed-use bars along Spandauer Strasse. Photo: Christian Gahl.

Center left and right:
Helge Sypereck, architect. Two examples of urban villas (Stadtvillen). Photos: Christian Gahl.

Bottom left:
Helge Sypereck, architect. Masterplan for Gartenstadt Falkenhöh (1991-2).

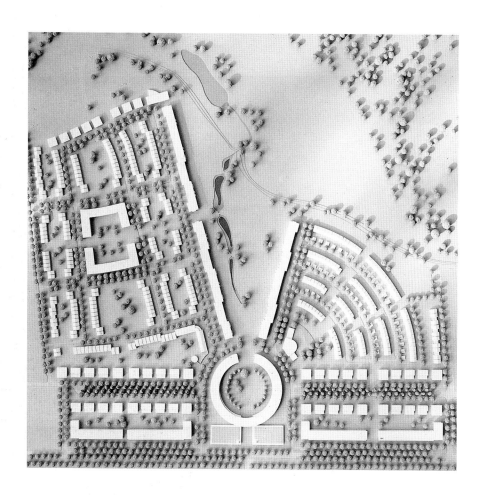

Data sheet:

Housing units: total of 1378 units, of which 680 will be privately owned.
Housing area: 125000 sq metre or 1339000 sq. feet.

Planning concept (1991). Beginning of construction (1992).

Urban design and coordination: Helge Sypereck (Berlin).
Construction plans: Christian Spath, Thomas Nagel (Berlin).
Landscape and gardens: Hannelore Kossel (Berlin).

Architects (for phases shown):
Helge Sypereck (Berlin) with as collaborators: Gabriele Mielke, Bernd Rüffer, Xavier Schneider (urban villas); Alexander Binder, Ursula Gottschick, Lee-Hsueh Hung, Stefan Müller, Klaus Pawlitzki (rotunda and shops).
Urs Müller, Thomas Rhode, Jörg Wandert (Berlin) with as collaborators: Silke Baumann, Clare Kemsley, Heike Landsberg, Uwe Minuth, Jörg Thiefenthaler.